THE
COMPLETE
BOOK *of*
FIVE RINGS

BOOKS BY KENJI TOKITSU

The Inner Art of Karate
Ki and the Way of the Martial Arts
Miyamoto Musashi: His Life and Writings

THE
COMPLETE
BOOK *of*
FIVE RINGS

Miyamoto Musashi

Edited and translated
by Kenji Tokitsu

SHAMBHALA
Boulder
2010

Shambhala Publications, Inc.
2129 13th Street
Boulder, Colorado 80302
www.shambhala.com

14 13 12 11 10 9

Design by James D. Skatges

Printed in the United States of America

Shambhala Publications makes every effort to print on acid-free, recycled paper.
Shambhala Publications is distributed worldwide by
Penguin Random House, Inc., and its subsidiaries.

Library of Congress Cataloging-in-Publication Data
Miyamoto, Musashi, 1584–1645.
[Gorin no sho. English]
The complete book of five rings/Miyamoto Musashi; edited and
translated by Kenji Tokitsu.
p.   cm.
Includes bibliographical references.
ISBN 978-1-59030-797-7 (pbk.: alk. paper)
1. Military art and science—Early works to 1800.
2. Swordplay—Japan—Early works to 1800.
I. Tokitsu, Kenji, 1947–   II. Title.
U101.M5913 2010
355.02—dc22
2010005134

CONTENTS

THE
COMPLETE
BOOK *of*
FIVE RINGS

Introduction

A LEGENDARY FIGURE

In popular Japanese culture, Miyamoto Musashi is a legendary figure. This warrior of the seventeenth century, a master of the sword but also a painter, sculptor, and calligrapher, left us a body of written work that has an important place in the history of the Japanese sword. His dense and brief *Gorin no sho*, or "Writings on the Five Elements," popularly known as *The Book of Five Rings*, is a summary of the art of the sword and a treatise on strategy.

Although the painting, sculpture, and calligraphy of Musashi are less well known, they are considered by connoisseurs to be of the first order.

Because of the extension of his art into so many domains and the way in which he explored the limits of the knowledge of his time, Miyamoto Musashi reminds us of Leonardo da Vinci. His personality and his adventurous life have been popularized by a famous novel and many films.

Here I present a completely new and annotated translation of the principal work of Miyamoto Musashi. Because of its concision, the *Gorin no sho* is a hard text for contemporary Japanese people to understand. The misunderstandings can only be greater for Westerners, who might draw the impression from the apparent clarity of the text that they are understanding it when in fact the author's essential ideas are eluding them. For this reason I have accompanied the text with clarifications, some of which are historic, others linguistic, and still others related to the nature of martial arts practice. I undertook this project even though several translations of the *Gorin no sho* already exist. Through carefully rereading the Japanese text, I discovered that these translations contained many errors or misunderstandings.

Translation of this work is a difficult undertaking because of the considerable evolution the Japanese language has undergone since Musashi's time, but even more so because of the major problem connected with the role—at once limited and important—played by verbal explanation in the traditional martial arts. That which is expressed in words is a little like the knot in an obi: only the knot is manifest, visible, but without the continuity of the belt, the whole thing would not hold together. What takes on meaning in the nodal point of the word is the entirety of a shared experience.

The principal mode of transmission of the martial arts was direct teaching. Words played a small role, and writing was confined for the most part to a simple enumeration of technical terms. This approach did not stem from respect for tradition; rather, it was connected with the very considerable difficulty of communicating techniques of the body and mind in writing. In the Scroll of Water, the second section of the *Gorin no sho,* for example, when Musashi explains techniques in words, it is difficult to understand, since the execution of each technique takes only a few seconds. The description in writing of a movement of the body that lasts only a few seconds is very complex—I continually have this experience in my own work. Nevertheless, at certain moments in the course of a student's development, a single word can trigger a profound understanding of the art by creating a new order for the experiences accumulated in the silence of physical practice. Musashi's words have this objective.

One of the big obstacles in translating the work of Musashi lies in this gap between his words and his body. I have attempted to bridge this gap through my own experience of *budo,* for the *Gorin no sho* is one of the books that serve me as a guide in the practice of the way of martial arts. The name and image of Musashi have been familiar to me from earliest childhood through stories, films, and, later, novels.

Musashi reappeared for me in the form of the *Gorin no sho* at a time when, after several years of practicing karate, I began to wonder about the relationship between this art and the tradition of the sword, which I saw as the essence of *budo*. It should be noted that from the cultural and ideological point of view, the tradition of karate is different in some respects from that of *budo*. Karate was a local practice transmitted secretly on the island of Okinawa (in the extreme south of Japan), and it was not included in the framework of *budo* until around 1930. The degree of technical refinement and depth that had been reached by karate at that time was nowhere near that of the Japanese art of the sword. Nonetheless, it quickly emerged, after the presentation of karate to the Japanese public, that this art fit in well with the modern life of the twentieth century and was capable of developing as a contemporary form of *budo*. For this discipline, newly a part of *budo*, the most important reference point was the Japanese art of the sword. By relying on this tradition, and particularly that of kendo and judo, karate found its *budo* form. Hence for Japanese karate practitioners, writings on the art of the sword became the cultural and technical reference points for their art.

As a result, the *Gorin no sho* has been my companion for the last twenty-five of my forty plus years of practicing *budo*. Of course, the intensity of my practice is not of the same order as Musashi's, but I have tried to bridge the gap between Musashi's words and the body through my own practice, however limited.

The other difficulty encountered in translating the *Gorin no sho* is more classical: How is it possible to bring out the proper sense of a word when the cultures involved are as different as those of the contemporary Western world and Japan of the seventeenth century? I will give just one example: In this work, Musashi very frequently uses the term *kokoro*, which is customarily translated "mind" or "heart." Many sentences, if translated literally, would yield expressions such as "Your mind must be resolute, tight, calm," and so on. Since the English language makes much greater use of expressions in which the person takes on the role of subject, the translation that seems to me to render these Japanese expressions the best is "Be determined, tight, calm," and so on. The idea expressed in Japanese by *kokoro* is included in the English personal form of the subject. In English when you say "Be calm," the underlying idea is that the mind should be calm, the primacy of the mind over the body being implicitly understood. In Japanese this primacy is not assumed in the same way. Musashi wrote: "The mind should not be pulled about by the body; the body should not be pulled about by the mind." This way of distinguishing the mind and body was established within the context of a way of thinking and a language in which the prevailing tendency is to mix the mind and body together nonhierarchically and in which an analytical effort has to be made to distinguish them. A superficial interpretation might see an affirmation of dualistic thinking in such remarks as Musashi's above, whereas, quite to the contrary, we find in such remarks efforts aimed at establishing distinctions that are not taken for granted.

All through this work, proper names have been given in the order customary in Japan, that is, with the patronymic preceding the personal name. For warriors, one or several personal names or names linked to their function may be added (in this society of warriors, the system of names was more complicated than it is in the present day). Patronymics and personal names are variable, being determined by several factors. For example, Musashi, during different periods of his life and in different circumstances, was referred to by the following family names: Hirata, Takemura, Shinmen, Hirao, and Miyamoto. To his personal name (Musashi), which was then a common personal name, he attached a warrior suffix, sometimes Masana, sometimes Masanobu. In addition, when a warrior claimed connection, by distant kinship, with one of the great historical clans, he also put a reference to this in his name. In the *Gorin no sho,* for example, Musashi refers to himself as Shinmen Musashi no kami Fujiwara no Genshin. Shinmen was the name of the lord of whom his family were vassals, and Fujiwara was the name of one of the most important clans starting in the seventh century; finally, Genshin was the personal name chosen by him or his family to designate him within this clan. (Genshin would be the Buddhist name for Musashi. [16, p. 13])

To simplify these very long names, after the second appearance I have designated a historical person by his personal name, since the personal name of a historical person was generally more specific and distinctive than his family name. Thus I have used Musashi rather than Miyamoto, since the name Musashi, for the Japanese, calls to mind most of the time Miyamoto Musashi; but if you write Miyamoto, you are not necessarily referring to Miyamoto Musashi.

Place names in Japanese include specifications such as "village," "island," or "temple." I also preceded the names with these specifications in my translations, in spite of the redundancy, in order to make things easier for those who do not know Japanese.

For dates, the number of the month has been kept, as in the Japanese system. In order to make the chronology clear for those who do not know Japanese, the years are given according to the Western system, despite the risk of some disparity. To be specific, the life of Musashi runs between the twelfth year of the Tensho period, which corresponds on the whole to the year 1584, and the second year of the Shoho period, which in the same way corresponds to the year 1645.

Reference numbers given in parentheses refer to the works listed in the bibliography.

The strategy of combat as well as reflection on it constitutes the basic background of Musashi's life and conferred on it several dimensions. It was his constant reaching toward creating an expression of his art in writing that gives a unique quality to Musashi's work.

In his youth, at around the age of twenty-two, Musashi wrote a scroll entitled "Writings on the Sword Technique of the Enmei Ryu" (*Enmei ryu kenpo sho*).[1] *Enmei ryu* was the first name Musashi used to designate his school. *En* means "circle" or "perfection"; *mei* means "light" or "clarity" (*ryu* means "school"). This image is derived from one of the techniques of the school, in which the practitioner holds his two swords in such a way as to call up the image of a circle. This work contains twenty-two instructions having to do exclusively with the art of the sword.

The *Gorin no sho* was preceded by other works that appear to function somewhat as sketches for it. In 1641 Musashi wrote the "Thirty-five Instructions on Strategy" (*Hyoho sanju go kajo*), a work written for Hosokawa Tadatoshi, the lord of Kumamoto on Kyushu, with whom Musashi stayed as a guest during the last period of his life. This scroll, composed of instructions on the art of the sword, is very similar to the *Gorin no sho*.

Finally, just before his death, Musashi composed another text, "The Way to Be Followed Alone" (*Dokkodo*), in which he distills his final thoughts.

Most of the time the reflection provoked by the in-depth practice of a martial art is allowed to feed back into the practice itself without being exteriorized, except perhaps in the form of brief aphorisms. As a practitioner of *budo*, I myself feel the difficulty of putting my experience into writing, as though having immersed myself in water, I were immediately to try to turn the pages of a book without getting them wet.

The work of Musashi stands out all the more because very few accomplished practitioners have written on the martial arts, especially during the period when the system of transmission was direct. This exceptional quality is borne out by the limited number of works on the art of the sword written during the two and a half centuries of the Edo period (1603–1867); the number appears very small in view of the large number of practitioners of the art.

There are several reasons why so few texts have been written on the arts of combat.

The Difficulty of Explaining the Practice in Words

Practitioners are generally content to progress on the way of practice without writing about it. Since intensive practice requires a person to immerse himself fully and deeply in his actions, an objective written description is difficult, for it requires one to assume some distance from the practice. If the practitioner has recourse to language, it is usually selectively, in order to bring out an intuition rather than pursue a line of logic.

Moreover, studying the practice of an art of combat in depth is not always compatible with writing about this art, for the process of going into the practice deeply means acquiring a capacity for sensory-motor reactivity that goes beyond the reach of mental reflection. Spontaneous movement and intuitive comprehension are reinforced, and one must avoid increasing the gap between perception and reaction by adding the pitfalls of intellectual speculation. Reflection is a part of *budo*, but it must be self-directed, introspective reflection that is not allowed to intervene in the moment of combat, where the spontaneity of movement is essential. However, as Musashi wrote, combat is not confined to the moment when it is actually taking place.

In Musashi's time, when confrontations were direct, it was enough for the majority of accomplished practitioners to immerse themselves deeply in their practice and limit themselves to a few words, just enough for quasi-sub-liminal hints intelligible to their students. In the transmission of a school's art, sometimes a language developed that was unintelligible to outsiders, based on a very broad intuitive register and seldom going in the direction of logical development. From that point of view, Musashi's work is exceptional. Nonetheless, looked at from our present point of view, his logic does not always seem coherent, and the meaning of his words is not always precise. If his words had been received directly from him in the flesh, with swords in hand, these verbal inexactitudes and ambiguities would not have been important, because Musashi's body and swords would easily have dispelled the ambiguities. However, three and a half centuries now separate us.

Someone who practices a martial art in depth and trains every day to the point of exhaustion has a tendency to develop a relationship with words that becomes prosaic or perfunctory at the same time as the intuitive aspect of his participation grows; he will tend to distance himself from long-winded objective reflection. He develops an intuition that can find a profound or manifold meaning in a single expression or a single ideogram. The sense of fullness that comes from these intensive physical exercises reduces the amplitude of logical sequences. It is only when the practitioner crosses the threshold of another dimension, where the sensation of fullness is realized through a stable treading of the way, that words will become more tangible. Thus it is no surprise that Musashi wrote his major work just before his death, even though he had been trying to write since his youth.

The Major Importance of the Art of Combat for Japanese Warriors

During Musashi's time, the tradition of a period of war was reflected directly in the way warriors practiced the sword. In the time that followed, with the coming of social stability, the symbolic aspect of the art of combat progressively increased in importance and the link between that art and a warrior's morality became more intimate. At the same time, the schools, now less involved in actual combat, became more dependent on feudal lords. These lords, to build up their prestige, emphasized the secrecy of the teachings of their schools. This secrecy might well have been compromised by the production of writings.

The Relationship between Speech and Action
among Japanese Warriors

The proverb "Speech is silver, silence is gold" is found in both the West and Japan, but it is interpreted and experienced in very different ways. The Japanese interpret this phrase as placing absolute value on silence and expressing contempt for eloquence—but this does not suggest contempt for words; on the contrary, it stresses the importance placed on every word. A worthy warrior spoke little, because he knew the importance of words. The word was conceived in terms of the role it might play in a possible chain of cause and effect, even if this were to remain virtual. Like a sword, a word can wound or kill, but as long as one does not touch the blade, the sword is no more than a smooth piece of metal. Someone who knows the qualities of a sword does not play with it, and someone who knows the nature of words does not play with them. Warriors attributed power and effective action to words, especially names. That is why the name of a technique was an important secret for someone seeking to understand the mind behind it. Anonymous transmission of a martial art did not exist, at least for warriors. For them the simple knowledge of how to do something was limited and incomplete. The ultimate transmission was in the name. For this reason the ultimate transmission of a school often took place through communication of the names of all the techniques, of which the practitioner had already for the most part attained mastery. One did not fully acquire the technique of a school until it had been named.

Miyamoto Musashi (1584–1645), a contemporary of René Descartes (1596–1650), lived at a turning point in the history of Japan—at the end of the period of feudal wars, at the moment when Japanese society was beginning to stabilize. Musashi witnessed the advent of the new system of warrior values, which was to be characterized by progressive internalization. Through his thought on strategy, which is pervaded by the philosophy of the period, we gain access to one of the roots of the culture of the Edo period.

The name of Miyamoto Musashi is known to Westerners through translations of the *Gorin no sho* and especially through the translation of the novel by Yoshikawa Eiji entitled *Musashi*. (62) Yoshikawa's novel ends with the famous duel between Musashi and Kojiro at Ganryujima. Musashi was twenty-nine at the time of this fight, which was the period of his youth concerning which we have the least imprecise documentation. The popularity Yoshikawa's image of Musashi has enjoyed over several generations shows that the novelist was able to distill in his character the ideal image of the samurai to which the Japanese people were attached.

Miyamoto Musashi had been renowned in Japan for a long time, but Yoshikawa's novel made him famous on a popular level, with the public as a whole. The author accentuated the introspective side of his personality. People sometimes say "Yoshikawa Musashi" to refer to the image that the Japanese public has of Miyamoto Musashi today. This novel was published as a serial in a daily paper from 1935 to 1939. It is, in a way, an expression of the position Yoshikawa took in the debate over Miyamoto Musashi's true qualities that was going on among Japanese writers at the beginning of the 1930s.

Naoki, a famous writer of samurai novels, triggered the polemic by writing that Musashi did not achieve excellence in the sword until a few years before his death. (21, pp. 39–42) His view is that in his youth Musashi was no more than an expert in publicizing himself and that his strength in the sword was not extraordinary. He takes as his proof Musashi's duel against Sasaki Kojiro, in which Musashi used a wooden sword so as to have a sword longer than Kojiro's; moreover, he deliberately delayed the time of the fight in order to disconcert his adversary. Naoki adds that although, as Musashi himself wrote, he had had more than sixty duels during his lifetime, most of them were against little-known samurai. This viewpoint is not entirely devoid of truth, but it is primarily based on suppositions.

Another writer attacked this position and defended Musashi's qualities. The debate grew, and Yoshikawa was drawn into the controversy. What was important about this debate is that it touched upon the way the Japanese cultural identity was being presented, a particularly sensitive issue at the moment when Japanese society was preparing for the Second World War.

Since Yoshikawa's book appeared, numerous works have been published on Musashi in Japan. The historical documents concerning Musashi are fragmentary but relatively numerous. They are not rich enough to allow us to construct a precise image of his personality, but they are sufficient to provide food for the imagination. These documents taken together seem to be equivalent to a small fragment of some piece of Greek pottery on the basis of which we might imagine a jar or a vase. Although the image of Musashi is vague, the features that emerge are very potent, strong in odor and color. It is difficult to maintain neutrality in the face of such an image. Either you like it or you do not. It seems to me that it is essentially primal attitudes of this sort that form the main basis for the disparate positions in the assessment of Musashi and his work evinced by contemporary Japanese authors.

The members of one group—for example, Ezaki Shunpei (15) and Naoki (21)—do not like or even detest the image they hold of Musashi. These writers consider him a cunning and accomplished practitioner but a second-class figure in the history of the Japanese martial arts. Some go so far as to characterize him as a paranoiac. In their view, the *Gorin no sho* is a rather mediocre work.

A second group—for example, Shiba Ryotaro (30), Tobe Shinichiro (31), and Saotome Mitsugu (59)—judges the work and martial art of Musashi positively but separates it from their assessment of him personally. In the view of these writers, Musashi was doubtless a great and accomplished artist and practitioner of the martial arts, but his personality is considered unbalanced by some of them and unwholesome by others. They do not like Musashi, but they do appreciate the quality of his accomplishments.

A third group—such as Fukuhara Josen (2), Imai Masayuki (3), Nakanishi Seizo (8), Terayama Danchu (11), Morita Monjuro (20), and Naramoto Tatsuya (58)—assesses both the accomplishments and the personality of Musashi positively. These writers consider his art (both martial and fine) as an overall reflection of his personality. The majority of works on Musashi belong to this category and in many cases display no critical distance.

A fourth group—for example, Takayanagi Mitsutoshi (10) and Watanabe Ichiro (13)—somewhat steps back from its personal appreciation of Musashi. These writers situate his works within their historical period and appreciate them particularly for their originality. Their attitude seems to be the most scientific, but in their method they do not go beyond brief commentaries on the texts. Thus for Takayanagi, the *Gorin no sho* is difficult to understand mainly because of the lack of organization in Musashi's writing, but despite this defect, Musashi's work is admirable when one takes into account the shortcomings of his time, in which the distinction between religion and science was not sufficiently developed.

Though it is perhaps still possible to criticize the swordsmanship of Musashi, since it belongs to the past, by contrast his calligraphies, ink paintings, and sculptures have come down to us. Their artistic quality is undeniable, and they are well known in the history of Japanese art. True, the *Gorin no sho* is difficult to understand, but its style appears relatively clear when compared with the works of Musashi's contemporaries; and as far as the content is concerned, only a great adept of the sword could have written it. As Musashi wrote: "Because I apply the principle of the sword to the other arts, I no longer have a need for a teacher in these other domains." The quality of his work taken overall indicates that he could only have excelled in the art of the sword.

My way of presenting Musashi takes historical research as its point of departure but is somewhat different from the approach of the historians, because I interpret the texts on the basis of my experience in the martial arts and attempt to derive from them teachings applicable to martial arts practice.

How Can We Assess Musashi's Practice of the Sword?

During this period, confrontations with the sword between practitioners of different schools in most cases meant death for one of the participants. The decision to make or accept a challenge demanded the utmost prudence. Mere bravado was not enough to survive a duel to the death. One had to have a level of accomplishment that was equal to that of the adversary. Now, it is undeniable that Musashi never made a mistake in accurately assessing the strength of an adversary—this made it possible for him to avoid fighting an enemy capable of defeating him. The word *mikiri* became the established term for characterizing this particular acuity of Musashi's perception. The origination of this term is attributed to him, but I have been unable to find it in his writings. The literal translation is: *mi*, "look" or "see"; and *kiri*, "cut." This means "to see with cutting minuteness" or "to cut through with a look," which amounts to "discerning the state of situations or things with incisive precision." In my view this precise discernment characterizes the sword of Musashi as well as his aesthetic expressions. If he judged his adversary as potentially his superior, he avoided fighting him. Discernment of incisive precision was, for Musashi, the basis of individual and collective strategy. *Mikiri* distills in one word one of the teachings of Sun Tsu: "If you know yourself and you know your enemy, you will not lose one fight in a hundred."

For Musashi, just being strong individually was not of such great value, because he knew that the strength of a single person is limited and even insignificant in the unfolding of a large battle such as those he participated in several times in the course of his life. He would have preferred to apply his talent fully on a larger scale, because he felt he had discovered a principle applicable to all phenomena of life.

From the end of his adolescence, Musashi began to travel and engage in many duels. The age of thirty marked a change in his life. He continued to travel in order to deepen his art of swordsmanship, but he no longer sought out duels as he had before. At the same time, he was looking for a feudal lord who would entrust him with the elaboration of large-scale strategies. However, Musashi's rigor and precision sometimes made as disquieting an impression as the blade of his sword. This is something that can also be seen in his works of art. This is without doubt one of the reasons he was not able to obtain the position he was looking for with one of the great feudal lords. I am convinced that Musashi was a very great master of the sword, but I also think that several masters in the history of Japanese swordsmanship attained a level that was equivalent or superior to his.

To reach an accurate evaluation of Musashi's martial art and personality, it seems indispensable to situate them within the history of the art of the sword in Japan. This is because—and Musashi's work is an expression of this—his period was the time at which the art of the sword began to pass beyond the sphere of military technique and merge with the practical notion of "the way." The art of the sword was on its way to becoming, both technically and morally, a formative element in the life of the Japanese warrior.

In accordance with the custom of the time, in referring to himself, Musashi used the term *bushi*, "warrior," which means "practitioner of arms." This was a reference to the division of Japanese society into four hierarchical social classes (warrior, peasant, artisan, and merchant), which the Tokugawa government had already firmly institutionalized by Musashi's time. By using the word *bushi*, warriors indicated their place in this hierarchy. This term appeared in the Nara period (eighth century) and progressively supplanted the older term *mononofu*, signifying men who knew how to use weapons and were courageous.

Samurai comes from *saburai*, the substantive form of the verb *saburau*, which means "to serve" or "to remain at the side of someone important" and was itself an evolved form of the older *samurau*. Starting with the Heian period (794–1145), *samurai* designated warriors who were in the service of nobles. Little by little, it came to be used by members of the other classes to refer to warriors in general. However, within the warrior class itself, it was used to refer to those most highly placed in the hierarchy. For example, the townspeople might call anybody who wore the two swords a samurai, but among warriors, this term was not applied to those who occupied the lower levels of the hierarchy. (106)

The power of the warriors became further established during the Heian period, especially starting with the tenth century, when the power of the government weakened in the provinces. The powerful *go zoku* (regional authority) families began to fight to protect and increase the territory they had acquired. They developed their military capability so they could govern the local peasants by themselves and protect themselves against rival powers as well as the representatives of the state. They built themselves up into larger groups united by ties of blood and also, for those who succeeded in becoming part of it, by a strong consciousness of belonging to the group. These armed groups, called *bushi dan*, developed in the provinces. Their moral values were based largely on the cult of ancestors and on family relations, which were expanded to form a clan hierarchy, as well as on values arising from the personal valor of combatants.

The warrior art to which warriors at first attached their identity was archery. *Yumiyatoru mi*, literally, "he who knows how to shoot a bow," designated men of war during the Kamakura period. *Yumi no ie* designated a family that excelled in the art of archery and thus a family of warriors. Such warriors fought from horseback, mainly with a bow. When the use of the sword on horseback spread, it brought about a modification in swords, which began to take on a curved form. The mode of combat changed progressively, and in the fourteenth and fifteenth centuries, the sword assumed first place among the arts of the warriors and became their emblematic weapon. However, it would be inaccurate to think that the Japanese art of the sword developed in isolation, because the metallurgy connected with it came from China via Korea, and in the wake of this, interaction with these countries increased further.

During Musashi's time, the art of the sword was dominant, and there were numerous schools teaching sword technique. Thus, in order to gain a clear understanding of the life of Musashi, who founded a school of swordsmanship several branches of which still exist today, it seems essential to situate him within the history of Japanese schools of the sword.

THE MAIN PERIODS IN THE HISTORY OF JAPANESE SCHOOLS OF SWORDSMANSHIP

The Formative Period (Fifteenth to Sixteenth Centuries)

A decisive period in the formation and evolution of the way of the sword extends from the end of the fourteenth century to the beginning of the seventeenth century. Later this period was to become a point of reference for masters and practitioners of the sword.

Of course, the art of the sword in Japan is much more ancient than this. In the course of the tenth century, the shape of swords was modified, and the curved sword gradually replaced the straight sword. These changes were a reflection of a development of techniques in which the action of slashing became increasingly important. The elevation of the social status of warriors went hand in hand with the evolution of combat techniques. By the eleventh century the change in the form and technique of the Japanese sword was becoming widespread. Before this the military force was overwhelmingly composed of foot soldiers who used the straight sword, mainly for stabbing. With the development of local military groups whose large estates permitted them to keep horses, mounted warriors assumed the primary place. The technique and form of the sword transformed little by little to facilitate the combat of fighters on horseback, for whom slashing is easier than stabbing. Curvature of the sword became important. The curved sword gradually came to be dominant, and slashing techniques were extended to combat on foot. The curved form of the sword stabilized beginning in the twelfth century, and the name *nihon to* (Japanese sword) was used to differentiate this curved sword from the straight sword, which preserved direct Chinese influence. The increase in the number of swords forged shows the dominance the sword was assuming, especially in the period from the twelfth through the fourteenth centuries. The *nihon to,* Japanese swords, made during the six centuries from the end of the tenth to the beginning of the seventeenth (the Keicho era) are classified as ancient swords and called *ko to.* They are of a high quality that has not been equaled since. We know the names of more than fifty-five hundred master smiths of ancient swords. According to Mitsuhashi Shuzo, there were

- 450 sword smiths from the tenth to twelfth centuries (Heian period)
- 1,550 sword smiths from the thirteenth to the middle of the fourteenth century (Kamakura period)
- 3,550 sword smiths from the middle of the fourteenth to the end of the sixteenth century. (41, p. 6)

In tandem with the evolution of the form of the sword, there was a remarkable surge in the development of sword technique. However, dependable documents on schools of swordsmanship do not go back beyond the end of the fourteenth century. Despite the fact that most schools like to claim that their roots go back to the Kamakura period (1185–1333) or still further back, the lineages of the main traditional schools of the sword can be traced with certainty only back to the middle of the fifteenth century.

From the last third of the fifteenth century until the end of the sixteenth, Japan was the scene of continual warfare among the feudal lords. It was through experience on the battlefield that the sword masters of that period developed their sword technique as well as their basic attitudes toward swordsmanship. The techniques of that period were relatively simple but forceful, since armor was worn in battle. Combatants used existing techniques but also carried on their own personal search for more effective ones, based on their own experience. While continuing to accept the idea that the true ability to fight comes from actual battlefield experience, some warriors began to attach importance to training, to daily preparation for combat. This included matches that often took place without armor, which resulted in the development of greater subtlety in technique. The practice exercises, called *kumitachi* or *tachi uchi,* consisted in reproducing combat techniques derived from the experience of various masters. These exercises, in which either a real or a wooden sword was used, became standardized.

Miyamoto Musashi lived at the end of this formative period of the classic schools of swordsmanship.

Period of Further Development
(Seventeenth and Eighteenth Centuries)

According to my analysis, we can consider the seventeenth and eighteenth centuries as the birth period of *budo.* This period, in which the art of the sword was developed further, extends from the second half of the seventeenth century to the beginning of the nineteenth century.

The shoguns of the Tokugawa family established and stabilized their power over the whole of Japan between 1600 and 1640. They imposed a strong rule that brought about a long period of peace, which lasted until the middle of the nineteenth century. This meant that warriors had to adjust progressively to a peacetime role.

At the time of the feudal wars, one could have summed up the value of a warrior's swordsmanship by answering the following question: How many heads can he cut off? In time of peace, this simple pragmatism transformed into an effort directed toward advancement in swordsmanship as an art. Since the way of action was closed to them, the sword masters internalized their art—it became a quest for the way, *do.* The level of commitment to this quest was deepened by the fact that the way, *do,* derived a part of its meaning from the relationship between the lord and his vassals.

The objective for the practitioner became finding a means to make progress in the way of the sword without really killing his adversary. From this point on, swordsmen no longer used armor, and sword technique was modified because there was no need for the forceful techniques that made it possible to kill an enemy through his armor. Masters developed subtle techniques that took into account the freedom of movement made possible by town clothes. The art of the sword reached its apex toward the end of this period.

In the middle of the eighteenth century, certain schools began to train with the *shinai* (bamboo sword) and to use armor again. These developments became general by the end of the eighteenth century. These safety measures were conducive to unlimited matches between practitioners, and this encouraged the elaboration of technique within each school. Autonomous trends within schools multiplied. At this point we can enumerate as many as seven hundred schools of the sword.

As the art of the sword became increasingly refined, it became a major vehicle for the energy of warriors within a Japanese society that was becoming closed toward the outside world. Warriors heightened their art while almost never using it in real confrontations. They killed each other every day in practice, but in reality they avoided death. Nevertheless, the idea that combat to the death could become an actuality at any moment remained the basic reference point for the warriors' state of mind. At the same time, through the elaboration of technique, the idea of harmony began to infiltrate deeper and deeper into the basic antagonism inherent in the use of weapons. The art of the warriors flourished under a variety of names (*bujutsu, bugei, kenjutsu, gekiken, to jutsu, ken po*). In all these disciplines, the energy of antagonistic confrontation remained dominant, symbolized by the wearing of the warrior's sword. The sword that accompanied a warrior everywhere still represented the fundamental idea of "kill or be killed."

The Flowering of the Art of the Sword (Nineteenth Century)

The third period of the history of schools of the sword encompasses most of the nineteenth century. The art of the sword flowered at the time when its power became a major factor in putting an end to the feudal period, which had been the period of the sword's dominance.

At the beginning of the nineteenth century, swordsmanship passed through a brief period of decadence, for as the period of wars became more remote, the sword became dissociated from the reality of combat, and the position of warriors became uncertain. But then, quickly, the threat represented by Westerners provided warriors with a renewed consciousness of their role. In the course of the second half of the century, Japan passed through a succession of troubles connected with the threat of invasion by Western powers. This was the time when the Japanese began to become aware of the power of the Westerners and to look for the most effective means of opposing them. This attitude and a new awareness of society as a whole was reflected in the manner in which warriors practiced swordsmanship. The art of the sword had reached a high point during the preceding period, but in becoming dissociated from the reality of combat it entered a decadent phase. The conflicts that pervaded Japanese society produced new needs, and the art of the sword then reached a level of fruition in which it produced sparks of steel between the two parties into which warriors were now divided—one defending the shogunate, the other seeking to oust this system of government.

The reign of the shoguns came to an end in 1867, and the new regime, as part of its plan to set up a modern military and industrial power, abolished the privileges of the warriors. In spite of these difficulties, some of those who had survived the confrontations of the period of transition continued the tradition and practice of the sword. They had to put up with the prohibition against carrying a sword and come to grips with the then prevailing tendency to discredit traditional culture, which was the support of their identity. The sword of the warrior disappeared at the end of the nineteenth century with the death of those who had lived through the last period of actual sword combat.

The notion of *budo* was born at the moment in which the class of warriors disappeared and the values of feudal society began to dissolve into the depths of modern society. (126) Even though *budo* takes tradition as its basis, it is a modern notion. It defines a practice that takes shape around a kind of dilemma. Arms are fundamentally offensive, but *budo*'s striving for quality in the art of arms contains within it an impulse directed toward the evolution of human beings as such, and this in turn implies a seeking for harmony, an element that is in apparent conflict with the objectives of combat. The ideal goal of *budo* is combat in which aggressive energy is perfectly balanced by its opposite component, harmony.

Kendo (Nineteenth and Twentieth Centuries)

The conception and practice of kendo developed and took on definitive form toward the end of the Meiji period (1868–1912), in the latter part of the nineteenth century and the first half of the twentieth. The name itself dates from this period. Kendo is a modern reformulation of the warriors' art of the sword, in which combat is practiced mainly with shinai and armor. Thus the kendo of today is not exactly the same art practiced by the sword masters of old.

Although this period was short, it was important because of the intermediary role it played between the kendo that was a continuation of the historical warriors' practice and modern kendo.

From 1945 to the Present

The destruction in Japan in 1945 was major, and in the shock of defeat, Japanese society as a whole was challenged. After the war, Japan was occupied, the pressure exercised by the Allies was heavy, and the practice of the martial arts was forbidden. Practitioners of karate were the first to get permission to resume their discipline, which they presented as a form of boxing. This comparison to Western boxing allowed them to put karate in the category of a sport. This did not work for kendo, for even when practiced with bamboo swords, it continued to evoke the strange barbarity of wartime Japan. Kendo practitioners tried to perpetuate kendo under the name *shinai kyogi*, "gamelike competition with *shinai*," by transforming the techniques of kendo to make it resemble a sportlike activity that would be acceptable in the eyes of the occupiers. To this end, they glossed over as much as possible the traditional aspect of the discipline, with its costumes and customs, and followed the model of European fencing. This experience continued to be one of the shaping factors in the transformations that led to contemporary kendo. Indeed, when kendo was able to resume in 1952, it was in the context of a society that had changed, and the spirit of the practice had been changed by integrating into it the modern idea of a combat sport.

In parallel with all this, a certain number of ancient schools of the sword continued, and continue down to the present day, to transmit their techniques in the traditional form but with a very limited number of practitioners.

Let us summarize the main lines of this history.

In the beginning, the nature of the sword was obvious. The blade was the main thing—it killed in a bloody way. Spirituality had little place in the practice of the sword.

In the next phase, the sword continued to be there, but it was in a scabbard. It killed less frequently, almost not at all. Sword practice was more a matter of technique, and it coexisted with spirituality. The notion of *do* developed in association with the consciousness of one's duty toward the ruler.

With the disappearance of the class of warriors and the prohibition against carrying a sword, the *shinai* supplanted the sword in the practice of the art, and a new conception of the way (*do*) was formed in connection with the idea of *budo*. This was a modern reforging of tradition that proposed as its overall objective the training of the human being as such in conformity with the expectations of nineteenth-century society.

CHRONOLOGY OF MUSASHI'S LIFE

Certain contradictions exist among the documents relating to Miyamoto Musashi's life. I have put together the following chronology by selecting the most plausible ones among the currently accepted hypotheses concerning the events of Musashi's life in view of the elements actually known to us.

According to the ancient system, a person is considered to be one year old during the course of the year following his birth. For example, according to the *Gorin no sho,* Musashi fought at the age of thirteen, but according to the modern system currently in use, this corresponds to the age of twelve. In references to Musashi's age in the following chronology, I have used the modern system.

1578
Birth of Jirota, older brother of Musashi, who died in 1660.
Musashi also seems to have had two sisters.

1584
Birth of the child who was to be known as Miyamoto Musashi, during the third month, in the village of Miyamoto-Sanomo (Mimasaka region). He received the name of Bennosuke. His father's name was Hirata Munisai and his mother's was Omasa. His mother died on the fourth day of the third month. Munisai then married the young Yoshiko, who would act as Bennosuke's mother.

1587 *(three years old)*
Around this time, Yoshiko divorced Hirata Munisai and left for the village of Hirafuku with Bennosuke. Her family having been scattered by war, she

was taken in by the adoptive son of her uncle, Tasumi Masahisa. Later he would marry her. He already had two sons by his first marriage.

Yoshiko, being uneasy about Bennosuke's future, placed him under the care of her uncle Dorin, who was a monk in the temple of Shoreian. Bennosuke received his education from Dorin and Tasumi.

1589 (five years old)

On the orders of his lord, Shinmen Iganokami, Munisai killed Honiden Gekinosuke (twenty-seven years old), who was one of his disciples in the study of strategy.

1592 (eight years old)

Certain documents record that Munisai died this year, but this is contradicted by other documents. It is probable that the person who died at this time was Hirata Takehito, not Hirata Munisai.

1596 (twelve years old)

Bennosuke fought a duel with Arima Kihei of the Shinto ryu (school). The fight took place in the village of Hirafuku-mura.

1599 (fifteen years old)

Bennosuke left the region. He visited his sister Ogin and her husband, Hirao Yoemon, who lived in the village of Miyamoto, and gave them the family possessions: weapons, furniture, the family genealogy, and so on.

In one of the documents of the village of Miyamoto, we find the following passage: "Musashi left this village ninety years ago. . . . He was accompanied by his friend Moriiwa Hikobei. At the time of their separation, the latter received from Musashi a *bokken* made of black wood. Musashi then went to the village of Hirafuku-mura to take leave of his mother Yoshiko and his stepfather Tasumi. He traveled to Tajima [Hyogo], where he fought a duel with a martial arts practitioner adept named Akiyama." (8, p. 43)

1600 (sixteen years old)

In the battle of Sekigahara, Musashi was part of the army of the West.

During the seventh month, he took part in an attack on Fushimi castle (his first battle).

During the eighth month, he took part in the defense of Gifu castle.

On the fifteenth of the ninth month, he took part in the battle of Sekiga-hara. The West lost in a few hours. Musashi was in the battalion of Lord Ukita, who was the liege lord of Lord Shinmen, of whom Musashi's family were vassals. Following this defeat, Shinmen Sokan took refuge on Kyushu. Musashi perhaps also traveled in the direction of Kyushu. One legend tells us that he trained on Mount Hikosan during his stay on Kyushu.

1604 (twenty years old)

On the eighth of the third month, Musashi engaged in a victorious duel with Yoshioka Seijuro in the hamlet of Rendaino on the outskirts of Kyoto.

Victorious duel against Yoshioka Denshichiro, younger brother of Seijuro, who had then challenged him.

Combat against the clan and dojo of Yoshioka at Ichijoji (Kyoto). Musashi won the victory and killed Matashichiro, the nominal head of the Yoshioka, aged twelve or thirteen.

According to certain documents, it was after these fights that Musashi went to Hozoin in Nara to engage in combat with the monks there, who were experts with the lance.

After Nara, Musashi went to Banshu (Hyogo) and stayed at Enkoji temple. The monk in charge of Enkoji liked the martial arts and had turned a part of the temple into a martial arts dojo. The monk's brother, Tada Hanzaburo, received teachings from Musashi in this temple. At this time Musashi called his school Enmei ryu, and Tada Hanzaburo received the certificate of transmission of this school from Musashi.

Later, Tada Genzaemon, the grandson of Hanzaburo, founded the Ensu ryu on the basis of the Enmei ryu and the art of swordsmanship called *mizuno iai jutsu* (the art of drawing the sword).

Musashi traveled in various regions of western Japan, using Enkoji as a base.

1605 (twenty-two years old)

One of the first certificates of transmission written by Musashi is dated this year. It ends as follows:

the one and only under the sky
Miyamoto Musashi no kami

Fujiwara Yoshitsune [signature] [hand-executed seal]
To Mr. Ochiai Tadaemon,
the auspicious day of the eleventh year of the Keicho era [1606].

1607 (twenty-three years old)

A certificate of transmission written by Musashi's father, Miyamoto Munisai, for his disciple Tomooka Kanjuro, is dated the fifth of the ninth month, 1607, which proves that he was still living that year.

Musashi went to Edo, passing by way of Nara and Yagyu. He fought a duel with Shishido Baiken, an expert with the *kusari gama* (a sickle to which a chain with a steel weight on the end is attached).

1607–1611 (twenty-three to twenty-seven years old)

Having arrived in Edo, Musashi fought a duel with two advanced practitioners of the Yagyu school, Oseto and Tsujikaze. In Edo he also fought Muso Gonnosuke, an expert in the art of the staff, whom he defeated without killing him. On the basis of his experience with Musashi, Muso developed his school of the art of the staff, the Shinto Muso ryu. Musashi remained in Edo three or four years, traveling from time to time in the vicinity.

1609 (twenty-five years old)

Musashi participated in the clearing of new fields, working the earth with the peasants of Gyotoku in Shimousa (Chiba). Another document puts this episode in 1611.

1611 (twenty-seven years old)

Musashi went to Kyoto. He visited the Myoshinji temple, where he practiced *zazen*. According to one document, at this temple he met Nagaoka Sado, a vassal of Lord Hosokawa Tadaoki, who became the lord of northern Kyushu after the battle of Sekigahara. Nagaoka had been a student of Musashi's father, Miyamoto Munisai, who had moved to Kyushu. It is possible that Musashi made Nagaoka's acquaintance when he visited his father on Kyushu. Nagaoka spoke to Musashi about an accomplished martial arts adept named Sasaki Kojiro and proposed that he organize a duel between Kojiro and Musashi. We may surmise that this was a political move against the Sasaki clan and not merely a matter of a duel.

1612 (twenty-eight years old)

Victorious duel against Sasaki Kojiro on the thirteenth of the fourth month, on the island of Funajima, north of Kyushu.

1613 (twenty-nine years old)

Musashi spent a period of time meditating at a temple on Mount Koyasan in Kishu (Wakayama prefecture). He later stayed in Nagoya and trained some disciples, among them Takemura, a practitioner of the art of the *shuriken*.

1614 (thirty years old)

Tenth month: the winter battle of Osaka. This was Musashi's fourth battle. The usual view is that Musashi was part of the Army of the West, but I believe he fought in the Army of the East under Tokugawa Ieyasu.

1615 (thirty-one years old)

Fourth month: summer battle of Osaka. In the course of the fifth month, the Army of the East won a decisive victory.

1616–1617 (thirty-two to thirty-three years old)

Musashi stayed at Akashi at the invitation of Lord Ogasawara. There he taught the sword and the art of the *shuriken*. He also participated in the construction of Akashi castle.

1618–1620 (thirty-four to thirty-six years old)

Musashi adopted a male child who later took the name Miyamoto Mikinosuke.

1621 (thirty-seven years old)

At Himeji, Musashi fought victoriously against Miyake Gunbei and three other adepts of the Togun ryu in the presence of the lord of Himeji. Musashi participated in the development of the plan of the town of Himeji. He also directed the creation of the gardens of several temples there.

1622 (thirty-eight years old)

Musashi's adoptive son Miyamoto Mikinosuke acquired the rank of vassal of the fief of Himeji. Musashi departed again on his travels.

1623 (thirty-nine years old)

Musashi went to Edo.

1624 (forty years old)

Musashi lived in Edo. He established relations with Hayashi Razan, a Confucianist scholar who was part of the shogun's government. Some historians advocate the theory that Hayashi recommended Musashi to the shogun as a sword master. At this time the shogun already had two principal sword masters, Ono Jiroemon and Yagyu Munenori. Musashi's application to the shogun ended in failure.

Musashi departed, traveling in the direction of Oshu (northern Japan). He got as far as Yamagata.

He adopted a second son, to whom he gave the name Miyamoto Iori. He traveled with Iori, passing through Edo, then Hokuriku, Kyoto, Ise, Kishu, finally arriving at Osaka, where he stayed for some time. According to one document, the adoption of Iori took place when he was at Yamagata; other documents indicate that Iori was his nephew and the adoption took place when he returned to the region of Banshu.

1625 (forty-one years old)

Meeting with Mikinosuke in Osaka.

1626 (forty-two years old)

In the course of the fifth month, Miyamoto Mikinosuke ended his life through *seppuku*, following his lord into death in accordance with tradition.

Miyamoto Iori entered the service of Lord Ogasawara of Akashi, probably in the course of this year.

Musashi again passed through Nagoya, where his attempt to become a vassal of the lord of Owari did not meet with success. This lord belonged to the family of the shogun and was one of its most powerful members. Musashi searched for a lord worthy of his level in strategy.

1633 (forty-nine years old)

Lord Hosokawa Tadatoshi left Kokura for the fief of Kumamoto. Lord Ogasawara Tadasane, coming from Akashi, succeeded him at Kokura. Iori, who was in the service of this lord with the rank of vassal, accompanied him.

According to certain documents, Musashi stayed at Izumo (Shimane), where he fought a duel with a vassal of the lord of Matsumoto castle, Matsudaira Naomasa, and then with this lord himself. The lord became his student.

Musashi remained for a time in this fief to teach. According to other documents, Lord Matsudaira established his residence in Izumo in 1638. If this is the case, the dates are in conflict.

1634 (fifty years old)

Musashi returned to Kyushu. He arrived at Kokura, where the lord was now Ogasawara Tadasane, to whom Musashi had taught the sword and the art of the *shuriken*.

Lord Ogasawara organized a duel for Musashi against a famous lance specialist, Takada Matabei. Musashi defeated him.

1637–1638 (fifty-three to fifty-four years old)

During the tenth month of 1637, the Christians of Shimabara (Kyushu) revolted against the regime, and the siege of Shimabara began. Musashi participated in the battles with Iori and directed Ogasawara's troops. Iori became the principal vassal of Lord Ogasawara. This was the sixth and final time Musashi participated in a battle.

A letter from Musashi to Lord Maruoka Yuzaemon dates to this year.

At this time, Nagaoka Sado, principal vassal of Lord Hosokawa, probably began applying to his lord to take on Musashi as a vassal.

1639 (fifty-five years old)

Nagaoka arrived in Kokura, charged with responsibility for the affairs of this fief. He visited Musashi, to whom he directly passed on an invitation from his lord that had already been indicated by letter. The time passed without a decision being made, and Hosokawa continued with his approaches to Musashi and also to Ogasawara.

1640 (fifty-six years old)

Musashi decided to go to Lord Hosokawa. At the end of the first month, he took up residence at Kumamoto.

Correspondence between Musashi and the representatives of Lord Hosokawa.

Lord Hosokawa Tadatoshi organized a duel for Musashi, meant as a means of training, against Ujii Magoshiro, principal martial arts master of this fief. Musashi was victorious.

1641 (*fifty-seven years old*)

In the course of the second month, Musashi wrote the *Hyoho sanju go kajo* for Lord Hosokawa Tadatoshi and practiced the arts: calligraphy, painting, tea ceremony.

During the third month, Hosokawa Tadatoshi died at the age of fifty-six. His eighteen vassals followed him into death (*junshi*).

Letter from Musashi recommending his third adoptive son, Hirao Yoemon, to one of the principal vassals of the Owari fief. Hirao Yoemon became Owari master of arms.

1642 (*fifty-eight years old*)

Musashi fell ill and suffered attacks of neuralgia.

1643 (*fifty-nine years old*)

Musashi departed for Mount Iwato, located near Kumamoto, where he began living in Reigando cave. He had a low table there, and on the tenth of the tenth month, he began to compose the *Gorin no sho*.

Letter from Musashi to Lord Hosokawa Mitsuhita, dated the eighth of the tenth month.

1645 (*sixty-one years old*)

Musashi lived at Reigando and composed the *Gorin no sho*, which he completed during the second month. Musashi sensed the approach of death. On the thirteenth of the fourth month, he wrote a letter of farewell to the three principal vassals of Hosokawa, Lords Shikibu, Kenmotsu, and Uemon, with whom he was particularly closely connected.

He dedicated his last work, the *Gorin no sho*, to his disciple Terao Magonojo, and gave the latter's younger brother, Terao Motomenosuke, his own copy of the *Hyoho sanju go kajo*.

On the twelfth of the fifth month, Musashi distributed his possessions among those close to him. During his final days, he wrote the twenty-one articles of the *Dokkodo*. He died on the nineteenth of the fifth month.

We do not know for sure whether Musashi died at his home or in Reigando cave. His hair was buried at Mount Iwato and his body, dressed in warrior's armor, was interred, in accordance with his wishes, near the main road, so that he would be able to greet the Hosokawa lords on their trips in the direction of Edo, where they periodically had to go to visit the shogun.

It was in a cave called Reigando (*rei*, "soul" or "spirit"; *gan*, "rock"; *do*, "cave") where Musashi, at the age of sixty, set himself up to write. He spent the last two years of his life there. This cave had long been considered a sacred place. It was in the most remote part of a group of lands belonging to Iwato-dera temple. It was deep in a mountainous setting, surrounded by rocks with vivid forms, between which water fell in cascades. Near the entrance to the cave, there were several statues of deities. It was an unfrequented spot, reserved for meditation.

Musashi indicated that he began writing the *Gorin no sho* in this place at four o'clock in the morning on the tenth day of the tenth month (of the twentieth year of the Kanei period [1643]).

Why did he choose this place and this moment to begin this work? To begin the main written work of his life in this manner says something about Musashi's art of swordsmanship. Beginning this work meant ending his life. And in fact, he died shortly after finishing it. To accomplish his endeavor in just the right way, he had to begin it in this place filled with the mysterious power of the mountain, before the break of day. He had to begin in a deep state of calm, by the light of a lamp, in the cool of the shadows. He welcomed the dawn by writing. This approach was indispensable for his act of writing to become one with the nature of the sacred beings. According to the beliefs of those days, morning is filled with positive yang energy, which is at the origin of creation; thus Musashi was not without reasons for choosing this hour. Through paying homage to heaven and bowing before Kannon and the Buddha, his act of writing became mingled with their presence. Through this it became a sacred act. But when he bowed to these sacred powers, it was not in the manner of a Christian bowing to an altar. In Japanese belief, the sacred takes on many forms that are accessible to human beings. By undertaking his writing in the way he did, Musashi entered the sacred world.

Before his death he wrote: "I respect the Buddha and the gods, but I do not rely on them." This sentence is found in a short text entitled "The Way to Be Followed Alone" (*Dokkodo*), which he wrote after the *Gorin no sho*. These two texts seem to have been written with the last of Musashi's life force, for it was only a week after having added to the end of his manuscript the name of his successor that Musashi died, on the nineteenth day of the fifth month of the second year of Shoho (1645).

Musashi bequeathed the *Gorin no sho* to one of his disciples, Terao Magonojo Katsunobu. Later this work would be copied by another of Musashi's disciples, who, on the fifth day of the second month of the seventh year of Kanbun (1667), gave this copy to his disciple, Yamamoto Gennosuke. It is through this copy that we know the work. The original of the *Gorin no sho*, written in Musashi's own hand, has never been found.

WRITINGS ON THE FIVE ELEMENTS (*Gorin no sho*)

Writings on the Five Elements
(*Gorin no sho*)

On problems of translation of the Gorin no sho *and on the meaning of some important terms, see appendix.*[1]

THE SCROLL OF EARTH

School of the Two Heavens United, Niten ichi ryu,[2] is the name that I give to the way of strategy.[3] In this text I am going to explain for the first time what I have been studying in depth for many years. At the beginning of the tenth month of the twentieth year of Kanei [1643], I came to Mount Iwato in the Higo[4] prefecture of Kyushu to write. I pay homage to heaven, I prostrate to the goddess Kannon, and I turn toward the Buddha. My name is Shinmen Musashi no kami, Fujiwara no Genshin,[5] and I am a warrior, born in the prefecture of Harima.[6] My life now adds up to sixty years.[7]

I have trained in the way of strategy since my youth, and at the age of thirteen I fought a duel for the first time. My opponent was called Arima Kihei, a sword adept of the Shinto ryu, and I defeated him. At the age of sixteen I defeated a powerful adept by the name of Akiyama, who came from the prefecture of Tajima.[8] At the age of twenty-one I went up to Kyoto and fought duels with several adepts of the sword from famous schools, but I never lost.

Then I traveled in several fiefs and regions in order to meet the adepts of different schools. I fought more than sixty times,[9] but not once was I beaten. All that happened between my thirteenth and my twenty-eighth or twenty-ninth year.

At the age of thirty I reflected, and I saw that although I had won, I had done so without having reached the ultimate level of strategy. Perhaps it was because my natural disposition prevented me from straying from universal principles; perhaps it was because my opponents lacked ability in strategy.

I continued to train and to seek from morning till night to attain to a deeper principle. When I reached the age of fifty, I naturally found myself on the way of strategy.

Since that day I have lived without having a need to search further for the way.[10] When I apply the principle of strategy to the ways of different arts and crafts, I no longer have need for a teacher in any domain. Thus, in composing this book, I do not borrow from the ancient Buddhist or Confucianist writings; I do not use ancient examples from the chronicles or the tradition of the military art.

I began writing on the tenth of the tenth month, at night, at the hour of the tiger,[11] with the aim of expressing the true idea of my school, letting my mind reflect in the mirror of the way of heaven and the way of Kannon.

Strategy is the practice that is necessary in warrior families.[12] A person who directs warfare must learn it, and soldiers must also be familiar with it. Nowadays those who know the way of strategy well are rare.

As far as the way is concerned, several of them exist. The law of Buddha is the way that saves people. The way of Confucianism is the way that leads to correctness in literature. Medicine is the way that cures illnesses. The poet teaches the way of poetry. There exist a number of ways in the arts—that of the man of taste,[13] that of the practitioner of archery, and those of other arts and crafts. Adepts train in these in their fashion, according to their manner of thinking, and are fond of them in accordance with their dispositions. But very few like the way of strategy.

First of all, warriors must familiarize themselves with what is known as "the two ways," literature and the martial arts. That is their way. Even if you are clumsy, you must persevere in strategy because of your position.

That which a warrior must always have in his mind is the way of death.

But the way of death is not reserved only for warriors. A monk, a woman, a peasant—any person—can resolve to die for the sake of a social obligation or honor. In the way of strategy that warriors practice, the aim of action must be to surpass others in all domains. A warrior has to win in combat against one or several opponents, bring fame to his lord's name and his own, and establish his position owing to the virtue of strategy. Some people perhaps think that even if they learn the way of strategy, it will not be useful in real practice. On this point, it is sufficient to train in it for it to be useful at all times and to teach it for it to be useful in all things. This is how the true way of strategy must be.

Concerning the Way of Strategy

From China to Japan, over a long time, a person who practices this way has been known as an adept of strategy. For a warrior, it is not possible not to study it.[14] Nowadays there are certain people to be found everywhere who declare themselves accomplished practitioners of strategy, but in general they practice only the sword. Recently the Shinto priests of Kantori and Kashima in the prefecture of Hitachi[15] have founded schools, saying that their art was transmitted to them by the gods, and they have propagated their art in various fiefs.

Among the ten talents and the seven arts that have long been known,[16] strategy is considered to be a pragmatic domain.[17] Since it is a pragmatic domain, it is not appropriate to limit it just to the technique of the sword. On the basis of the principles of the sword alone,[18] you will not be able to understand the sword well, and you will be far from being in accord with the principles of strategy.

There are people who make a profession out of selling the arts. They treat themselves as articles of merchandise and produce objects with a view to selling them. This attitude is tantamount to the act of separating the flower from the fruit. And it must be said that the fruit in this case does not amount to much. They adorn the way of strategy with flowery colors, lay out a display of techniques, and teach their way by creating first one dojo, then another. Someone who might want to learn such a way with the goal of making money should keep in mind the saying "Strategy, inadequately learned, is the cause of serious wounds."[19]

In general, four ways exist for traversing human life: those of the warrior, the peasant, the artisan, and the merchant.[20] The first is the way of the peasant. Peasants prepare various tools and are vigilant with regard to the changing of the seasons, year after year. That is the way of the peasant.

The second is the way of the merchant. A manufacturer of sake, for example, buys the necessary materials and makes profits that correspond to the quality of his product—this is the way he goes through life. All merchants pass through human life making more or less profit from their businesses. That is the way of business.

The third is the way of the warrior. Warriors must make various weapons and know the richness[21] of each weapon. That is the way of the warrior. Without learning how to handle weapons, without knowing the advantages of each of them, a warrior is lacking somewhat in education.

The fourth is the way of the artisan. A carpenter follows his way by skillfully making various tools and knowing well how to use them. He correctly lays out construction plans using black cords and a square.[22] He goes through life with his art without wasting a moment.

This is the way the four ways should be, those of the warrior, the peasant, the artisan, and the merchant.

I am going to speak of strategy by comparing it to the way of the carpenter. This comparison has to do with a house constructed by carpenters. We speak, for example, of a noble house, a warrior house,[23] or the Four Houses.[24] We also speak of the decline or continuation of a house; in the realm of art, we also speak of a house in the sense of a school or a style.[25] It is because the term *house* is used in these ways that I make the comparison with the way of the carpenter.

The word *daiku*, carpenter, is written *dai*, "fully," *ku*, "to be very clever at." In the same way, the way of strategy is built upon ingenuity of great fullness and scope. That is why I compare it to the way of the carpenter. If you want to learn strategy, you must contemplate these writings and train ceaselessly, the master and disciple together, so that the master is like the needle and the disciple is like the thread.

Comparison of the Way of Strategy
with the Way of the Carpenter

A general, like a master carpenter, should know the overall rules of the country and adjust the rules of his own province to fit with them, just as the way of the master carpenter consists in regulating the measurements of the house he is going to construct.

The master carpenter learns the structural pattern for building a tower or a temple and knows the construction plans for palaces and fortresses. He builds houses by making use of people. In this way the chief carpenter and the chief warrior resemble each other.[26]

In constructing a house, one must first choose wood that is suitable. For the front pillars, wood is chosen that is straight, without knots, and of good appearance. For the rear pillars, one chooses wood that is straight and sturdy, even if it has a few knots. It is appropriate to use woods that are less strong but of handsome appearance for the sills, the lintels, the sliding doors, and the shoji.[27]

The house will last for a long time even if knotted or twisted wood is used, on the condition that the strength needed for the different parts of the house is accurately assessed and the qualities of the wood used are carefully examined. It is appropriate to use somewhat weak, knotty, or twisted wood for scaffolding and then afterward for heating.

In using men, the master carpenter must know the qualities of the carpenters. In accordance with their high, medium, or low ability, he must assign them different tasks, such as construction of the *tokonoma*;[28] of the sliding doors and the shoji; or of the sills, lintels, and ceilings. It is appropriate to have support framing done by those with not much skill, and wedges made by the most unskillful. If one is able to discern the qualities of men in this manner, work progresses quickly and efficiently.

Being fast and efficient; being vigilant with regard to the surroundings;[29] knowing substance and its function;[30] knowing the high, medium, or low level of ambient energy;[31] knowing how to energize the situation; and knowing the limits of things: Above all, a master carpenter must possess all those. It is the same for the principle of strategy.

The Way of Strategy

Both a vassal and a soldier are similar to a carpenter.[32] The latter sharpens his tools, makes other tools, and carries them in his carpenter's box. Following the orders of the master, he accomplishes his work efficiently; his measurements will be exact for the smallest detail work as well as for the long external corridors.[33] Sometimes he roughs out the pillars and beams with his adze or planes the posts of the *tokonoma* and the shelves; sometimes he carves openwork in planks or sculpts wood. Such is the law of the carpenter. If he learns to practice the techniques of woodworking and also learns how to draw up plans, he can later become a master.

A carpenter must keep his tools well sharpened and always maintain them. Only a specialist in woodworking knows how to make a precious box for a statue of the Buddha, a bookshelf, a table, a stand for a lamp, all the way down to a chopping block or a lid. Either a vassal or a soldier is similar to a carpenter. They should ponder this well.

A carpenter must always keep his mind attentive to the following things: The wood must not lose its shape, the joints must hold, he must plane well but avoid oversmoothing, the wood must not warp later on.

If you study the way of strategy, it is necessary to examine attentively what I write here, down to the least detail.

I Write on Strategy in Five Scrolls

I write my work in five scrolls, the scrolls of Earth, Water, Fire, Wind, and Heaven, in order to show clearly the qualities of each of the five ways.[34]

In the Scroll of Earth, I present an overall vision of the way of strategy and the point of view of my school. It is difficult to arrive at the true way relying on the way of the sword alone. It is appropriate to understand details on the basis of a broad vision and to attain depth by beginning on the surface. It is necessary to plot a straight path through terrain that has been leveled. That is why I have given the name Earth to the first scroll.

The second is the Scroll of Water. You should learn what is essential regarding the state of the mind from the nature of water. Water follows the form of a square or round vessel. It is a drop and also an ocean. The color of its depths is pure green, and taking this purity as my inspiration, I present my school in the Scroll of Water.

If you succeed in clearly discerning the general principle[35] of the art of the sword and in this manner easily defeat one person, you can defeat any opponent. The mind is the same whether it is a matter of defeating one person or a thousand or ten thousand enemies.

The strategy of a general consists in applying on a large scale what he has studied on a small scale. This is the same thing as designing a large statue of the Buddha on the basis of a model[36] of thirty centimeters. It is difficult to explain it in detail, but the principle of strategy is to know ten thousand things from a single thing. It is in this way that I write about the content of my school in the Scroll of Water.

The third scroll is that of fire. In this scroll I write about war, for fire symbolizes a blazing mind, whether small or large. The way of war is the same if the situation is one against one or ten thousand against ten thousand. This should be examined well, making the mind now large, now small.

Seeing what is large is easy, seeing what is small is difficult. It is difficult to change strategy quickly when you are many, whereas a single person quickly changes his tactics in accordance with his state of mind; that is why for such a case it is difficult to foresee the minute details. This should be examined well.

That which I write about in the Scroll of Fire happens in a short time.[37] Therefore it is necessary to train in it and habituate oneself to it every day so that an immutable mind can become the ordinary thing. This is an essential point of strategy; it is in relation to this mind that I write about war and individual combat in the Scroll of Fire.

The fourth is the Scroll of Wind. What I write in this scroll is not about my own school but deals with the strategies of other present-day schools. We use the expressions the ancient wind and the modern wind, and also the wind of such and such a family.[38] I explain the strategies of the other schools and their techniques in the Scroll of Wind.

Without knowing others, one cannot really know oneself. In the practice of all the ways and in all manners of working with things, the danger exists of deviating from the true way.[39] Even if you practice the way daily and think you are on the right track, it is possible to deviate from the true way if your mind has turned away from it. You can recognize this if you know how to observe on the basis of the true way. If you are not progressing along the true way, a slight twist in the mind can become a major twist. This must be pondered well.

In other schools it is thought that just the way of the sword constitutes strategy, and not without reason. But what I understand by the principle and the techniques of strategy is quite different. I write about the other schools in the Scroll of Wind so as to acquaint you with their strategy.

The fifth is the Scroll of Heaven [or Emptiness].[40] With regard to that which I mean by heaven, how could one distinguish between the depth of it and its entrance,[41] since what we are talking about is emptiness? After having realized the principle of the way,[42] it becomes possible to move away from it—you will find yourself naturally free in the way of strategy and you will naturally reach a high level of ability.[43] You will naturally find the cadence that is appropriate to the moment, and the stroke will appear all by itself and strike home by itself. All of that is in the way of emptiness. I write in the Scroll of Heaven of the manner of entering naturally into the true way.

I Give My School the Name School of Two Swords

I describe my school in terms of two swords, since all warriors, from the vassal to the ordinary soldier, must wear two swords firmly at their sides.[44] Formerly, these two swords used to be called *tachi* and *katana;* today they are called *katana* and *wakizashi.* It goes without saying that all warriors wear these two swords[45] in their belts. Whether they know how to use them or not, in our country, carrying the two swords is the way of the warrior. It is in order to make the advantage of carrying the two swords understood that I describe my school in terms of the two swords. The lance and the *naginata*[46] are weapons to be used outside, on the field of battle.[47]

In my school a beginner learns the way by taking the large sword and the small sword in his hands at the same time.[48] This is essential. If you are going to die in battle, it is desirable to utilize all the weapons you are carrying. It is deplorable to die with weapons left in their scabbards without having been capable of using them.[49]

But if you have a sword in each hand, it is difficult to handle each of the two swords as you wish. That is why you have to learn to wield the large sword with just one hand. It is normal to wield a large weapon like the lance or the *naginata* with two hands, but the large sword and the small one are weapons to be utilized with just one hand.

Holding a large sword with two hands is a disadvantage when fighting on horseback, when fighting on the run, when fighting in marshy terrain, in a deep rice paddy, on stony ground, on a steep road, or when you are in the midst of a melee. When you are holding a bow,[50] a lance, or any other weapon in your left hand, you must hold the sword with the right hand.[51] That is why holding a sword with two hands is not appropriate in the true way. If you do not succeed in killing your enemy with just one hand, it is enough to use two hands at that point. It is not a very complicated matter.

It is in order to learn to handle the large sword easily with one hand that we learn to wield the two swords.[52] At the beginning everyone has difficulty handling the large sword with just one hand because of its weight. It is the same thing in any form of new beginning. For a beginner it is hard to draw a bow, and handling a *naginata* is also hard. Whatever the weapon, the important thing is to get used to it. In this way you may succeed in drawing a strong bow, and by exercising every day, you will achieve the ability to wield the sword easily by acquiring the strength that is fitting for the way.

The way of the sword is not a mere matter of the swiftness of the strike. I will explain this precisely in the second scroll, the Scroll of Water. The large sword is used in an open space and the small sword in a confined space—that is the starting point[53] of the way.

In my school one must win with a long weapon as well as a short one. That is why I do not fix the length of the sword. To be ready to win with all the weapons—that is the essence of my school. The advantage of using two swords instead of one becomes manifest when one is fighting alone against many adversaries and when one is fighting in a closed-in place. It is not necessary to write more about this now. It is necessary to know ten thousand things by knowing one well. If you are to practice the way of strategy, nothing must escape your eyes.[54] Reflect well on this.

Knowing the Meaning of the Two Ideograms *Hyo Ho*[55]

Customarily in this way, someone who knows how to handle a sword is called a man of strategy. In the way of the martial arts,[56] someone who knows how to shoot a bow is called an archer, someone who knows how to shoot a gun is called a gunner, someone who is skillful with the lance is called an expert with the lance, and someone who handles the *naginata* well is called an expert with the *naginata*. Thus someone who excels in the techniques of the sword should be called an expert with the long sword or an expert with the short sword. The bow, the gun, the lance, and the *naginata* are all weapons of the warrior; each one of them is part of the way of strategy. Nevertheless, strategy is usually used to designate the art of the sword. There is a reason for this.

It is through the virtue of the sword[57] that one rules a country and that one behaves in a fitting manner oneself. The sword is at the origin of strategy. By mastering the virtue of the sword, one person can defeat ten. If one can defeat ten, a hundred can defeat a thousand, and a thousand will defeat ten thousand. It is in this sense that in my school the principles are the same for one as for ten thousand, and what I mean by strategy includes the practices of all warriors.

We may speak of the way of the Confucians, of the Buddhists, of tea masters, of masters of etiquette, or of dancers, but these ways are distinct from the way of the warrior. Nonetheless, anyone who understands the way in great depth will find the same principle in all things. It is important for each person to persevere[58] in his own way.

Knowing the Advantage of Each Weapon in Strategy

If you know well the advantages of the different weapons, you can use any weapon appropriately[59] in accordance with the situation of the moment.

The small sword is advantageous in a confined place and when you get close to your opponent. The large sword is suited to nearly all situations and presents advantages in all of them. On the battlefield the usefulness of the *naginata* is slightly less than that of the lance, for if you compare the two, the lance allows one to take the initiative better.[60] If there are two practitioners of the same level and one has a lance and the other a *naginata*, the one with the lance will have a slight advantage. The effectiveness of the lance and the *naginata* depends on the situation of combat; they will not be very effective in a confined space nor when you are surrounded by enemies in a house.[61] They are weapons especially for the battlefield, indispensable in situations of war.

You can learn and develop the subtleties of technique indoors,[62] but they will not be appropriate if you forget the true way. The bow is appropriate[63] when you are moving troops forward or back in the strategy of battles. It makes possible rapid fire in parallel with the use of lances and other arms. It is therefore particularly useful on battlefields in open terrain. But its effectiveness is insufficient for attacking fortresses or for combating enemies who are farther than thirty-six meters away.[64]

At the present time, there are many flowers and little fruit in archery—this goes without saying, and goes for the other arts as well. If an art is nothing but that, it cannot be useful in a really important situation. The interest is great.[65]

From within a fortress, there is no weapon more effective than a gun. On the field of battle also, the interest of the gun is great before an encounter. Once, however, the encounter has begun, its effectiveness diminishes. One of the advantages of the bow is that the trajectory of the arrow is visible, and the deficiency of the gun is that the ball cannot be seen. It is appropriate to examine well this aspect of things.

As far as the horse is concerned, it must be strong, resilient, and without bad habits. Generally, as for all the weapons of war, you should choose horses that are large and good for marching. The swords, both the short and the long, should be large and sharp,[66] the lance and *naginata* large and well honed. You must have bows and guns that are powerful and are not easily ruined. You should not have a predilection for certain weapons. Putting too much emphasis on one weapon results in not having enough of the others. Weapons should be adapted to your personal qualities and be ones you can handle. It is useless to imitate others. For a general as for a soldier, it is negative to have marked preferences. You should examine this point well.

Cadences in Strategy

Cadence is inherent in all things, especially as far as strategy is concerned.[67] It is not possible to master cadence without thorough training.

In this world we can see that different cadences exist. The cadences of the way of the dance and of musicians with their stringed or wind instruments are all concordant and without distortion.[68] Going through the various ways of the martial arts, there are different cadences depending on whether you are shooting a bow, firing a gun, or riding a horse.

You must not go against cadence in any of the arts, nor in any handcraft. Cadence also exists for that which does not have a visible form.[69] Regarding the situation of a warrior in the service of a lord, according to the cadences he follows, he will rise or fall in the hierarchy, for there are cadences that are concordant and others that are discordant.

In the way of business, there are cadences for making a fortune and cadences for losing it. In each way, there exist different cadences. You must discern well the cadences in conformity with which things prosper and those in conformity with which things decline.

In strategy, different cadences exist. First it is necessary to know the concordant cadences and then to learn the discordant ones.[70] Among the large or small and slow or fast cadences, it is indispensable for strategy to discern striking cadences, interval cadences, and opposing cadences.[71] Your strategy cannot be sure if you do not succeed in mastering the opposing cadence.

At the time of strategic combat, you must know the cadences of each enemy and utilize cadences that they will not think of. You will win by unleashing the cadences of emptiness that are born from those of wisdom. In each scroll, I will write about cadence. Examine these writings and train well.

If you practice diligently, from morning till night, the way of strategy I teach, your mind will spontaneously broaden. I am transmitting to the world my strategy in its collective and individual dimensions. I am expounding it for the first time in writing in these five scrolls of Earth, Water, Fire, Wind, and Heaven.

Those who would like to learn my strategy should apply the following rules in order to practice the way:

1. Think of that which is not evil.[72]
2. Train in the way.
3. Take an interest in all the arts.
4. Know the way of all professions.
5. Know how to appreciate the advantages and disadvantages of each thing.
6. Learn to judge the quality of each thing.

7. Perceive and understand that which is not visible from the outside.
8. Be attentive even to minimal things.
9. Do not perform useless acts.

You must train in the way of strategy keeping these general principles in mind. Particularly in this way, if you do not know how to see the right things in broad perspective, you will not be able to become an accomplished practitioner of strategy. If you master this method,[73] you will not lose, even alone against twenty or thirty opponents. First of all, because you maintain your vital energy constantly in your strategy[74] and you practice the direct way, you will win through your techniques and also through your way of seeing. Since you have free mastery of your body[75] as a result of your training, you will win through your body; since your mind is accustomed to this way, you will also win through your mind. Once you reach this stage, how can you be defeated?

Regarding grand strategy, you must be victorious through the quality of the people you employ, victorious through the way in which you utilize a great number of people, victorious by behaving correctly yourself in accordance with the way, victorious by ruling your country, victorious in order to feed the people, victorious by applying the law of the world in the best way. Thus it is necessary to know how not to lose to anyone—in any of the ways—and to firmly establish your position and your honor. That is the way of strategy.

The twelfth of the fifth month of Year 2 of Shoho [1645]

SHINMEN MUSASHI

For the Honorable Lord Terao Magonojo

The fifth of the second month of Year 7 of Kanbun [1667][76]

TERAO YUMEYO KATSUNOBU

For the Honorable Lord Yamamoto Gensuke[77]

THE SCROLL OF WATER

The mind of strategy of my School of Two Swords takes water as its fundamental model.[78] Therefore I title this text the Scroll of Water, because the idea here is to practice a method of pragmatic effectiveness.[79] For this reason I elucidate the sword techniques of my school in this part of my writing. It is difficult, in writing, to explain this way in detail as I would like to do. Even where words are inadequate, you should understand the principle intuitively.[80] It is necessary for you to pause and reflect on each of the words and ideograms I have written in this text. If you read superficially, you run a great risk of deviating from the way.

Regarding the principle of strategy, even though I may describe [the situation] as though talking about individual combat, it is essential to understand this with broad vision—as the principle of a battle among tens of thousands of people. You are in danger of falling into a bad way if you wander and choose the wrong path, for the slightest error in judgment can have grave consequences, especially in this way. If you content yourself with reading what I write here, it will be impossible for you to reach a high level in the way of strategy. Read this text thinking that it is written for you;[81] do not think that you are just reading or learning written things. Instead of imitating what I write, make this text yours, like a principle that you have brought forth from your own thought. It is necessary to ponder well by putting yourself into the situation.

State of Mind in Strategy

In the way of strategy, one's state of mind[82] need not be distinct from the ordinary one. In daily life as well as in strategy, it is necessary to have an ample and broad mind and to carefully keep it very straight, not too tight and not at all loose. In order not to have your mind too much off to one side, it is necessary to place it in the center and move it calmly so that it does not cease to move even in moments of change.[83] All that has to be examined well.

Even at a calm time, the mind is not calm; even at a moment of great speed, the mind is not at all fast. The mind must not be carried along by the body, nor the body by the mind. The mind must be wary when the body remains unguarded. The mind must not be insufficient or even a little bit too much. When the surface of the mind is weak, its depth must be strong so that the opponent cannot perceive one's state of mind. Those who are small [either in size or in number] must know well those who are large [in size or number], and those who are large must know those who are small. The large as well as the small must keep their mind straight and not overestimate themselves.

It is necessary to keep the mind pure and broad, and wisdom will find its place within this breadth. The important thing is to polish wisdom and the mind in great detail. If you sharpen wisdom, you will understand what is just and unjust in society and also the good and the evil of this world; then you will come to know all kinds of arts and you will tread different ways. In this manner, no one in this world will succeed in deceiving you. It is after this stage that you will arrive at the wisdom of strategy. The wisdom of strategy is entirely distinct. Even right in the middle of a battle where everything is in rapid movement, it is necessary to attain the most profound principle of strategy, which assures you an immovable mind. You must examine this well.

Posture in Strategy

Regarding posture,[84] it is appropriate to keep the face neither lowered nor raised, nor leaning nor frowning; to keep the eyes unperturbed, the forehead without wrinkles but with creases between the brows; not to move the eyeballs and not to blink, though keeping the eyelids slightly lowered. In this way you shape a beautiful, luminous face, keeping the nose straight and the lower jaw slightly protruding.

Keep your neck straight, putting some force in the hollow of the nape; lower your shoulders, with the sensation that the torso from the shoulders down forms a unity; keep the back straight, do not stick out your buttocks, push your force downward from your knees to the tips of your toes. Advance the belly slightly forward so that the pelvis does not lose its stability; remember the adage "squeeze from one corner," which recommends pressing the scabbard of the small sword (*wakizashi*) firmly against the belly so that your belt does not loosen up.

In sum, it is necessary for you to have as your posture for strategy just the ordinary one, and it is essential that the posture of strategy be the ordinary one for you. This must be examined well.

The Way of Looking in Strategy

Your look must be broad and ample. Looking and seeing are two different things.[85] Look powerfully, see gently. It is necessary to look at what is distant as something that is close and what is close as something that is distant—this is essential for strategy. It is fundamental in strategy to know the sword of the adversary without ever looking at it. You must exercise well in this. Whether it is a matter of strategy on the individual scale or strategy on the large scale, the way of looking is the same. It is essential to look to both sides without moving your eyes.[86] But without preparation, you will not be able to achieve this way of looking at the time of combat. That is why you had better study well what I write here; you must accustom yourself to looking all the time in this way in order to be able to keep this way of looking in any situation. Examine this well.

The Way of Gripping the Sword

You should grip the sword holding the thumb and index finger as though they were floating, the middle finger neither tight nor slack, the ring and little fingers very tight. It is bad to have an empty space inside your hand. Hold the sword with the thought of slashing your opponent. When you slash your opponent, the posture of the hand remains the same, and your hands must not tense up. It is with the sense of just slightly moving your thumb and index finger that you beat back your opponent's sword, that you receive it, strike it, or exert pressure on it. In all these cases, you should grip the sword with the thought of slashing. Whether you are training at slashing an object or in the thick of combat, the way of holding the sword remains the same—it is held with the intent of slashing your opponent. In sum, it is not good to let the hand or the sword become fixed or frozen.[87] A fixed hand is a dead hand; a hand that does not become fixed is alive. It is necessary to master this well.

The Way of Moving the Feet

To move from one place to another, you slightly raise your toes and push off your foot from the heel, forcefully. According to the situation, you move your feet with a large or a small step, slowly or rapidly, but always in the manner of walking. There are three ways of moving it is necessary to avoid: jumping, moving with a floating step, stomping heavily.[88] The essential instruction related to moving from place to place is alternate movement of the two feet,[89] positive foot and negative foot. Which means you should not move just one foot. When you slash, when you back away, when you parry, you must always move the right and left feet alternately. You must never move only one foot. This should be examined with care.

The Five Guard Positions

The five guard positions are the high, middle, low, and those of the two sides, left and right. Five guards can be distinguished, but all of them have as their goal to slash the opponent. There is no guard position other than those five. Whatever guard position you assume, do not think of taking a position, instead think of being ready to strike.

The choice of a wide or narrow guard depends on your assessment of the situation. The high, middle, or low guard positions are the substantial positions, and the side positions, right and left, are circumstantial ones.[90] Thus, when you are fighting in a place of limited height where one of the two sides is obstructed, take the side guard position, either right or left. You choose between the right and left in accordance with the situation.

Do not forget this instruction: The middle-level guard position is fundamental. In fact, the middle-level position is the original guard.[91] Observe that as you broaden your strategy, you will understand that the middle-level guard position corresponds to the place of the general. Four other positions come after that of the general. You must examine this well.

The Pathway of the Sword (*Tachi no Michi*)

Here is what I call knowing the pathway (*michi*)[92] of the sword: When you handle the sword that you carry all the time, you can handle it freely even with only two fingers if you know well the pathway (*michi*) of the sword. If you are preoccupied about moving the sword fast, the pathway of the sword will be troubled and that will cause you difficulties. It is enough to move the sword appropriately and calmly. If you attempt to move the sword fast like a fan or a small knife, you will have difficulties, because you are straying then from the nature (*michi*) of the sword. You cannot slash a man by thrashing about with your sword as though you were chopping something with a knife. If you strike downward from above, you raise the sword up again, following a pathway that naturally reflects the reaction of the force. Likewise, if you strike horizontally, afterward you bring the sword back along the horizontal following a suitable pathway. In all cases, you must move the sword broadly and powerfully, amply extending your arms.[93] That is the way (*michi*) of the sword.

If you master the five formulas of technique of my school, you will strike well, because the path (*michi*) of your sword will be well stabilized.[94] It is necessary to train well.

The Series of Five Technical Forms[95]

First Technical Form

Take the middle guard position and point your two swords at your opponent's face—confront your opponent in this manner. When he launches an attack, deflect his sword to your right and, pressing on it, make your attack with the point of your sword.[96] If your opponent attacks you again, strike him from above downward, turning the point of your sword one quarter of a circle, and leave your sword in the position it has reached. If your opponent attacks once again, cut his arm starting with your sword in this low position.[97] All of this constitutes the first form.[98]

It is not possible to understand the five forms just by reading; it is necessary to assimilate them by practicing them with your swords in hand. By making a thorough study of these five forms of the sword, you will understand the way of your own sword, and consequently you will be able to face all kinds of attacks on the part of your opponents. Know that there are no other forms apart from these five in the School of the Two Swords. It is necessary to train in this.

Second Technical Form

In the second form, you hold the two swords high and strike with a single blow at the moment your adversary launches his attack. If your blow is deflected, leave your sword in the position it has reached and strike from below upward at the moment your opponent launches another attack. Do the same if this situation repeats.[99]

This form includes different ways of directing your mind and various cadences. If you exercise in the techniques of my school, striking according to this form, you will be able to attain precise mastery of the five principles (*michi*) of the sword and you will obtain the ability to win, no matter what your way of doing it is. It is necessary to train in this well.

Third Technical Form

In the guard position of the third form, you hold the sword with the point down, as though it were hanging, and you strike the wrist of the adversary from below at the moment he attacks. If the adversary parries and tries to force your sword down by striking it, you turn your sword aside with a passing cadence[100] and cut his upper arm horizontally. The essence of this formula is to win with a single blow starting from the low guard position the instant your opponent launches his attack. In training in the way, you will encounter this low guard position, which is used when combat is fast as well as when it is slow. You must exercise in it with your swords in hand.[101]

Fourth Technical Form

In the guard position of the fourth form, you hold the two swords horizontally on your left side and strike the wrist of your opponent with an upward motion[102] at the moment he launches his attack. If he attempts to knock down your upward-moving sword, you follow your intention of striking his wrist in accordance with the way of the sword,[103] and you extend the stroke obliquely up to the height of your own shoulder.[104] This technique conforms to the way of the sword. If your adversary launches another attack, you will defeat him in the same manner in accordance with the way of the sword. You must examine this well.[105]

Fifth Technical Form

The fifth form has to do with a guard position where you hold the swords in the right-side guard position, horizontally. Relating to the opponent's attack, starting from this position low and to the side, you strike diagonally upward and then slash directly downward from above. This form is also important for knowing the way of the sword well. If you train in handling the swords in accordance with this form, you will reach the point of being able to move the heavy swords easily.[106]

Giving more details regarding these five forms is not necessary. Above all, it is through continuously applying the techniques of these five forms in their full depth[107] that you will learn the whole of the way of the sword of my school, master the general cadences, and perceive the qualities of the sword of your opponents. At the time of combat against opponents, you will thoroughly and fully apply these sword techniques, and you will win, in whatever way, by employing various cadences in response to the intentions of your opponent. You must learn well how to see with discernment.[108]

The Teaching of the Guard without a Guard[109]

Here is what is called the guard without a guard—this is not having in your mind the idea of adopting a guard position. Nevertheless, the five positions that I have mentioned can become guard positions. You will find yourself placing your sword in a variety of positions depending on the openings furnished by your opponent[110] and depending on the place and the situation of combat—but no matter what the situation, you must always hold the sword in such a way you that can slash well at your opponent.

You hold your sword in the high position, and if in accordance with the moment you lower it a little, your guard will become that of the middle level, and then if it becomes advantageous to raise it a little, your guard will again become the high one. In the same way, if in responding to the occasion you slightly raise your sword from the low position, that will become the middle-level guard. If you hold the sword to the right or the left, and in response to situations you move it inward, you will pass into the middle or low guard. It is in this sense that I recommend the guard without a guard. Whatever the situation is, you hold the sword so that you can slash your opponent.

You parry your opponent's sword, which is coming to strike you; you touch, press against, or graze it—all that becomes the occasion for you to strike him.[111] You should keep that clearly in mind. If you think of parrying, if you think of striking, if you think of touching, of pressing, of grazing, you run the risk of your slashing action being inadequate. The essential is to think that anything you are doing has to become the occasion for slashing. You must examine this well.

As for group strategy, the placement of troops corresponds to the guard position, and what is necessary is to aim at creating an opportunity to win. Letting a situation fixate[112] is bad. You should work this out well.

A Single Cadence for Striking Your Adversary[113]

Here is what I call the single-cadence strike: You are near your opponent, at a distance apart at which you can just reach each other, and you strike very rapidly and directly without moving your body,[114] not letting your will to attack become attached anywhere, seizing the instant when he does not expect it. You strike him with a single blow just at the instant when he is not even thinking of pulling back his sword or moving it out of the guard position or attacking. After having learned this cadence well, you must train in striking rapidly with the interval cadence.[115]

The Passing Cadence in Two Phases

Here is the passing cadence in two phases:[116] You are just about to attack and your opponent backs away or parries quickly. You feint striking him and then actually strike him at the moment when he relaxes after having started a parrying movement or after having backed up. That is the passing cadence in two phases. It is difficult to master this strike just from reading this text, but you will understand it immediately when it is taught to you directly.

The Strike of Nonthought[117]

In a situation where both you and your adversary are just about to launch an attack, make your body into a body that is striking, make your mind into a mind that is striking. Then your hand will strike spontaneously out of emptiness, with speed and power, without taking note of the starting point of the movement. This is the strike of nonthought. It is of prime importance. You will often encounter this kind of strike. You must study it and train in it well.

The Flowing-Water Strike

Here is what I call the flowing-water strike:[118] You are fighting an equal battle with your opponent and each of you is searching for an opening. In this situation, when your opponent tries in haste to back off or to disengage his sword or to push yours back, you expand your body and your mind. You strike broadly and powerfully by moving your body forward first and then your sword, with a movement that is apparently quite slow, like flowing water that seems to be stagnating.[119] By mastering this technique, you will gain ease and confidence. It is indispensable here to discern the level of your opponent.[120]

The Chance-Opening Blow[121]

When you strike, your opponent tries to parry by blocking or hitting your sword. You put yourself fully and completely into the action of striking with your sword and you strike whatever you encounter in your path, whether it is the head, the arms, or the legs [of your opponent]. Strike in this way, following the single way of the sword—this is the chance-opening strike.[122] If you learn this approach well, you will find an application for it at all times. You must minutely discern the details in the course of training bouts.

The Blow Like a Spark from a Stone[123]

In a situation in which your sword and your opponent's are about to cross, strike extremely hard without raising your sword at all. That is the blow like a spark from a stone. To execute this technique, you must strike quickly with the three combined forces of your legs, your body, and your hands.[124] This blow is difficult to execute if you do not exercise in it frequently. With diligent training you will be able to increase the force of its impact.

The Crimson-Leaves Strike[125]

You cause your adversary's sword to drop by striking it, then you immediately bring yourself back to a readiness to strike. That's what I call the crimson-leaves strike. When the opponent assumes a guard position facing you, at the moment he is thinking of striking, hitting, or parrying, you strike his sword either with the strike of nonthought or with the strike like a spark from a stone. You strike with force, and if you extend the force of your strike[126] by executing it so that the point of your sword is directed toward the ground, your opponent's sword will definitely drop. By training assiduously, you will arrive at being able to make your opponent's sword fall with ease. You must train well.

The Body Replacing the Sword

Instead of "the body replacing the sword,"[127] I could as well say "the sword replacing the body." In general, when you strike, the movements of body and sword are not simultaneous. Taking advantage of the opportunities created by your opponent's strikes, first you put your body in striking position, and your sword will strike without taking your body into account. It can also happen that you strike solely with the movement of the sword without moving your body, but generally first you put your body in a striking position, and the sword will strike afterward. As you learn the strikes, you must examine this well.

The Strike and the Hit

A strike and a hit[128] are two different things. Striking is striking consciously, deliberately, whatever the manner of the strike. The hit is like a chance encounter, and even if it is strong enough so that your opponent dies from it at once, it is a hit. Whereas a strike is carried out with awareness. This must be examined. A hit might get to the adversary's arm or leg, but this hit must be followed by a potent strike. A hit means having the sensation of touching [by chance]. As you learn this, the difference becomes obvious. Work this out well.

The Autumn Monkey's Body

The autumn monkey's body[129] expresses a combat posture in which you do not use your hands. In getting in close to your opponent, do not think of using your hands. Think of quickly getting your body in close[130] before striking your opponent. If you think of reaching out with your hands, your body will inevitably remain distant.[131] That is why you must think of getting your whole body in close quickly. When you are at a distance[132] at which you exchange sword blows, it is easy to get in close to your opponent.[133] You must examine this well.

The Body of Lacquer and Paste[134]

By speaking of lacquer and paste, I teach getting very close to your opponent and staying stuck to him. When you get in very close to your adversary, behave as though you were strongly glued to him with your head, your body, and your feet. In general, fighters have a tendency to put their heads and feet forward, but the body often hangs back. You must try to paste your body against your opponent's without leaving any place where your bodies are not touching. You must examine this well.

Comparing Heights

Here is what I call comparing heights:[135] When you get in close to your opponent, whatever the circumstances, penetrate forcefully and avoid shrinking; as though you were comparing heights, stretch the limbs, the pelvis, and also the neck. Set your face over against that of your adversary and enlarge yourself, as though to defeat him in a comparison of heights. It is important to move forward forcefully with this attitude. Work this out well.

Making Your Movements Stick[136]

In a situation where you and your opponent are both striking with your swords, when your opponent parries your attack, you stick your sword to his and get in close to him while maintaining this sticky quality. This stickiness should produce the sensation that your swords are difficult to separate, and you must get in close without having too much of a feeling of forcing. When you stick your sword to your opponent's and maintain this adhesion, it is possible for you to get in close to him with complete confidence.

There is a difference between sticking and getting tangled up. Sticking is powerful, getting tangled up is weak. These should be distinguished.

Banging into Your Opponent[137]

At the moment of coming in close to your opponent, you bang into him. You tilt your face slightly to the side, stick out your left shoulder,[138] and bang into his chest. In banging into him, you fill your entire body with force, and you strike with a cadence of concordance with the breath[139] and with a sensation of rebounding. By mastering this technique, you can strike so violently that your opponent will be knocked back a distance of two or three *ken*.[140] Your impact can be such that your opponent dies of it. You should train well.

The Three Parries

Here are what I call the three parries:[141] When you come in close to your opponent, if he strikes at you, you parry his sword with a movement as of stabbing[142] his eye with your large sword, thus deflecting his sword over your right shoulder.

Here is what I call the stabbing parry: You parry the sword of your adversary, who is attacking you, as though you were going to stab his right eye, with the sensation that you are going to slit his throat with the continuation of this movement.

Finally, at the moment when your opponent attacks, you parry with your short sword as you come in close to him, doing this as though you were going to punch him in the face with your left fist and without giving any thought to the length of the blade of the sword you are holding. For this third parry,[143] you should think that you are delivering a punch with your left hand.[144]

You should train in these well.

Piercing the Face

Here is what I call piercing the face:[145] In the course of combat, the two combatants are face-to-face, separated by a certain distance, each holding his
sword pointing toward his opponent. At this time it is essential to think constantly of piercing the face of your opponent with the point of your sword.
By applying your mind to piercing the face of your opponent in this way, his
face and body will be pushed back.[146] After having repulsed the adversary in
this manner, different opportunities to defeat him will present themselves.
You must work this out well. During the combat, if you succeed in pushing
back the body of your opponent, you will already have won. That is why you
must never forget what I call piercing the face. You must acquire this approach in the course of your training in strategy.

Piercing the Heart

Here is what I call piercing the heart:[147] When the place of combat is tight with
regard to height and breadth and you have difficulty in executing slashing
movements, stab your opponent. Elude his strike with the sensation of directly showing him the back of your sword,[148] then bring the point of your
sword back into a straight line and from this position stab him in the chest.[149]
You should apply this technique when you are tired or when your sword is
not cutting well anymore. You must understand this well.

Katsu-totsu

Here is what I call katsu-totsu:[150] When you attack, driving your opponent
back, or when he tries to riposte in response to your attack, you lift your
sword from below upward as though to stab him, then you reverse this
movement—lowering your sword—in order to strike him. In all cases, you
strike with a rapid cadence, katsu-totsu—that is, you raise your sword upward
in order to stab, katsu, and then you strike, totsu. In the course of combat, you
will very often encounter this cadence. You execute katsu-totsu by first raising
the point of your sword as though to stab your opponent and then lowering

it immediately in order to strike him. You must train well in this cadence and examine it.

The Parry with the Flat of the Sword

Here is what I call the parry with the flat of the sword:[151] In the course of combat, when the exchanges of attacks and defenses between adversaries become stagnant and repetitive in a cadence of *totan-totan*,[152] you parry an attack with a slap of your sword, which you apply to the sword of your opponent side against side, and afterward you strike. Do not slap too hard and do not think about parrying. The proper way to react to your opponent's attack is to slap his sword and strike him immediately as an extension of the same effort. You must take the initiative through the movement of slapping your opponent's sword and take the initiative through the strike. If you slap his sword with the right cadence, with the sensation of stretching your arm slightly,[153] even if your opponent's strike is very strong, the point of your sword will not be knocked down. You must study this well and examine it.

Conduct against Many Adversaries

What I call "conduct against many adversaries"[154] applies when you are fighting alone against many adversaries. Draw both your large and small swords and take up a guard position with them held wide apart, as though you were tossing them horizontally to both sides of you. Even if your opponents come at you from four sides, you will fight them by driving them back in a single direction. Distinguish clearly in the conduct of your opponents the order in which they are launching their attacks; you face first those who come at you first. Look all around, strike at the same time in opposite directions with the right sword and the left sword in response to the tactics of your adversaries. It is bad to wait after having struck. Immediately resume your guard position on the two sides, and as soon as someone advances, strike him forcibly and in this way shake your opponents. Extending this momentum, assault those who advance each time with the intention of making them crumble. Continually make every effort to push your opponents back so they will be forced into one rank, one behind the other, like fish strung on a line. As soon as your opponents pile up one behind the other, sweep them away by slashing with force, without letting this moment escape. It is not very effective to continue to beat back opponents who form into a compact group. It is also ineffective to face off with adversaries each time they approach you, because you then place yourself in a situation of waiting. Perceive the cadences of your adversaries, recognize the moment in which they will crumble, and you will be victorious.

Train from time to time with many partners and exercise in the way of driving them back. If you grasp this nuance, you will be as at ease fighting against ten or twenty opponents as against a single one. You must train well, then examine.

The Principle of Combat

In strategy it is by the principle of combat[155] that you will know victory with the sword. I do not have to write about the details. The important thing is to train well and learn how to win. This has to do with sword techniques that express the true way of strategy. The rest must be transmitted orally.[156]

The Single Strike

Gain the capacity to win with certainty by keeping in your mind the single strike.[157] It is impossible to acquire this strike without studying strategy thoroughly. It is by training in this strike that you will achieve a free mastery of strategy. This is the way of victory at will in any combat. You must exercise well.

Direct Communication

The mind of transmission of direct communication[158]—that is what I will transmit to he who has received the true way of my School of Two Swords. It is essential to train well so that your body becomes strategy. The rest will be communicated orally.

I have written above in this scroll the general teaching of my school of the sword.

In strategy, to know how to win with the sword, it is necessary first to learn the five forms of striking in conjunction with the five guard positions. Mastering by this means the pathway *(michi)* of the sword, the body will be free and the mind will come alive to grasp the cadences of the way *(michi)*. Your sword and your technique will be naturally remarkable, since your body will be available from head to toe to move with free mastery. It is in this way that you will be victorious first over one, then over two, and that you will finally be able to understand what is good and what is bad in strategy. Train by following one by one the instructions I have written down in this text, and you will progressively obtain the principle of the way *(michi)* by practicing combat with different opponents. Never fail to have this attitude of mind, go forward without hurry, learn the essence of things through frequent experiences, taking advantage of every occasion. Fight against all kinds of people and be aware of their mind. Follow a road that is a thousand leagues long one step at a time. Be without haste and be convinced that all these practices are the duty of a *bushi*. Be victorious today over what you were yesterday; tomorrow be victorious over your clumsiness and then also over your skill. Practice in accordance with what I have written without letting your mind deviate from the way.

Even if you gain victory over the most formidable of adversaries, unless it is in conformity with the principle, this victory cannot be considered part of the true way *(michi)*.[159] By assimilating this principle, you will become able to conquer several tens of adversaries. Then, through the wisdom of the art of the sword, you will be able to master individual strategy and group strategy.

A thousand days of training to develop, ten thousand days of training to polish. You must examine all this well.

The twelfth of the fifth month of the second year Shoho [1645]
SHINMEN MUSASHI
For the Honorable Lord Terao Magonojo

The fifth of the second month of the seventh year of Kanbun [1667]
TERAO YUMEYO KATSUNOBU
For the Honorable Lord Yamamoto Gensuke

THE SCROLL OF FIRE

I write about battle and combat in this scroll of fire,[160] for it is through the image of fire that I think of battle in the strategy of the School of Two Swords.

In this world, people are alike in having too limited a conception of strategy. Often strategy is thought of in a small way. Some seek trivial advantages by using the ends of their fingers and an area of the wrist of five or three *sun* in length.[161] They know how to be victorious in combat through movements of the forearm that they teach with a fan. Others teach the advantages of slight increases in speed with a *shinai*[162] through developing techniques of the arms and legs, and they attribute the greatest significance to any increase in speed, as slight as it might be.

I have engaged in combat many times in accordance with my strategy, at the risk of my life. I have discerned the principle that makes it possible to situate oneself between life and death, and I have learned the way of the sword. I have also learned to recognize the strength and weakness of the adversary's sword, and I have understood the meaning of the edge and the back of the sword.[163] In training to strike your adversary a mortal blow, you cannot even think of small and feeble techniques. Especially if you are seeking to gain advantage in combat where armor is worn,[164] you cannot even think about small techniques.

The way of my strategy, again, is to know with certainty the principle (*michi*)[165] that makes it possible to be victorious alone against five or against ten opponents when your life is at risk. Where, then, is the difference in the principle of the way[166] between "winning one against ten" and "winning a thousand against ten thousand"? That must be examined well.

However, in ordinary training it is impossible to exercise in the way with a thousand or ten thousand people. That is why, in single combat, you probe the tactics of each of your opponents, you try to be aware of the strength and weakness of their techniques; in this way you will understand how to win against any person,[167] thanks to the wisdom of strategy. In this fashion you will become an accomplished practitioner of this way.

Thinking, "Who besides me in the world is going to attain direct communication[168] in strategy?" and also "I will surely achieve this one day," train from morning till night. When in this manner you have finished polishing, you will spontaneously acquire freedom and excellent ability, and in this way you will be able to gain access to supernatural power.[169] This is the vital essence[170] of the practice of the method of the art of war.

Regarding the Place of Combat[171]

Regarding the evaluation of the place, a first teaching is to situate yourself with your back to the sun; assume a guard position with the sun behind your back. Depending on the situation, if it is impossible to place yourself with your back to the sun, you should place yourself with the sun on your right.

The same goes for light when you are fighting in a house. Place yourself with the light behind you, and if not, on your right. It is preferable to place yourself without having your back right up against the wall, leaving some space on the left side and not leaving any space on the right side.[172]

At night, if your opponents are visible, you should also situate yourself with your back to the light or with the light on your right, keeping present in your mind your guard position as in the previous situations.

You should try to situate yourself on higher ground, however slightly; this is what is called "looking at your opponents from above." If you are in a house, consider the rear of it as the high place.[173]

In the course of combat, you should try to direct your opponents toward your left side and drive them back in such a way that they have their backs to the difficult place. In any case, it is important to drive your opponents toward a difficult place. Drive them back without relenting, so that they will not have a chance to turn their heads to recognize the difficulty of the place. When fighting in a house, drive them back in the same way without allowing them to turn their heads so that they cannot recognize that they are getting close to the threshold, the lintel, the sliding door, the porch, or a pillar.

In all cases, you should force them in the direction where the terrain is bad, where there are obstacles. Taking the advantages and disadvantages of the location clearly into account, you must try to win first through your grasp of the site. You should examine this all well and train.

The Three Ways of Taking the Initiative (Sen)

In combat there are three ways of taking the initiative (sen).[174]

The first consists in attacking before your opponent. I call this "attacking before your opponent" (ken no sen).[175]

The second consists in taking the initiative when your opponent attacks first. I call it "taking initiative at the time of an attack" (tai no sen).

The third consists in taking the initiative when the two adversaries are getting ready to attack each other. I call it "the initiative at the time of a reciprocal attack" (tai-tai no sen).

These are the three ways of taking the initiative.

Whatever the form of combat, there does not exist any other way of taking the initiative once the fighting has started apart from these three. Taking the initiative is essential for strategy, since it is through this that a quick win in combat will be determined. There are details to be mastered in relation to taking the initiative, but it is pointless to describe them, because it is a matter of winning through the wisdom of your own strategy by discerning the intentions of your opponent and choosing the way of taking the initiative that is appropriate to each moment.

First, attack before your opponent does (ken no sen). When you want to attack, you remain calm at the beginning, then you take the initiative of attacking all of a sudden. Take the initiative with a state of mind that remains calm in its depth while being strong and fast on the surface. Maintain a mental disposition that is very strong, move your feet somewhat more quickly than usual, and as soon as you near your opponent, take the initiative by acting very fast.[176] All through the combat, preserve an untroubled mind[177] with the sole idea of crushing your opponent; in this way you will gain a victory with a mind that is strong to its depth. All these examples are ways of taking the initiative by attacking before your opponent does.

Second, taking the initiative at the time of an attack (tai no sen).[178] When your opponent attacks you, pretend to be weak and remain without a reaction. At the moment when he approaches, make a broad and vigorous move back, then, with a leap, feint an attack, and the instant he relaxes, strike him, straight on and with force. Take the initiative to win in this way. When the adversary attacks you, oppose him with the greatest vigor—he will modify the *hyoshi* of his attack; take control of him in this moment of change and defeat him. Such is the principle of taking the initiative at the time of an attack.

Third, taking the initiative at the time of a reciprocal attack *(tai-tai no sen).*[179] When your opponent attacks fast, face him calmly and powerfully. Then at the moment he gets near you, pretend suddenly to abandon your riposte. From this, the instant your opponent relaxes in anticipation of an illusory victory, you gain the victory by striking directly. Against an opponent who attacks you calmly, attack in a lively manner, rather quickly—approach him and exchange a series of sword blows. Following his reactions, you will defeat him with strength. These are two ways of taking the initiative at the time of a reciprocal attack *(tai-tai no sen).*

It is not possible to give the details in writing. You must find out for yourself along with reading this text. You will be able to execute these three ways of taking the initiative by adapting to the evolution of the situation and applying the principles. Although you may not necessarily be able to attack first, it is preferable to try to force your opponent to move through your initiative. In any case, in order to be able to take the initiative, train your mind well to strive toward a flawless victory by employing the wisdom of strategy.[180]

Holding Down on the Headrest

What I want to express by "holding down on the headrest"[181] is a way of conducting yourself in combat in which you do not allow your opponent to raise his head. In the combat of strategy, it is harmful to allow yourself to be led by your opponent and to place yourself on the defensive. It is necessary at all costs to work to lead your opponent in accordance with your will. However, if you are thinking that, your opponent is thinking that also. It is therefore impossible to lead him in a way that is favorable for you unless you are able to foresee his actions. You block a strike, you parry the sword that is coming to stab you, or you get loose when your opponent is holding you—you are then behind your opponent in strategy.

What I mean to say by "holding down on the headrest" is different. If you are fighting as one having arrived at the true way (*michi*), you can perceive the will of your opponent before he makes a move.[182] If he intends to strike, you grasp the first letters of strike—*stri*—and you do not allow him to complete his striking movement. That is the sense of "holding down on the headrest." For example, when your opponent means to attack, you grasp the letters *att* in *attack,* when he means to jump, you take hold of the *ju* in *jump,* when he means to slash, you seize the *sla* in *slash.* All these have the same sense. In the course of combat, you allow him to do useless things while preventing him from doing anything effective. This is essential in strategy.

However, working to prevent each movement your opponent tries to make is following his initiative. The essential is for you to exercise in all the techniques following the way correctly, and in this manner you will come to the point where you can foresee the will of your opponent and prevent him from actualizing it by rendering all of his movements ineffective. Dominating your opponent in this manner proves that you are a true adept who has spent long years in training. You should examine well what I mean by holding down on the headrest.

Getting Over a Critical Passage

Here is what I call "getting over a critical passage."[183] I will take the example of navigation at sea. In certain straits the currents are fast, and a distance of forty or fifty leagues constitutes a critical passage. Also in traversing life,[184] a person encounters numerous critical passages.

In navigating at sea, it is necessary to know the dangerous places, the position of the ship, and the weather. Without having a pilot ship, it is necessary to know how to adapt to each situation. The wind might blow from the side or from behind or even change. You must have the determination to row for a distance of two or three leagues in order to reach port. That is the way you can get over a critical passage in a ship at sea. This way of being also applies to traversing life. You must get over a critical passage with the idea that this event is unique.[185]

It is important during a combat of strategy, also, to get over critical passages. You get over them by precisely evaluating the strength of your opponent and your own capacity. The principle of this is the same as for a good captain who is navigating a passage at sea. Once the critical place has been passed, the mind becomes calm. If you get past the critical point, your opponent will come out of it weakened, and you will begin to take the initiative. You have then practically already won. In group strategy and in individual strategy, it is essential to be determined to get over the critical passage. You should examine this well.

Realizing the Situation

Here is what I call "realizing the situation."[186] In group strategy it is necessary to recognize the moments when your opponents are at a high point and when they are at a low point, to know their numbers and their intentions, to take into account the conditions of the place, and to discern their situation clearly. You must be able to deduce from these things a way to direct your forces applying the principle of strategy, which will lead with certainty to victory, and to fight knowing how to take the initiative.

In individual strategy, you must have knowledge concerning your opponent's school,[187] discern his personality, and find his strength and his weakness. Use tactics that thwart his intentions,[188] and it is important to seize the initiative of attack by perceiving the rises and falls of your opponent's combativeness and by knowing well the cadences of his intervals. If the strength of your wisdom is sufficient, you can always perceive what the situation is. If your body moves freely in the realm of strategy, if you accurately probe the mind of your adversary, you will find many ways of winning. You must work this out.

Crushing the Sword with Your Foot

"Crushing the sword with your foot"[189] is an expression that is unique to strategy.

In group strategy the adversaries first shoot with bows and guns or attack in some other way. If you make your assault after their bow and gun volleys, it is difficult to succeed in penetrating by force, because they have time to draw their bows again and to refill their guns with powder. That is why it is necessary to make a rapid assault while your adversaries are shooting their bows or firing their guns. As soon as the enemy acts, break their actions by reacting in accordance with principle. Thus you will obtain victory.

In individual strategy, if you strike by responding after each of your opponent's attacks, the combat will stagnate and become a repetition of the same cadences.[190] If you think of crushing your opponent's sword under your foot, you will vanquish him the instant of his first attack so as to take away his chance of acting a second time.

You do not crush only with your foot; you must also know how to crush with your body, with your mind, and also, of course, with your sword[191] in order to interdict any second move by your adversary. It is in this way that you can take the initiative (sen) in each situation. You act at the same time as your opponent not in such a way as to collide with him but so as to pursue him after the encounter.[192] You must examine this well.

Recognizing the Instant of Collapse[193]

For each thing there exists an instant in which it collapses. A house, a person, an adversary, collapses over the course of time following discordances in cadence.[194]

In group strategy, once you have grasped the cadence of collapse of your adversaries, it is essential to place them under attack without leaving them a single instant's interval. If you let them have a breather when they are about to collapse, you will give them a chance to recoup their forces.

In individual strategy, it may happen that during the combat your opponent begins to collapse as a result of a discordance in cadence. But if you slack off at this moment, you will give him an opportunity to reestablish himself, and you will lose a chance to defeat him. At the moment your opponent fails to collapse, persist in pushing him back by means of firm attacks so that he has no further chance of raising his head. Drive him back with a direct and powerful mind and strike him in a way that makes the blow carry a long way, so that he will not be able to recover. You must understand well this strike that causes the blow to carry a long way.[195] If you do not put some distance between you and your opponent, this strike is difficult to execute.[196] This must be worked out.

Becoming Your Opponent

Here is what I call "becoming your opponent."[197] This is the thinking you do when you put yourself in his place. In life there exists a tendency to overestimate the power of the adversary. Take for example a robber who, not having succeeded in fleeing, locks himself up in a house. If you put yourself in his place, surrounded, with all society as his enemy, you are desperately upset. Someone who locks himself up this way is a pheasant, and the person coming in to kill him is a falcon. You should think all that over well.

In group strategy, there also exists a tendency to overestimate the strength of your adversaries and to assume too prudent an attitude. You do not have to be afraid if you have a sufficient number of soldiers, if you know the principle of strategy, and if you know how to create an opportunity to win.

In individual strategy also, you must think on the basis of putting yourself in your opponent's place. Having to face an adept of *hyoho* who has perfectly mastered the principle and the techniques, he will consider himself to have lost in advance. You should examine this well.

Undoing Four Hands

Here is what I call "undoing four hands."[198] If you and your opponent are both doing the same thing, pushing one another back, the combat will not unfold to your advantage. As soon as you feel that you are being drawn into restraining your opponent by making an effort similar to his, drop what you are doing and seek to win by another means.

In group strategy, if you fight with the approach of the fight of four hands, you will not be able to come to a favorable result, and you will lose troops. It is important to drop this approach quickly and to win through means that your adversaries have not thought of.

In individual strategy, as soon as you feel that you are fighting in the manner of four hands, change your attitude. You must win by employing a radically different means, recognizing clearly the state of your opponent. You must understand this well.

Moving Your Shadow

Here is what I call "moving your shadow."[199] This is to be applied when you are unable to discern what is in the mind of your opponent.

In group strategy, when the state of your adversaries is unfathomable, pretend to attack forcefully and you will discover their tactic. Once you have discovered their tactic, it will be easy to defeat them through the use of an effective means[200] adapted to it.

In individual strategy, when your opponent takes up a guard position with his sword held back or to one side,[201] feint an attack and his mind will then be reflected in the movement of his sword. Having unveiled his state of mind, you will employ an effective means against him, and you will surely win. But if, in doing this, you let yourself relax, you will lose the appropriate cadence. Examine this well.

Constricting the Shadow

Here is what I call "constricting the shadow"[202] when you see that your adversary intends to act.

In group strategy, you constrict the instant your adversaries are about to launch their action. If you show forcefully that you are constricting the effective means used by your adversaries, they will change their tactic, because they will be constricted by your strength. At this moment you change your own tactic and gain the victory by taking the initiative of attack with an empty (ku) mind.[203]

In individual strategy, at the moment your opponent is about to attack you with a strong will, you get him to give up his action by using an effective cadence. During the cadence of his retreat, you find an effective means to defeat him, and you take the initiative of attacking. You must work this out well.

Infecting

Here is what I call "infecting."[204] This exists in everything: Sleep is infectious, yawns are infectious, and this goes for time too.[205]

In group strategy, when you perceive in your adversaries a quality of indecision and haste, pretend not to notice it and act extremely slowly; that will influence your adversaries and they will relax their attitude. When you judge that you have infected them sufficiently, seize this opportunity to win by attacking fast and strong with an empty (*ku*) mind.

In individual strategy, it is important to win by attacking powerfully and fast in order to grasp the initiative by seizing the moment in which your opponent has relaxed because he has been infected by the relaxed quality of your body and your mind.

You can also intoxicate your opponent by a similar process. Here you introduce dreariness, indecision, and weakness into his mind. You should work this out well.

Irritating Your Adversary[206]

One can become irritated in different ways, for example, as a result of the feeling of brushing the limits of danger, of facing the impossible, or of surprise. You should examine this well.

In group strategy, it is important to know how to irritate your adversaries. Launching a violent assault at a place your adversaries have not thought of, before their minds have a chance to stabilize,[207] take the initiative of attack, making the best of this advantage. To win in this way is essential.

In individual strategy also, show yourself as slow to begin with, then attack abruptly with force, and following the ups and downs of your opponent's concentration and movements, take advantage of this opportunity to defeat him without slacking off even to the slightest extent.[208] This is essential. You should examine it well.

Frightening[209]

Anything can frighten. One allows oneself to be frightened by what one does not expect.

In group strategy, you can frighten your adversaries not only by a direct action but also sometimes by making noises, sometimes by making a small thing look large, sometimes by making sudden attacking movements off to the sides. You should gain victory by relying on the advantage offered to you by the cadence of your adversaries' fright.

In individual strategy, you can frighten with your body, with your sword, and also with your voice. It is essential to win directly by taking advantage of the opportunity that arises at the moment when your opponent is frightened by acts that he will not have imagined. You should examine this well.

Coating

Here is what I call "coating."[210] When your adversary approaches you and you clash with him forcefully and then the development of the combat stagnates, coat your adversary as though you constituted but one single body. Try to find a chance to win in this melee.

In group strategy and also individual, when the combat stagnates because the two opponents are clashing equally, coat your opponent in such a way that it is impossible to distinguish yourself from the other. In this situation seize the opportunity to win and gain the victory with power. Examine this well.

Hitting a Corner

Here is what I call "hitting a corner."[211] You cannot always cut something down directly, especially if it is powerful.

In group strategy, first you must look at the number of enemies and create an opening by beginning attacking at the point where the enemy force forms a protrusion. If a corner is weakened, the whole will be influenced by this and weaken. While one corner is deteriorating, it is important again to find other corners where you can apply the same tactic in order to win the victory.

In individual strategy, if you wound a corner of your opponent's body, this will weaken him, however slightly, and he will begin to crumble. It is then easy to win. You should examine this well in order to master the principle of winning.

Troubling

Here is what I call "troubling."[212] It is preventing the adversary from having a confident mind.

In group strategy, probe the mind of your adversaries on the field of battle; trouble them with the skillfulness of your strategy. Draw them here and there, make them think this and that, make them sometimes think slowly and sometimes think fast. Make the most of the cadence of their troubled state to defeat them with certainty.

In individual strategy, vary your techniques according to the moment. Feint striking, stabbing, getting in close. Grasp the manner in which your opponent's mind is becoming troubled and win with ease. This is essential for combat; you must examine it well.

The Three Types of Cries

The three types of cries,[213] those for the beginning, middle, and end of a combat, are distinct. Depending on the situation, it may be important to sound a cry. Cries come from a surge of energy—people cry out at the time of a fire, in the course of a storm when there is wind and waves. You can tell someone's force from their cry.

In group strategy, at the beginning of a battle it is necessary to cry out as loudly as possible,[214] beyond what could be imagined; during the confrontations, it is appropriate to cry out in a low tone that comes from the bottom of the belly; and after having won you should make great, powerful cries.

In individual strategy, cry out *ei*[215] while pretending to attack in order to cause your opponent to make a move, and strike with your sword after this cry. Sound a cry also after having won in order to declare your victory. These two cries are called "cries of before and after."[216] Do not sound a great cry at the same time as you strike with your sword. If you cry out during combat, the cries should fit in with your cadence and be low ones. You should examine this well.

Concealing Yourself

Here is what I call "concealing yourself."[217] When two large groups oppose each other in battle, if your adversaries are powerful, conceal yourself by attacking first in one direction, then, as soon as you find your adversaries beginning to crumble, leave them as they are and redirect your attack toward other powerful groups. Move more or less as though you were zigzagging down a slope.[218]

This strategy is important when you are fighting alone against many opponents. Do not try very hard to win on each side, but as soon as you have made one side fall back, attack on another side where your opponent is strong. Perceiving the cadence of your adversaries, move with the cadence that suits you, from left to right as though you were zigzagging down a slope, while following the reaction of your opponents. When, after having discerned the force of your opponents, you go in among them to strike them, you must not in any way have the slightest notion of backing off, and you will obtain the opportunity of winning with strength. This strategy can also be applied when you are facing a single powerful adversary in order to get close to him.[219] To conceal yourself, you must not have in your mind the least thought of backing away. You must understand clearly what is meant by, "going forward while concealing yourself."

Smashing

Here is what I call "smashing."[220] For example, it is important to have in mind to smash the adversary, determinedly considering him to be weak while viewing yourself as strong.[221] In group strategy, if the adversaries are few in number or even if they are many, they are in a state of weakness when they are moving about indecisively in a disoriented condition. Smash them, starting with the head, adding to this an oppressive burst of energy[222] that has the sensation of pushing them and smashing them. If you do not smash them enough, it is possible they may regain their strength. So smash them as though you held them in your hands. You must understand this well.

In individual strategy, when you are fighting against an inferior opponent or when your opponent backs away as the result of a discord in his cadence, it is important not to give him a moment to breathe and, without meeting his glance, to continue straight on and smash him completely. It is of vital importance not to give him the least opportunity to recover, however slightly. You should examine this well.

Change from the Mountain to the Sea[223]

Here is what I call "the mind of the mountain and the sea." It is harmful to do the same thing several times in the course of combat. You can do the same thing twice but not three times. If you fail with a technique, you can begin it over again once more, but if you do not succeed this time, abruptly apply another, completely different technique. In this way, if your opponent is thinking of the mountain, you apply the sea; if he is thinking of the sea, you apply the mountain. Such is the way of strategy. You must examine this well.

Ripping Out the Bottom

Here is what I call "ripping out the bottom."[224] When you fight against an opponent, it might happen that you get the impression of having won on account of the advantage of the way, but it could be that the mind of your adversary has not been broken and that his defeat has been superficial, while in its depth his mind has not been defeated. In this case, abruptly renew your mind and batter him until his mind has been broken and he feels completely defeated.[225] It is essential to ascertain this.

You rip out the bottom [of his resistance] with your sword, with your body, and also with your mind. It is not appropriate to think of this in just one way. It is when he has collapsed from the very bottom that you no longer need to maintain your vigilance—otherwise, you must maintain it. But as long as in its depth he maintains his mind, it is difficult to bring him to collapse. In group and individual strategy, you should train well in order to learn how to rip out the bottom.

Renewing Yourself

Here is what I call "renewing yourself."[226] If at the time of a combat, you feel yourself entangled with your opponent and the fight is stagnating, you throw off your preceding sensations and renew your thoughts as though you were doing everything for the first time. In this way you employ a new cadence to achieve victory.[227]

As soon as you feel a grating indecisiveness in your contact with your opponent, immediately renew your mind so you can make use of a completely different opening in order to win. In group strategy as well, it is important to know how to renew yourself. This is something you will find immediately through the wisdom of strategy. You should examine it well.

A Mouse's Head and a Bull's Neck

Here is what I call "a mouse's head and a bull's neck."[228] In the course of a combat, it sometimes happens that the two combatants become entangled because both of them have gotten hung up on details. In this situation you should always keep in mind that the way of strategy is like a mouse's head and a bull's neck, and while you are fighting with small techniques, all of a sudden enlarge your mind and transform those small techniques into big ones. This is an integral part of strategic thought. It is important for a warrior to think every day that a person's mind is like a mouse's head and a bull's neck. For group and individual strategies, it is necessary always to have this way of thinking present. You should examine all this well.

The General Knows His Soldiers

Here is what I call "the general knows his soldiers."[229] This is applicable in all battles. If you practice this method unremittingly and if you succeed in realizing the way as you understand it, you will obtain the power of the knowledge of strategy. You will then be able to consider all your opponents as your own soldiers, with whom you can have done whatever you like. You will have the sense of directing your opponents according to your will. You are then the general and your adversaries are your soldiers. You must work this out well.[230]

Letting Go of the Sword Handle

What I call "letting go of the sword handle"[231] has several senses. It is the state of mind of winning without having a sword and also the state of mind of not winning with the sword. I shall not write down all the ways of conducting oneself that flow from this mind. You should train well.

The Body of a Rock

Here is what I call "the body of a rock." He who has mastered the way of strategy can immediately become like a rock. At that point he will never receive a sword blow and nothing will be able to move him.[232] The details will be given orally.

I have written in the foregoing what I think uninterruptedly in the practice of the sword of my school. This is the first time I have written on this principle. There are therefore confusions in the organization of the sentences, and I have not been able to express myself down to small details. Nonetheless, this text will serve to guide the mind of those who study this way.

I have devoted myself to the way of strategy since my youth. I have exhausted the knowledge of the hand and body in all the techniques of the sword, and my thought has passed through several stages. I have visited a variety of schools and I have seen in some of them skillful explanations being given and in others subtle techniques of the hand being shown. They have a nice appearance, but none of them manifests a correct mind. I think it is possible to develop a certain skill of body and a certain finesse of mind by learning these techniques, but all this training becomes, for the way, a source of faults. These persist without ever disappearing, and because of them, the correct way of strategy fades away and the way is lost.

For mastering the true way of the sword and for defeating your adversary in combat, the principle is in no way different. If you obtain the power of the knowledge of my strategy and if you act correctly, there will be no doubt of your victory.

> The twelfth of the fifth month of the second year of Shoho [1645]
> SHINMEN MUSASHI
> To the Honorable Lord Terao Magonojo

> The fifth of the second month of the seventh year of Kanbun [1667]
> TERAO MUSEI KATSUNOBU
> To the Honorable Lord Yamamoto Gennosuke

THE SCROLL OF WIND

Knowing the Way of Strategy of Other Schools

I write the Scroll of Wind[233] on the subject of the other schools of strategy in order, in this scroll, to explain what they are. You cannot know with certainty the way of your own school without knowing the way of others.

I have visited and observed other schools of strategy. In one school they use a large sword of great length and merely seek for power in their technique. In another school the way is practiced with a small sword called a *kodachi*. Another school has elaborated many varied techniques; there the way is transmitted with different guard positions for the sword, and they distinguish between surface training and depth training.[234] In this scroll I write the reasons why all these trends are not the true way and I explain their advantages and disadvantages.

The principle of my school is quite different. In the other schools, techniques are displayed like merchandise adorned with colors and flowers, so they can be turned into a way of making a living, which is not the true way. The strategies propagated in this world are limited to the single small domain of the art of the sword,[235] and it is thought that to win it is enough solely to acquire techniques by training in handling the sword and in movements of the body. Neither of these two ways is a sure one.

I explain here what is lacking in the other schools. It is necessary to thoroughly examine all of this together as a whole in order to understand the advantage of my School of Two Swords.[236]

Schools That Use a Particularly Long Large Sword

There are schools that prefer a particularly long large sword.[237] From the point of view of my strategy, these are weak schools. For their preference for the long large sword comes from the idea of trying to win by placing oneself far from the sword of your opponent; they think that this is the advantage of a long sword. This attitude comes from a misunderstanding of the principle that consists in defeating the adversary no matter what the situation is.

People say that the longer one's limbs are, the better it is,[238] but this idea comes from those who are ignorant concerning strategy. Instead of relying on the principle of strategy, they try to win by means of length and situating themselves far away from their opponent. This approach comes from mental weakness; it is in this sense that I consider their strategies to be weak.

If you fight from a short distance away, at a distance from which you might well be able to close in to a hand-to-hand range, the longer your sword is, the less well you are able to strike, the less well you are able to swing it around—and a long sword becomes a weight on you. Someone who has a small sword,[239] or even someone who has nothing in his hands, can have the advantage in this sort of situation. Those who prefer a long sword may be able to justify their choice, but their reasoning is valid only for themselves. If you look from the point of view of the true way of this world, there is no reason for that. How can you say that with a small sword you will inevitably lose against someone with a big sword? When you fight in a space that is tight in width or height, or when you are in a house where it is permitted to carry only a small sword, preference for a large sword has bad consequences, because this preference comes from uncertainty about your own strategy. In addition, some people do not have the main force to handle a large sword.

As a proverb has it—"something large can replace something small"—so I do not unconditionally reject length, but, rather, it is the prejudice in favor of length that I repudiate. In group strategy, the large sword corresponds to a large number of troops and the small sword to a small number. Is it impossible for a small number to fight a large number? We know of several examples where a smaller force has carried off the victory. In my school I reject this sort of narrow preconceived outlook. You should examine this well.

Schools That Use the Sword with Brute Force[240]

It is not appropriate to set up a distinction between a strong sword and a weak sword. If you strike with the intention of producing force, your sword technique will be crude, and it is difficult to achieve victory with crude technique. If you try hard to cut through a human body using force, you will not succeed. If you try to cut through various objects,[241] you will see that it is bad to strike with force.

In fighting a mortal enemy,[242] no one would think of cutting him down weakly or strongly; when you want to kill someone, you do not do it strongly, and of course not weakly, but simply in such a way that he dies.

In practicing the sword with brute force, if you slap the other's sword forcefully in making a parry,[243] the force will spill over, and that is always bad. If you hit the other's sword with a great deal of force, your sword might break in two.[244] Thus it makes no sense to advocate using the sword with brute force.

In group strategy, if you try to win in a battle through sheer power—with strength in troops—then your opponents will also try to have strength in troops and they will want to fight with brute force. The two sides will thus be thinking the same way. It is impossible to win in any domain without the principle of the way.[245] In the way of my school,[246] you must never consider the impossible and you must learn to win in all ways thanks to the power of the knowledge of strategy. You must work this out well.

Schools That Use the Short Sword

Trying to win with only the short sword[247] is not the true way. From ancient times the large and the small sword have been talked about; this clearly expresses the usefulness of having a long and a short one. In this world a strong person can easily handle a large sword; there is no point in limiting him to a short sword. When you need a long weapon, you can even take a lance or a *naginata*.[248] With a small sword, trying to look for a fault in your opponent's attack in order to cut him down, trying to penetrate in close by leaping, or making an attempt to catch hold of the body of your opponent—all these approaches are partial and no good. Looking for a fault as the opening for your attack amounts to submitting to the initiative of the other[249] and should be avoided, because you run the risk of becoming entangled with him.

When facing many opponents,[250] if you have a short weapon in your hand, the idea of getting close enough[251] to them to fight hand to hand or to catch hold of them is ineffective. If you are particularly trained in the use of the short sword, even when you want to drive back many adversaries by slashing at them, or when you want to leap about freely or spin energetically, all of your sword technique becomes defensive, and you have a tendency to fall into confusion. Therefore this is not a sure way.

To the extent to which it is possible, you must repulse your opponents by getting them to jump about and become disconcerted, while you yourself keep straight, with power, in order to obtain the victory with certainty. This is the way. The principal is the same for group strategy. To the extent to which it is possible, the essence of strategy is to crush your enemies immediately through the power of great numbers by driving them back all of a sudden.[252]

In this world, if you continually accustom yourself in the course of your apprenticeship to certain techniques of parrying, dodging, disengaging, and warding off an attack, your mind will be steered by these ways of doing things (*michi*),[253] and you will run the risk of letting yourself be controlled by others. Since the way of strategy is straight and true, it is important to dominate your adversary by harrying him with the true principle. You should examine this well.

Schools That Have a Large Number of Techniques

Teaching people a large number of sword techniques[254] is turning the way into a business of selling goods, making beginners believe that there is something profound in their training by impressing them with a variety of techniques. This attitude toward strategy must be avoided, because thinking that there is a variety of ways of cutting a man down is evidence of a disturbed mind. In the world, different ways of cutting a man down do not exist. Whether you are an accomplished adept or a noninitiate, a woman or a child, the ways (*michi*) of striking, slapping, and cutting are not all that numerous. Apart from these movements, there are only those of stabbing and slashing broadly on the horizontal. Because what is primarily at issue is the way (*michi*) of cutting someone down, there cannot be many differences.

All the same, whatever the place and situation of combat might be, for example, a place that is closed in with regard to height or width, one must hold the sword without being discomfited by the place. It is from this necessity that the five ways of holding the sword come. All five are necessary.

Apart from that, it is not fitting to the true way to cut someone down by pivoting one's wrists, twisting one's body, jumping, or pulling back.[255] Because you cannot perform the act of cutting a man down by pivoting, twisting, jumping, or pulling back. These are entirely futile movements.

In the strategy of my school, keep your body and mind straight and make your opponent go through contortions and twist about. The essence is to defeat him in the moment when, in his mind, he is pivoting and twisting. You should examine this well.

Schools That Insist on the Importance of the Guard Position in the Art of the Sword[256]

It is erroneous to think that the guard position is essential in the art of the sword. In this world it is when there is no adversary that one can establish a guard position.[257] The reason is that, in the way of combat, there is no place for the setting up of laws, whether they relate to current custom or present-day rules. In strategy the point is to do whatever creates a disadvantage for the adversary. What is called the guard or guard position involves having recourse to immobility. For example, to construct a fortress or establish the order of a battle, one must have a powerful and immovable mind, even if the enemy attacks; this is a fundamental attitude. Whereas in the way of strategic combat, it is necessary to take initiative after initiative in any situation. Now to assume a guard position is to wait upon the initiative of the other. You must work this out well.

In the way of strategic combat, you shake the other's guard; you employ techniques he is not thinking of; you get him to panic, to become irritated, frightened; and you defeat him by becoming aware of the cadence in accordance with which he is getting lost in the situation of combat. In this practice it is bad to take up a guard position, which is waiting upon the other's initiative. It is in this sense that I insist in my school on the guard without a guard,[258] that is to say, even if there is a guard, it is not a rigid guard.

In group strategy, you must be informed of the number of your adversaries and the conditions of the place and know your own numbers and the abilities of your camp. The essential is to have an idea of the potential import of these elements when you begin combat maneuvers with your troops. Between the two situations, that in which your adversary has seized the initiative of attack and that in which you have taken the initiative, the disadvantage and the advantage vary from single to double.

Firmly setting up a guard position as a preparation to blocking the sword of your opponent and thoroughly beating it back amounts to moving a lance or a *naginata*[259] about in such a way as to set up a barrier.[260] If you strike your opponent, it is best for you to take the approach of pulling up a stake from the fence to use it as a lance or *naginata*. You should examine this well.

Schools That Teach Particular Ways of Gazing[261]

Certain schools teach particular ways of directing the gaze. This teaching varies from one school to another—you are to focus your gaze on the sword, the hand, the face, or the feet of the adversary. But to fasten the eyes in this way on a particular spot is liable to interfere with the mind and is a fault in strategy.

I will explain myself by giving some examples: Someone playing ball[262] kicks without fixing his gaze on the ball. Sometimes he kicks as he is stroking his temples,[263] sometimes while catching up to the ball on the run, sometimes as he spins. Once accustomed to it, he has no need to maintain a fixed gaze. The same is true of an acrobat.[264] An expert in this art is capable of juggling several swords while balancing a door over his nose.[265] Things are seen naturally as a result of unremitting training and not on account of looking at them fixedly.

In the way of strategy, by accumulating experiences with different opponents, you will learn the lightness or weight of the mind of each one. By practicing the way in this manner, you can see everything that is far away or close and also assess the speed or slowness of the adversary's sword. Generally, in strategy you place your gaze on the mind of your opponent.[266] In group strategy your gaze is directed onto the situation and the state of the enemy troops. There are two things you can do: looking and seeing.[267] It is necessary to look hard, to the point of perceiving the mind of your adversary and the condition of the site. It is also necessary to look broadly in order to perceive the dynamic state of the battle and the strength and weakness of the moment. You must win like this, in the right way. In group strategy and also in individual strategy, it is out of the question to fix one's gaze narrowly. As I have already said, as a result of narrow and minutely detailed vision, you will let something big escape you, and your mind will become uncertain, which will lead you to let a sure chance of winning get away from you. You should examine these reasons well and train well.

Schools That Teach Various Kinds of Footwork[268]

There are schools that teach different ways of moving the feet so as to vary movements from place to place and make them faster. These are, for example, floating foot, leaping foot, hopping foot, stamping foot, and crow's foot.[269] From the point of view of my strategy, all these movements have deficiencies.

Floating foot is to be avoided because in situations of combat, there is always the tendency to have the sensation of floating in the feet; therefore one should move with firm steps.

Leaping foot is not good because at the moment of leaping, there is a pushing-off movement, and you make a movement to dampen the impact at the moment of landing on the ground that holds the body back.[270] There is no reason to leap several times in a row during a battle. Therefore leaping foot is to be avoided.

With hopping foot, the mind will be hopping too, and you will not be able to fight effectively.

Stamping foot is particularly bad, since it involves a wait.[271]

There is also crow's foot and several other ways of moving rapidly.

But sword combat can take place in a variety of conditions, for example, in a marsh, in a deep rice paddy, or in the mountains; on the banks of a river, in a stony field, or on a narrow path. In some places you cannot leap or hop, and you will not be able to move rapidly either.

In my strategy the way of moving is no different from normal walking on a road.[272] You move rapidly or calmly in accordance with your opponent's cadence. In all cases, move without the movement of your feet being disturbed, without missing a step, without any excess in your step, with a suitable body posture.

Movement from place to place is equally important in group strategy, for if you launch an attack without knowing the intention of your adversary, with imprudent speed, your cadence will be thrown off, and it will be difficult to gain victory in these conditions. If your steps are too slow,[273] you will not be able to find the moments when your adversaries become troubled and are on the verge of collapse—one of the elements of victory will elude you and you will not be able to win quickly. Discern the moment when your adversaries become troubled and are foundering, and do not give them the least chance to catch their breath. Winning in this way is essential. You must train well in this.

Schools That Stress Speed[274]

Speed is not part of the true way of strategy. When you say "fast," this means a lag has occurred in relation to the cadence[275] of things; that is what is meant by "fast" or "slow."

In whatever the domain, the movements of a good, accomplished practitioner do not appear fast. For example, there are messengers who cover forty or fifty leagues at the run in a single day, but they do not run fast from morning till night. Whereas, a beginner cannot cover such a long distance, even if he has the wind to run the whole day.

In Noh theater, when a beginner sings following a good, accomplished practitioner,[276] he has the impression of lagging behind and sings with the feeling of haste. In the same way, in the drumbeat for "Old Pine" ("Oimatsu"),[277] which is a slow melody, a beginner has the feeling of lagging behind and having to catch up. "Takasago"[278] is a rather fast song, but it is not appropriate to play the drum too fast. Speed is the beginning of a fall, because it produces a deviation in the cadence. Of course, excessive slowness is also bad. The movements of a good, accomplished practitioner look slow, but there is no dead space between his movements. Whatever the domain, the movements of an expert never appear hurried. Through these examples, you should understand a principle of the way.

In the way of strategy, it is bad to try for speed. I will explain. In places such as a marsh or deep rice paddy, you cannot move either your body or your legs fast. This is all the more true for the sword—you must not try to cut with speed. If you try to cut with a fast movement, the sword—which is neither a fan nor a knife—will not cut because of the speed. You must understand that well.

In group strategy also, it is bad to think of hurrying up in order to attain speed. If you possess the attitude of mind of "holding down on the headrest," you will never be late. If your adversaries act too fast, you apply the opposite approach, you calm yourself and avoid imitating them. You must train yourself well in developing this state of mind.

Schools That Distinguish Depth and Surface

In questions of strategy, what is meant by surface and what is meant by depth?[279] In the different arts, there is a manner of distinguishing the depth from the entry[280] that refers to the ultimate teaching or the secret transmission.[281] But as to the principle that comes into play at the time of combat with an adversary, you cannot say that you fight him with techniques of the surface and cut him down with those of the depth.

In my school's teaching of strategy, you teach techniques that are easy to assimilate for those who are beginning in the study of the way, giving them an explanation that they can understand right away. Observing the degree of their advancement,[282] you progressively give them explanations that direct them toward more and more profound principles. However, in general you teach them things that correspond to situations they are really in; there is no need to distinguish between depth and entry in the teaching. This can be connected with the adage according to which if you continue to go deeper and deeper into the mountains, you will come out by a different entry.[283]

In all the ways, it might turn out that the depth technique is effective or that the entry technique is.[284]

With this principal of combat, why should you hide one thing in order to show another? That is why, in the transmission of my school, I do not have written oaths, accompanied by penalties.[285]

Observing the student's level of intelligence, you teach him the correct way and help him to free himself of the five or six bad ways of strategy.[286] You cause him to enter naturally into the true way that conforms to the principles of the warriors, so that his mind will be free from doubt. Such is the way (*michi*) of teaching strategy in my school.

You should train well in this.

In the Scroll of Wind I have written succinctly about the strategy of other schools in nine sections. I should have written about each of these things in greater detail, going from the entry to the depth, but I intentionally avoided mentioning the names of the schools and the names of the techniques. For in every school, the ideas and the explanations concerning such and such a way can vary from person to person in accordance with the way he understands, and every person has his way of reasoning. Thus there are small differences in thought within a single school. That is why I mentioned neither the name nor the techniques of the schools, thinking about their development in the future.

I have outlined the general characteristics of the other schools in these nine sections. If we observe things from the point of view of the way of the world and also from that of correct human reasoning, these schools follow partial ways, because one of them is attached solely to length, another touts the advantage of the short sword, and the others are partial because of one single preoccupation, whether it is strength and weakness or coarseness and fineness. I do not need to be specific about whether I am talking about the entry or the depth of such and such a school, because everybody knows.

In my school there is neither depth nor entry for the art of the sword, and there are no fixed guard positions. The essence of strategy is solely that the mind learns virtue from it.

The twelfth of the fifth month of the second year of Shoho [1645]
SHINMEN MUSASHI
For the Honorable Lord Terao Magonojo

The fifth of the second month of the seventh year of Kanbun [1667]
TERAO MUSEI KATSUNOBU
For the Honorable Lord Yamamoto Gensuke

THE SCROLL OF HEAVEN

In this scroll of heaven,[207] I elucidate the way of strategy of the School of Two Swords. The meaning of emptiness is space where there is nothing, and I also envisage emptiness as that which cannot be known. Emptiness, of course, is where there is nothing. Knowing that which does not exist while knowing that which exists—that is emptiness.

In this world, some people think of emptiness in an erroneous fashion, interpreting it as not distinguishing anything. This is the product of a mind gone astray. It is not true emptiness.

In addition, for the way of strategy, emptiness does not mean disregarding the law in order to practice the way of the warrior. Some also speak of emptiness as existing where they find nothing to do because of many doubts, but that is not true emptiness.

The warrior must learn the way of strategy with certainty by practicing the different disciplines of the martial arts, and he should not disregard anything connected with the practice of the way of the warrior. He should put it into practice from morning till night without tiring and without letting his mind wander. He should polish his mind and his will and sharpen the two visions—the one that consists in looking and the one that consists in seeing. He should know that true empty space is where the clouds of uncertainty have completely dissipated.

As long as you remain ignorant of the true way, even if you think you are on a sure way and that you are doing well in accordance with Buddhist laws or in accordance with the laws of this world, you will deviate from the true way, because you overestimate yourself and your way of seeing is distorted. You understand it if you see things with the direct way of the mind and take into account the great code of this world.

Know this state of mind and take as fundamental that which is straight, conceive of the way with a sincere mind, practice strategy broadly, think on a large scale with accuracy and clarity, think of *void* as the way and see the way as *void*.

In emptiness the good exists and evil does not exist.

Knowing exists, the principle exists, the way exists, and the mind—is void.

The twelfth of the fifth month of the second year of Shoho [1645][288]
SHINMEN MUSASHI
For the Honorable Lord Terao Magonojo

The fifth of the second month of the seventh year of Kanbun [1667]
TERAO MUSEI KATSUNOBU
For the Honorable Lord Yamamoto Gensuke

The Texts Preceding
THE *Gorin no sho*

The Texts Preceding
the *Gorin no sho*

"THE MIRROR OF THE WAY OF STRATEGY" (*Hyodokyo*)

1. The state of mind of strategy
2. The way of looking
3. The way of holding the sword
4. About sword combat
5. The way of moving from place to place
6. The way of holding the body
7. The way of cutting
8. How to change the situation in the midst of combat
9. Getting the other to drop his sword
10. Yin in combat
11. Yang in combat
12. How to discern the other's state
13. Delivering a blow
14. How to take the initiative
15. Striking while turning the point of the sword
16. Attacking the legs
17. Attacking the hand
18. How to avoid the point of the adversary's sword
19. How to pass above the adversary's sword
20. Moving with sliding steps

21. Discerning the real intention
22. The two swords
23. How to throw a *shuriken*
24. Fighting against many opponents
25. Using the *jitte*
26. How to draw the various swords
27. The ultimate strike
28. The state of direct communication (*jiki tsu*)

> Miyamoto Musashi no kami, Fujiwara Yoshitsune,
> the Enmei Ryu,
> the Best Adept in Japan
> To Mr. Ochiai Chuemon,
> the auspicious day of the tenth year of the Keicho period [1605]

"The Mirror of the Way of Strategy" (*Hyodokyo*) is Musashi's first work. It is a work of his youth, written between the ages of twenty-one and twenty-four. Two copies of it are extant today. Each is addressed to a different person and carries a different date. One of them is composed of twenty-one articles and the other of twenty-eight articles. I have given a partial translation of the latter.

I have translated only the article titles of this work because its content is less developed than that of the *Gorin no sho*, and it would seem repetitive here. The work is confined to the practice of the sword in individual combat, but the subject matter that would be developed in the *Gorin no sho* is present in embryonic form.

I consider this text a proof that Musashi was not self-taught. It seems impossible to me that a young man of twenty-two, living in the conditions of his time, could have acquired the whole of the art of sword combat through his own experience and formulated it in such a systematic form. This text appears to me to be a proof that Musashi had received the general transmission of a school, which could only have been that of his own family. This hypothesis is reinforced by the fact that in the twenty-fifth article, Musashi mentions the *jitte*, a weapon of which his father was a master. Thus Musashi had already received a systematic teaching, which he tried to reproduce when he granted a certificate of transmission to his first student.

"THIRTY-FIVE INSTRUCTIONS ON STRATEGY"
(Hyoho sanju go kajo)

In 1641, two years before beginning to write the *Gorin no sho,* Musashi wrote a work called "Thirty-five Instructions on Strategy." It was written for Lord Hosokawa, whose guest Musashi was. The *Gorin no sho* can be considered an elaboration of this work.

If we wish to get a closer idea of Musashi's thought, it seems essential to bring together these two works, which were written some years apart. We find several articles whose subject matter is identical, but with variations in expression and also some different ideas. Comparison of the two works is useful for an in-depth reading of the *Gorin no sho,* because Musashi sometimes uses different words to express the same idea, which makes it possible to get a clearer impression of his meaning. However, in some cases it is not clear whether Musashi was using a different word or whether a copyist's error has occurred (for example, *jiki tsu* for *jikido*).

We should not forget that Musashi's works were not intended for the public and that each of them was addressed to a specific person. This is something that should be borne in mind when comparing the two texts. For this reason, even if certain passages are repeated in both, it is not accurate to consider the *Hyoho sanju go kajo* purely as a work preparatory to the *Gorin no sho.* It has an original character of its own.

The *Gorin no sho* was written by Musashi for Lord Hosokawa Tadatoshi. At the end of his life, Musashi accepted the invitation of Hosokawa Tadatoshi, a lord of the south of Japan (Kyushu), to live at his court. But he was received there as his guest, not as his vassal. Lord Hosokawa practiced swordsmanship himself. In his youth he had lived for several years in Edo, where he practiced the art of the sword of the Shogun Tokugawa school. From the principal master of this school, Yagyu Munenori, he received the transmission of the school's highest level of accomplishment. When he returned to his fief in Kyushu, he practiced the sword with a certain pride and self-confidence. When he received Musashi in his fief, he faced him himself in order to gauge his level. He was mastered in just a few seconds and immediately became aware of Musashi's exceptional ability. Hosokawa also greatly appreciated Musashi's great talent in a very broad range of activities. They were both about the same age and entered into a friendship of sorts in spite of their separation in the hierarchy. That is why Hosokawa received Musashi as a guest rather than a vassal. To take Musashi in and offer him a fixed income (as he would have done for a vassal) would have been in some sense to buy him at a certain price. Whereas a guest is priceless. For this reason Hosokawa refrained from offering Musashi a position as his retainer.

Quickly persuaded of Musashi's qualities as an adept of strategy and as a man, Hosokawa became his student. After a year of practicing with Musashi, Lord Hosokawa had not succeeded in grasping the essence of his school, so he asked Musashi to compose a text to guide his practice. Musashi then began to compose the *Hyoho sanju go kajo,* which he presented to the lord a year later.

In the translation that follows below, I confine myself to giving only the titles of those articles that more or less replicate ones in the *Gorin no sho.* I have translated the others and, in my commentary, situated them in relation to the *Gorin no sho.*

To help understand the nature of this text, it should be pointed out that in his introduction Musashi uses a special verbal form to express his respect for Lord Hosokawa. This is a nuance that is difficult to render in an English translation.

I write for the first time here, in your honor, on my School of Two Swords, which is the result of many years of training. Considering that it is you I am addressing, this text is insufficient to communicate that which is difficult to say. It deals with how one must handle oneself with a sword in the strategy that you usually practice. I write below about the principal aspects of this in the way that they come to my mind.

1. Why I Named My School "School of Two Swords"

The ideas in this article are presented again and further developed in the Scroll of Earth of the *Gorin no sho*. However, after explaining why he uses two swords and indicating that it is through training that one becomes capable of handling a heavy sword with ease, Musashi adds:

Among the people also, a sailor with a rudder or oars or a farmer with a spade and a hoe each in his way succeeds in accustoming himself to his action. You too can acquire strength through regular exercise. Nonetheless, it is appropriate for each person to choose a sword that corresponds to his strength.

2. The Manner of Understanding the Way of Strategy

The way is identical for group strategy and for individual strategy. I am writing here about individual strategy, but it is appropriate to look at this keeping in mind, to take an example, the image of a general—the limbs correspond to vassals and the torso corresponds to soldiers and to the people. It is thus that one must govern the country and one's own body. In this sense I say that the way is the same for group strategy and for that of the individual.

To practice strategy it is necessary to integrate the whole of one's body, without having any imbalances. Nobody is strong and nobody is weak if he conceives of the body, from the head to the sole of the foot, as a unity in which a living mind circulates everywhere equally.

3. The Way of Holding the Sword

After a brief description of the way of holding the sword, similar to that in the *Gorin no sho* (the Scroll of Water), Musashi continues:

Life and death exist for the sword as well as for the hand. When you adopt a guard position or parry an attack, if you forget to slash your opponent, your hand is going to forget an essential dynamic and will become fixed. That is what is called a "dead hand." A living hand is one that does not become fixed in a gesture. You will then be at ease with the possibility of slashing properly, since both the sword and the hand will be adapting flexibly to successive actions. I call that "living wrists." The wrist must not be slack, the elbow must not be too tense nor too bent. A sword should be held with tension in the lower part of the arm muscles and relaxation in the upper part of these muscles. You should examine this well.

4. Posture

It is appropriate to hold the head neither lowered nor raised. The shoulders are neither raised nor contracted. The belly is forward but not the chest. The buttocks are not drawn in. The knees are not fixed. The body is placed in a facing position, so that the shoulders appear broad. The posture of strategy should be well examined so that it also becomes one's ordinary posture.

5. Movement of the Feet

This section is nearly identical to the *Gorin no sho* (the Scroll of Water, "The Way of Moving the Feet").

6. The Way of Looking

This is almost identical to the *Gorin no sho* (the Scroll of Water, "The Way of Looking in Strategy").

7. Sizing up the Ma

Different schools give different instructions on the way to assess the *ma*, but I find that they tend to fix or rigidify your strategy; that is why I advise you not to take into consideration what you have learned before.

Whatever the discipline may be, it is by repeating exercises that you arrive at the point of being able to assess the *ma*. In general you should think that when your sword reaches your opponent, he can also reach you. When you want to kill an opponent, you have a tendency to forget your own body. You must reflect well on this.

Let us recall that *ma* is not exactly distance but is a description of the space-time of a relationship. *Ma* also refers to the action of the mind by which this spatial and temporal phenomenon is grasped.

In this text Musashi is doubtless alluding to the habits acquired by Lord Hosokawa in the Yagyu ryu.

8. Regarding State of Mind

The mind should be neither solemn nor agitated, neither pensive nor fearful; it should be straight and ample. This is the state of mind that should be sought after. The will should not be heavy, but the depth of one's awareness should be; in this way you make your mind like water that reacts appropriately to shifting situations. Whether it is a drop or an ocean with blue depths, it is water. You should examine this well.

9. Knowing the Three Levels of Strategy

Someone who adopts guard positions in strategy and displays different guard positions while handling the sword sometimes slowly, sometimes fast, practices strategy of a low level.

Someone who has refinement in strategy and who appears magnificent due to the subtlety of his techniques, who is a master of the cadences and has an elegant bearing, practices at an intermediate level.

The supreme strategy appears neither strong nor weak, neither slow nor fast, neither magnificent nor bad, but broad, straight, and calm. You should examine this well.

In Musashi's text the three levels—low, intermediate, and high (or supreme)—are expressed by the terms *ge*, "low," *chu*, "intermediate," and *jo*, "high." When these words are associated, the usual order is *jo-chu-ge*; this expression refers to level or quality.

10. A Graduated Cord Measure

You must always have a graduated cord measure in your mind. If you measure your opponent by adjusting the cord to him, you will be able to ascertain clearly his strength and weakness, his straightness and crookedness, where he is relaxed and where he is tense. With this measure you must size up all aspects of your opponent—round, square, long, short, crooked, or straight. You should examine this well.

> "A graduated cord measure," *ito gane: Gane* is the connecting form of the word *kane,* which means "metal ruler"; the expression refers to a cord that is used as a measure.

11. The Pathway of the Sword

Without knowing the pathway of the sword, you cannot handle it freely. You cannot properly slash your opponent if you put too much force into it, if you do not have a sense of the back and side of the blade, if you shake the sword around like a knife or a spoon for serving rice. You must train in hitting your opponent well, always knowing the pathway of the sword and moving it calmly, following its weight.

12. The Strike and the Hit

> This is almost identical to the *Gorin no sho* (the Scroll of Water).

13. The Three Kinds of *Sen*

> This is almost identical to the *Gorin no sho* (the Scroll of Fire).

14. Getting Past a Critical Passage

You often find yourself in a situation where you and your opponent can reach out and touch each other. In this situation, you strike. And if you see before finishing the strike that your opponent is in the process of avoiding your sword, get up as close as possible to him, moving your body and your feet.

If you get past this critical moment, you are in no danger. For this you must understand well what I have written concerning how to take the initiative.

15. The Body Replacing the Sword

This idea is developed more completely in the *Gorin no sho* (the Scroll of Water).

16. The Two Steps

You should move your feet in two movements (one foot, then the other) in making a single strike. This is what I call "the two steps." When you parry, pressing on your opponent's sword, or when you move forward or backward, you must move your feet in two steps, as though one foot were taking over from the other. If you move with a single step when making a strike, your body will be held by this movement and it will be difficult for you to react immediately for the next movement. Ordinary walking is the basis for the two steps. You should examine that well.

17. Breaking the Sword with Your Feet

This is almost identical to the *Gorin no sho* (the Scroll of Fire).

18. Leaning on the Shadow

Here is what I call "leaning on the shadow." If you observe clearly what is happening in the body of your opponent, you can discern where his mind is excessively full and where it is absent. If you place your sword on the shadow of the place where his mind is absent, while at the same time vigilantly watching the place where it is overly full, your opponent's cadence will be disturbed, and your victory will be facilitated by this. Nonetheless, it is important never to miss a strike as a result of attaching your mind to your opponent's shadow. This must be worked out.

19. Moving Your Shadow

This idea is more completely developed in the *Gorin no sho* (the Scroll of Fire).

20. Disconnecting the Cord

There are situations in which it seems you are attached to your opponent by a cord that is pulling you together. At this point you disconnect the cord. You must disconnect it without delay, as much with your body as with your sword, as much with your feet as with your mind. It will be easy for you to disconnect it if you make use of that which your opponent does not have in mind. This must be worked out.

21. The Teaching of the Small Comb

The idea of the small comb is to disentangle. You have a small comb in your mind and you should disentangle yourself each time your opponent snags you with a thread. Snagging with a thread and pulling with a cord are similar, but pulling is strong and snagging is weaker. You should examine that well.

22. Recognizing a Gap in a Cadence

A void in a cadence should be discerned in relation to your opponent, who could be either fast or slow.

When you are fighting a slow opponent, without moving your body at all and without letting him see the beginning of your sword movement, you strike him fast on the basis of the void. This is the cadence "in one" (*ichi hyoshi* or *hiotsu hyoshi*).

Against a fast opponent, you feint a strike with your body and with your mind, your opponent will move, and you will strike after his movement. This is the double *hyoshi* for passing over the top, *koshi*.

Your body is ready to strike, your mind and your sword are kept back, you strike with force starting from the void—at the instant when a gap (*ma*) arises in the will of your opponent. This is the "strike of nonthought" (*munen muso*).

When your opponent is ready to strike or parry, you make a striking movement that is deliberately slow, braking the movement during its trajectory, and you strike at the point where a void (*ma*) appears in his attention. That is the delayed cadence (*okure hyoshi*).

You should examine that well.

| The term *ma* is used here in the sense of a gap or a void in perception.

23. Holding Down on the Headrest

24. Recognizing the State of Things

25. Becoming Your Opponent

| The ideas in the previous three articles are developed more completely in
| the *Gorin no sho* (the Scroll of Fire).

26. Holding and Letting Go of One's Mind

Depending on the situation and the moment, you must either hold your mind or let go of it. In general, when wielding a sword, you must launch your will but hold on to the depth of your mind. When you strike your opponent with certainty, you must let go of your mind deep down and hold your will. These two states of mind, holding and letting go, can take on different forms, depending on the situation. This must be worked out well.

| "Holding the mind," and "letting go of the mind" in Musashi's text trans-
| late *zan shin* and *ho shin*, respectively. These terms are used in contempo-
| rary martial arts.

27. The Chance-Opening Blow

28. Paste and Lacquer

29. Body of the Autumn Monkey

30. Competition in Size

| The ideas in the previous four articles are developed more completely in
| the *Gorin no sho* (the Scroll of Water).

31. The Door Teaching *(Toboso)*

When you are glued to your opponent, take a position in which you straighten up your body and accentuate its breadth, as if you were covering the sword and the body of your opponent with your body, without leaving any gap between him and you. Then pivot, keeping your profile quite straight and making it as narrow as possible. Then deliver a powerful blow to your opponent's chest with your shoulder so as to knock him over. You must train well in this.

> Regarding "the door teaching," *toboso no oshie, toboso* refers to the mechanism for holding in place and closing a door that pivots on a central axis. It is composed of two pivot points situated in the middle of the door on the floor and above the door.

32. The General and His Troops

> This is almost identical to the *Gorin no sho* (the Scroll of Water, "The General Knows His Soldiers").

33. The Guard without a Guard

> This idea is developed more completely in the *Gorin no sho* (the Scroll of Water, "The Teaching of the Guard without a Guard").

34. The Body of a Rock

The body of a rock is the state of an unmoving mind, powerful and large. Something inexhaustible that comes from the universal principle exists in the body. It is through this that the power of the mind resides in every living being. The grass and trees, which do not have a consciousness, are powerfully rooted in the earth. This mind is also found in the rain and the wind. You must examine well what is meant by "the body of a rock."

35. Spotting Opportunities

You must know how to spot opportunities: those that come sooner or later, the opportunity to escape or not escape. In my school the ultimate teaching consists in spontaneous emanation of the universal energy, *jiki tsu*. The details of this teaching are given through oral transmission.

All reasons and principles come from emptiness. The meaning of this sentence is impossible to explain—be so good as to reflect on it yourself.

I have described above the principal aspects of my conception of strategy and state of mind in thirty-five articles. A number of sentences are inadequate, but it all has to do with what I have already explained to you. I have not written down the technical details of my school, which I teach you directly and orally. If you run across an obscure passage, be so kind as to permit me to explain it to you directly.

The auspicious day of the second month
of the eighteenth year of Kanei [1641]
Shinmen Musashi Genshin

"FORTY-TWO INSTRUCTIONS ON STRATEGY"
(Hyoho shiju ni kajo)

Nowadays, few people know of the *Hyoho shiju ni kajo*, and even fewer read it attentively. It is true that Musashi's thought is presented in the most comprehensive manner in the *Gorin no sho*, and people generally are content with reading that alone.

The "Forty-two Instructions on Strategy" (*Hyoho shiju ni kajo*) is a copy of the "Thirty-five Instructions on Strategy" supplemented by additional articles. It was handed down by Terao Motomenosuke, one of Musashi's disciples.

As I already explained, the "Thirty-five Instructions on Strategy" (*Hyoho sanju go kajo*) was written at the request of Lord Hosokawa Tadatoshi. Musashi presented this work to him in 1641; Hosokawa died that same year.

We might surmise that Musashi, as was the custom at the time, made a copy of his manuscript and gave it to one of his disciples before he died, in this case, Terao Motomenosuke. Terao Motomenosuke was the younger brother of Terao Magonojo, to whom Musashi bequeathed the *Gorin no sho*.

Musashi seems to have had great confidence in these two brothers. A few years before his death, he wrote:

> Up to this point I have traveled in more than sixty provinces, and I have transmitted my art to those who desired it. But I never met a person to whom I could pass on the transmission of my whole school. I was thinking, with regret, that my way was going to pass away with my own death until the day I met a disciple like Moto-menosuke. Thanks be to heaven I had a student like him.

We can imagine from this expression the confidence Musashi must have had in Terao Motomenosuke.

The two texts, the "Thirty-five Instructions on Strategy" and the "Forty-two Instructions on Strategy," are composed, to a great extent, of identical articles. The second contains everything from the first with the exception of the fourteenth instruction ("Getting Past a Critical Passage") and contains eight additional articles as well. Here is the translation of those eight.

Making Your Movements Stick

You and your opponent attack each other. At the moment when he blocks your sword, you close in on him and make your sword stick to his. You must glue your sword to his as though it were impossible to make it come unstuck, but without putting too much force into it. In making your movements stick, you can never be too calm. You must distinguish between sticking and becoming entangled. Sticking is strong, becoming entangled is weak.

> "Making Your Movements Stick," *nebari o kakuru:* The description here is simpler than in the article of the same name in the *Gorin no sho* (the Scroll of Water), written four years later.

Regarding the Place of Combat

Combat against Many Adversaries

> The previous two articles are more or less identical to those in the *Gorin no sho* (the Scroll of Fire and the Scroll of Water, respectively).

Regarding the Five Directions of the Guard

The five articles below are grouped under the title "Regarding the Five Directions of the Guard" *(Goho no kamae no shidai)*. The five guard positions described here are not the same as in the *Gorin no sho*.

1. *The middle guard position* (kanjitsu no kamae) *with your blades held slightly at an angle*

When your opponent is far away, you approach him just to the limit of his range of attack, holding your swords slanting downward and keeping your body straight. You situate yourself facing him and adopt a guard position as follows:

You raise your arms, with your elbows neither raised nor lowered, and cross your large and small swords in a forward position and at a middle level, broadly but without putting them too far forward. The point of the large sword is tilted slightly upward and placed above the line that runs between the middle of your body and your opponent's. The blades of your swords are neither raised nor held flat on the horizontal. They should be held on an angle.

In this position, keep your will mobile and the depth of your mind stable. Avoid your opponent's attack by detecting the movement of his will. Jab the point of your sword toward his face; this will disconcert him, and on account of that he will be drawn into launching his attack. At that point strike his arm from top to bottom by bringing the point of your sword back into position. After striking, leave this sword at the point it has reached, as though you had abandoned it, without moving your feet. And when your opponent attacks again, strike his arm from bottom to top in such a way as to hit him when he is a third of the way into his movement of attack.

Generally speaking, it is appropriate to keep your attention on the unleashing of your opponent's will to attack. You can then detect what he is about to start doing. This is a situation that is encountered all the time. You must understand it well.

2. *The high guard position of* gidan (gidan no kamae)

Place your right hand at the level of your ear, slanting your large sword slightly toward the inside—this is what I call the guard position of *gidan*. You hold the sword neither too tight nor too loose, with the point of the sword aimed toward the center line of your opponent's body. You strike, depending on your opponent's attack, either low, at the middle level, or high. The speed, depth, and force of your strike depend on his.

To dominate your opponent from the outset, strike his wrist by moving your large sword forward. But you must not strike downward. Strike with the feeling of piercing your opponent's hand, being quite sure of the direction of the blade of your sword. Then, whether your opponent parries or not, you immediately raise your sword, striking from below upward. To carry out this technique, you must hold the sword correctly and strike swiftly. It contains a sequence in the course of which it is possible to have a chance to cut your opponent down. But at a short distance, this technique is difficult to execute; in this case you must try to achieve dominance after having parried. You must use your judgment.

3. The right-side guard position (uchyoku no kamae)

Hold your large sword down on the right side and your small sword up, as though you were going to make a broad horizontal slashing movement.

When your opponent attacks, you strike him in such a way as to hit him when he is a third of the way through his move. If he tries to strike your small sword so as to make you drop it, you lower it slightly to make him cut in the void, then you slash your opponent by straightening the direction of the blade of your own sword. Speed is necessary for this strike. You must watch to make sure you keep the direction of the blade of your sword correct at the moment when you turn the point.

4. The left-side guard position (juki no kamae)

There are two kinds of left-side guard positions. For the first you move your right hand, which is holding the large sword, to the left, with the point of the sword forward and rather low, directed to the right. When your opponent attacks, you strike a third of the way through his movement. Your striking movement is as follows: You raise the sword, reaching with your arm in such a way that your hand goes beyond the point of your opponent's sword. After this strike, you must immediately turn the blade of your sword over.

For the second, you hold your sword rather low with the point directed to the left. Your hand then touches your right leg, and the blade of your sword is turned toward your opponent. You strike him as soon as he shows his intention to attack. Adjust the depth and force of your strike depending on your opponent. You must examine this strike well.

5. *The low guard position* (suikei no kamae)

You hold the two swords with the points coming near one another, downward and toward the inside, with the elbows broadly separated, without extending the arms. In this position, the small sword is placed forward. That is the low guard position.

When your opponent attacks, as you cross his sword you strike him on the central line, raising your sword up to the level of his forehead. You must strike broadly and fully, straight ahead. It is bad to cross the adversary's sword by moving your sword from the left side. After this strike, you must immediately turn the blade of your sword over. Depending on the situation, you could then adopt the right-side guard position. You must use your judgment.

With these five guards you can deal with all situations. Without conforming to the principle of the nature of the sword, you will not be able to cut down your opponent.

> The following final sentences are no longer present in the *Hyoho sanju go kajo*.

I have written here the general principles of my school. To learn the principle of victory with the sword through strategy, you must master the five guards by means of five technical forms. Through this you will be enabled to recognize the nature of the sword and you will obtain flexibility of body. You will be able to find cadences that conform to the way on any occasion.

> These five articles are not found in any of Musashi's other writings.
>   According to Ozawa Masao (9, p. 251), six articles were added by Terao Motomenosuke to the "Thirty-five Instructions on Strategy" (*Hyoho sanju go kajo*), and together these constitute the "Forty-two Instructions on Strategy" (*Hyoho shiju ni kajo*), which he passed down to his disciples. Ozawa does not explain his reasons for this assertion, which is not very precise,

because the difference between the two documents involves eight articles and not six. [Ozawa counts the title as one article.] By contrast, Mitsuhashi Kanichiro, a kendo master of the end of the nineteenth century, claims that this text was written by Musashi himself for his favorite disciple.

Several hypotheses are possible:

1. Musashi wrote the *Hyoho shiju ni kajo* in tandem with the *Hyoho sanju go kajo*. He gave the latter to Lord Hosokawa, and by adding a number of articles to this, he generated the copy intended for his disciple.
2. Musashi wrote out two or more copies of the *Hyoho sanju go kajo* and he bestowed one of these on his disciple.
3. Before presenting the *Hyoho sanju go kajo* to Lord Hosokawa, Musashi allowed his disciple to copy down its contents.

We have no historical basis for concluding in favor of any one of these three hypotheses. Nevertheless, I have to say that the five last articles added in "Regarding the Five Directions of the Guard," which I have translated above, are particularly difficult to understand. In addition, if these are compared with all the other texts by Musashi, their style is found to be quite different. Why is Musashi's writing so unclear in these five articles? Translating the entirety of his works makes the difference in style between these five articles and the rest of his works stand out quite clearly. But does the English, which forces one to give a certain logical construction to the text, show this difference clearly?

In view of this difference in style, I adopt the hypothesis that these articles were written by Terao Motomenosuke.

The text is followed by a postface in which Terao, as was the custom, affirms the authenticity of the transmission, mentioning the founding master of the school.

Postface

What I have written above comes from my master Genshin [Musashi]. The master persevered from his youth in the way of strategy and was able to attain the ultimate level in all the domains of the art, thanks to the principle of strategy. He engaged in more than sixty combats, either with the sword or with the *bokuto* (wooden sword), without ever losing. In this way he defeated the most famous adepts of all Japan. He continued to look for a more profound way, training from morning till night. Only after the age of fifty did he attain the ultimate state from which an extraordinary energy spontaneously emanates, and from that day on, he no longer had the need to go deeper.

The master did not write anything about his art until he met Lord Hosokawa Tadatoshi of Hishi [Kumamoto], who pursued this way. This lord had studied the strategy of several schools and had received the highest transmission from Yagyu Tajimanokami [Munenori], the most celebrated master of strategy in Japan. The lord secretly believed he had attained the highest level. At the time of his meeting with the master, they fought and the lord was completely dominated. He was astonished at the master's ability, and he asked him a number of questions.

The master then replied: "As far as the principle of strategy is concerned, this is true for all the schools: if the way of ultimate sincerity does not become one with what one is trying to do, it is not a true way."

The lord said, "Although I am not very skillful, I will persevere until I arrive at this way."

That is how the Master came to begin teaching him the way in private, and he presented to him his first writing. The lord swiftly attained mastery, thanks to his previous achievements in strategy.

The lord said, "I have persevered in the art of the sword (*kenjutsu*) from the time of my youth and I have studied several schools in a conscientious manner, but I have understood that none of this was part of the true way. Everything that I had learned over a long period of time turned out to be useless and disappeared." In this, his joy was great.

As for me, thanks be to heaven, I was able to meet my master, who granted me his special attention, and I was able to benefit from the depth of this relationship. I was able to attain the way by drinking at the spring of my master's mind by means of training.

The master complimented me, saying, "Until now, I have taught a great number of people, but none of them was able to enter into the real way. Without attaining a true way, it is impossible to give a real transmission. Nobuyuki [Terao's name], you have great intelligence in strategy, and you can understand ten things on the basis of one. And thanks to your exceptional ability, you have reached the state where an extraordinary energy spontaneously emanates from your person."

But this way is not a mere method of the sword (*kenjutsu*), and very few people pursue it. Even if there are people who search for it, if they do not do so with a sincere mind and with great perseverance, it is better not to speak to them of anything, because they will never arrive at it. I passed a number of years without ever showing my art to anybody, saying to myself that teaching my art amounted to touching my nose to indicate my mouth.

In this situation I have a trustworthy friend, Yasumasa, with whom I have been training for a long time, and I wish to be able to continue to do so for the rest of my life. I know the real sincerity of his mind, through which he inevitably reaches success, and how could he fail? Therefore I have transmitted everything to him, and he has attained the ultimate state of the way. It is for this reason that I bestow on him this text that comes from my master. This is an extraordinary occasion.

The school that will be perpetuated for all eternity is called *Niten ichi ryu* (the School of Two Swords toward the Sky). This is the strategy of the reality that has the fullness of a circle. The master gave it this name because "all principles arise from emptiness. If there is no communication, there is no response."

The fifteenth of the eighth month of the sixth year of Kanbun [1666]
TERAO MOTOMENOSUKE NOBUYUKI

"THE WAY TO BE FOLLOWED ALONE" (*Dokkodo*)

1. Do not go against the way of the human world that is perpetuated from generation to generation.
2. Do not seek pleasure for its own sake.
3. Do not, in any circumstance, depend upon a partial feeling.
4. Think lightly of yourself and think deeply of the world.
5. Be detached from desire your whole life long.
6. Do not regret what you have done.

7. Never be jealous of others, either in good or in evil.
8. Never let yourself be saddened by a separation.
9. Resentment and complaint are appropriate neither for yourself nor for others.
10. Do not let yourself be guided by the feeling of love.
11. In all things, do not have any preferences.
12. Do not have any particular desire regarding your private domicile.
13. Do not pursue the taste of good food.
14. Do not possess ancient objects intended to be preserved for the future.
15. Do not act following customary beliefs.
16. Do not seek especially either to collect or to practice arms beyond what is useful.
17. Do not shun death in the way.
18. Do not seek to possess either goods or fiefs for your old age.
19. Respect Buddha and the gods without counting on their help.
20. You can abandon your own body, but you must hold on to your honor.
21. Never stray from the way of strategy.

"The Way to Be Followed Alone" was written by Musashi in the few days preceding his death. We presently have two versions of the *Dokkodo*. One has nineteen articles and the other twenty-one. Articles 4 and 20 are absent from the shorter version.

We know of certain moments in Musashi's life from a later text entitled *Nitenki* (Writings on the Two Heavens), according to which, one week before his death, Musashi gave away his personal objects to people close to him. On that occasion he composed the twenty-one points entitled *Dokkodo* (the way where one walks alone), which are a reflection on his life at the moment of death. He dedicated these thoughts to his disciple Terao Magonojo, to whom he had also addressed the *Gorin no sho*. Terao Magonojo took them as precepts.

The sentences in the *Dokkodo* are short, concentrated expressions. That is why their meaning is difficult to understand in the original text. Unless some commentary is added, the translation might be somewhat incomprehensible or lead to misunderstandings.

These twenty-one thoughts of Musashi's require us to unpack the meaning of each word in order to get a sense of their overall signification, since each sentence distills Musashi's thought in a very few words and contains a great number of implicit notions meant to be understood by someone who has received his teaching at firsthand. For this reason a literal translation of this text, even if very well done, does not permit us to get at its meaning. Strictly speaking, Musashi himself and the disciple to whom these words were addressed doubtless remain the only ones able to decipher their meaning fully. We can get more or less close to the meaning of the text by elucidating the implicit notions the text contains.

For each precept I give the Japanese pronunciation, because the sonority of the words contributes to their message. I then explain the meaning of the main words, situating them in relation to their context.

1. Do not go against the way of the human world that is perpetuated from generation to generation (*yo yo no michi o somuku koto nashi*).

Yo: "society" or "the world of human beings," and in a broader sense, "the world." The repetition of the term denotes the idea of succession and movement over time.

Michi: "the way" or "principle."

Somuku: "to go against."

Koto nashi: a negation applied to a verb. *Nashi* corresponds to the negation ("not"), and *koto* to the nominative form taken by the verb in this sentence.

Yo yo no michi: "the way of the human world that is perpetuated from generation to generation." According to Imai Masayuki, the present-day and tenth successor of Musashi, this expression designates the way of wisdom, the true way that traverses time from the past to the future. This idea belongs to the tradition of Buddhism. According to Imai Masayuki, this sentence indicates the state of a man who is independent yet, acting freely, conforms to a truth of human nature.

2. Do not seek pleasure for its own sake (*mi-ni tanoshimi o takumazu*).

Mi: "the body," "oneself."

Tanoshimi: "pleasure," "enjoyment."

Takumazu: negative form of the verb *takumu,* which means "to elaborate, look for a good means."

In this precept it is not only physical pleasure that is meant but, in a more general sense, that which is pleasant and which Musashi has given up seeking intentionally. Would it be accurate to describe this ascetic attitude as masochism, as certain contemporary critics do? In my view labels of this type result in hiding the true image of Musashi behind a smoke screen of current-day thinking. This may produce a clear image, but it is an illusory one.

Renouncing pleasure, for Musashi, is a basic condition for arriving at what is essential. In this he is following the path that has been followed by other great accomplished practitioners of the martial arts. Asceticism of this sort is connected with a view of life that sees the agreeable aspects of existence as obscuring its depth, which is hard and heavy. Musashi seeks to avoid being detained at the level of pleasure, which would only distract him from the essential. His idea is to confront the deeper and weightier aspect of life directly in order to attain the essence of his art, which is inseparable from life itself. Such a conception of life is derived from a synthesis of Buddhist thought with more ancient Japanese notions of nature and the world. One of the contributions of Buddhism to this synthesis is the notion that life contains apparently contradictory aspects that are nevertheless inseparable from one another: There is old age in youth, death in life, hatred in love, separation in meeting, bitterness in pleasure, and so on. In his effort to see the true face of existence, Musashi goes directly toward this most pithy and substantial aspect of it. Becoming detached from the power of his own desire enables his mind to discover true emptiness (*ku*)—on that basis a new dimension opens before him. Although Musashi does not mention Buddhist doctrine (in which the notion of emptiness is another key element), his orientation is deeply permeated by Japanese Buddhism.

3. Do not, in any circumstance, depend upon a partial feeling (*yorozu ni eko no kokoro nashi*).

Yorozu: literally, "ten thousand; a very large number of things or phenomena; everything."

Eko: "dependency; that on which one is dependent; partial point of view; personal interest."

Kokoro: "heart, mind, thought."

The point here is to have an attitude toward all things and all persons that is neither dependent nor partial nor egotistic. This clear-sighted attitude, applied even to those close to one, might give an impression of coldness, and this is indicated by some documents on the subject of Musashi.

4. Think lightly of yourself and think deeply of the world *(mi o asaku omoi, yo o fukaku omou).*

Mi: "the body, oneself."

Asaku, asai: "not deep, shallow."

Fukaku, fukai: "deep."

Omoi: "to think, to consider."

First we should point out the opposition here between self and the world. The word-for-word translation of the beginning of this sentence would be "think not deeply with regard to oneself."

Musashi is telling us here that the proper way to look at things is not putting oneself at the center of them and not overestimating the weight of one's own existence. Such a self-centered view is often dominated by ego-centric ideas and desires. He is inviting us to meditate on our own small-ness in relation to a world that is moving in time, in eternity.

5. Be detached from desire your whole life long *(issho no aida yokushin omowazu).*

Issho: "all one's life."

Aida: "during."

Yokushin: "cupidity, lust."

Omowazu: "not thinking of, not having in mind, being detached from."

According to Imai Masayuki, man is tormented by lusts of the follow-ing three kinds: the desire to be viewed favorably by others; the egotistic desire for material riches; the desire to surpass others, to defeat them. Ac-cording to Imai, the point here is to live in a state of detachment from these kinds of desire.

6. Do not regret what you have done *(waga koto ni oite kokai o sezu).*

> *Waga koto:* "one's own affair, what one has done." These ideograms can also be read *ware koto.* In this case, *ware* is the subject, and the meaning is approximately the same.
> *Oite:* "in, concerning."
> *Kokai:* "regret."
> *Kokai o sezu:* "do not regret."

7. Never be jealous of others, either in good or in evil *(zen aku ni ta o netamu kokoro nashi).*

> *Zen aku:* "good and evil, in any case."
> *Ta o:* "toward others."
> *Netamu:* "to be jealous."
> *Kokoro:* "heart, mind, thought."
> *Nashi:* "do not have."

8. Never let yourself be saddened by a separation *(izure no michi nimo wakare o kanashimazu).*

> *Izure no michi nimo:* "in all ways, whatever the situation in which one finds oneself."
> *Wakare:* "separation."
> *Kanashimazu:* "do not be saddened"; this is the negative form of *ka-nashimu.*
>
> The sadness of momentary separation or the separation of death is considered in Buddhism to be one of the causes of being drawn away from the essential. It arises from the illusion of seeing as immutable that which is transient. Let us not forget Musashi's own experience—he spent the greater part of his life traveling.

9. Resentment and complaint are appropriate neither for yourself nor for others *(ji ta tomoni urami kakotsu kokoro nashi).*

> *Ji:* "oneself."
> *Ta:* "others."
> *Tomoni:* "both together, as well as."
> *Urami:* "resentment."

Kakotsu: "complaining."
Kokoro: "heart, mind, thought."
Nashi: "negation."

10. Do not let yourself by guided by the feeling of love *(renbo no michi omoi yoru kokoro nashi).*

Renbo: "love (being in love)."
Michi: "road, way, direction, orientation."
Omoi yoru: literally, "to think of and come near, to incline one's feeling toward a person."
Kokoro: "heart, mind, thought."
Nashi: "negation."
Musashi never had a child. The documents we have do not tell of his having relations with a woman. Some interpret this as a will to control his desire so as to dedicate himself to the way; others see it as a sign of homosexuality. This dictum militates in favor of the first hypothesis.

11. In all things, do not have any preferences *(mono goto ni sukikonomu koto nashi).*

Mono goto: "each thing."
Ni: "in, concerning."
Sukikonomu koto: "preference, predilection."
Nashi: "negation."

12. Do not have any particular desire regarding your private domicile *(shitaku ni oite nozomu kokoro nashi).*

Shitaku: "domicile" or "private house."
Ni oite: "in."
Nozomu: "to desire."
Kokoro: "heart, mind, thought."
Nashi: "negation."
For Musashi it was necessary to be able to live wherever he was, whatever the conditions were. It was not a question of seeking out discomfort but of not being attached to the quest for comfort in a dwelling place. There is no hindrance here to appreciating good things, but one must not

be attached to them. All through his life, Musashi had to be able to be at home wherever he was, whether it was in a house or in a natural setting with the sky as his roof. Realizing this may help us to understand why he chose to spend the last two years of his life in a cave, although he had a comfortable house at his disposal.

13. Do not pursue the taste of good food *(mi hitotsu ni bishoku o konomazu).*

> *Mi:* "one's body, oneself."
> *Hitotsu:* "alone."
> *Bishoku:* "delicacy, good meal."
> *Konomazu:* "do not prefer, do not love."

This means not allowing oneself to be drawn by the taste of a good dish and being able to nourish oneself, whatever the nature of the food available. In the life of a *bushi,* it was necessary to face situations of war in which material conditions could reach levels of extreme privation. One had to be able to avoid being weakened by unfavorable material conditions. In addition, daily life was regarded as a preparation for war. In Musashi's time, wars began to occur more rarely, and keeping oneself in condition to deal with war became an ethical matter.

Another interpretation is possible. For a follower of the way like Musashi, the taste of sophisticated cuisine would be a negative element, because it would run counter to his effort to relate to the profound nature of things, which is better reflected by the taste of simple food not requiring fussy preparation.

14. Do not possess ancient objects intended to be preserved for the future *(suezue shiromono naru furuki dogu shoji sezu).*

> *Suezue:* "in the future, posterity."
> *Shiromono:* "merchandise, object."
> *Furuki:* "ancient, old."
> *Dogu:* "object, utensil."
> *Shoji sezu:* "do not possess."

One becomes attached to an old object and tries to preserve it. One can possess an object but can also be possessed by an object.

A man might possess an object that came into his hands in a certain particular way and attach a special value to it for that reason, especially if that object came down to him from his ancestors.

One must be wary of this sort of attachment, particularly if it comes into play in choosing a weapon. An antique object may be precious, but what is important here is usefulness. Therefore it is necessary to free oneself from conditioning that is based on a value that is perverted from the point of view of one's primary goal.

15. Do not act following customary beliefs *(wagami ni itari monoimi suru koto nashi).*

> *Wagami:* "my body, myself."
> *Ni itari:* "concerning."
> *Monoimi:* "to avoid something because of a belief."
> *Suru koto:* "doing" (nominative form)
> *Nashi:* "negation."

There are many customs of *monoimi* in traditional Japanese usage. For example, one must not choose a course of action or a date without taking into account mandatory divinatory indications. For another example, it is believed that a person must preserve the purity of the body in order to please the gods, and numerous purificatory procedures exist. For this reason also, a person must avoid certain places and certain acts. As an expression of mourning, close relatives are required to remain shut up indoors for a longer or shorter period, from a week up to a hundred days. A number of these ancient beliefs are still observed in present-day Japan.

The important point here is that in a period in which most Japanese were subject to a great number of superstitious beliefs, Musashi dared to reject them in order to try to see the world as it is.

16. Do not seek especially either to collect or to practice arms beyond what is useful *(hyogu wa kakubetsu yo no dogu tashinamazu).*

> *Hyogu:* "arms, weaponry."
> *Kakubetsu:* "particularly, especially."
> *Yo no:* "supplementarily, in surplus, outside of."
> *Dogu:* "utensil, object."

Tashinamazu: negative form of *tashinamu,* "do not like to practice or collect."

For Musashi, under no circumstances were weapons collectible objects, even if they had great aesthetic qualities. One had to know how to use them correctly and have the ones that were necessary. If they were not available, one had to know how to make them oneself. Musashi himself handmade a considerable number of weapons.

17. Do not shun death in the way *(michi ni oitewa shi o itowazu omou).*

Michi: "the way."

Ni oitewa: "in."

Shi o: "toward death."

Itowazu: negative form of *itou,* "do not detest, do not avoid or shun."

Omou: "to think, to consider."

Musashi also presents this idea in the Scroll of Earth in the *Gorin no sho.*

18. Do not seek to possess either goods or fiefs for your old age *(rogo ni zaiho mochiyuru shoryo ni kokoro nashi).*

Rogo ni: "having grown old, being old."

Zaiho: "treasure."

Mochiyuru: "to possess."

Shoryo: "fief."

Kokoro: "heart, mind, thought."

Nashi: "negation."

19. Respect Buddha and the gods without counting on their help *(busshin wa totoshi, busshin o tanomazu).*

Busshin: "Buddha and the gods."

Totoshi: "respectable."

Tanomazu: "not depending on, not counting on someone," negative form of *tanomu.*

20. You can abandon your own body, but you must hold on to your honor *(mi o sutetemo myori wa sutezu).*

Mi: "the body, oneself."

Sutetemo: "even if one abandons" (*suteru:* "to abandon").

Myori: "reputation, honor."

Sutezu: "to not abandon" (negative form of *suteru*).

21. Never stray from the way of strategy (*tsune ni hyoho no michi o hanarezu*).

Tsune ni: "always, at any moment."

Michi: "the way."

Hanarezu: "to not stray from, not deviate from" (negative form of *hanareru*).

The *Dokkodo* brings out the asceticism that Musashi advocates in connection with the way of strategy. The life and works of Musashi have been the object of systematic eulogies and passionate critiques. Thus some of our contemporaries have described him as obsessive, paranoid, and the like. But these judgments do not take into account the lifestyle of his period. Nonetheless, we can also adopt a critical attitude.

Musashi represents a form of fruition of the practice of the arts of his time, and the works he left behind are a reflection of this. In order to understand Musashi's personality, we must see what he did in relation to what he was seeking to do and also take into account the innovative qualities of his quest when seen within the context of this period in history. His writings show that his mental and spiritual stance does not arise from the context of the ordinary preoccupations of ordinary people; rather, his entire life was structured around the extended dynamics of the way of strategy. However, we shall see from other examples that this total concentration of his on the way, as rare and exceptional as it was, had an exemplary value for the society in which he was living. Is strategy not a positive way of shaping the human energy of society as a whole, a way that does not hide either from life's harshness or from death?

Thus, both in connection with the martial arts and in terms of daily life, it would be unjust to judge Musashi's thought on the basis of the forms of security and comfort that we are familiar with, on our values and our conception of death.

APPENDIX

Notes on the Translation of the *Gorin no sho*

The Text of the *Gorin no sho*

The text of the *Gorin no sho* used in this book throughout is from the 1942 edition of the most common version, the one edited by Takayanagi Mitsutoshi. (10) This edition is based on the text handed down in the Hosokawa family.

In making my translation, I compared different versions and different transcriptions into modern Japanese of Musashi's texts. Where these versions presented significant differences, I have so indicated in a note.

Translation of the *Gorin no sho*

In my translation of the *Gorin no sho* I made every effort to render as faithfully as possible the meaning such as it appeared to me from reading the Japanese text and continually referring to the practice of the martial arts. Difficulties in comprehending Musashi's text are numerous, even in Japanese. At the end of his edition of the *Gorin no sho*, Watanabe Ichiro wrote:

> The *Gorin-no-sho* was written by Musashi on the basis of the *Hyoho sanju-go-kajo* in the strained psychological conditions of the end of his life. He did not have enough time to reexamine the text; that is why all through it we see traces of confusion and repetition. Nevertheless, this has the advantage of

showing, in the manner of a sketch, the thoughts on the martial arts and on life that he had come to after more than fifty years of practicing swordsmanship. But if we read it from the point of view of the technique and original principles of the School of Two Swords, we cannot help but recognize that it is too abstract and general, lacks concrete detail, and leans too far toward the psychological aspect. (13, p. 172)

In the epilogue to his work on the *Gorin no sho*, Takayanagi Mitsutoshi writes:

In any event, the *Gorin-no-sho* is a work that is difficult to read. In general, works on art and technique are difficult. . . . It is by knowing kendo that the *Gorin-no-sho* can be fully understood. It must be admitted, therefore, that it is normal for this work to be difficult for us to understand. But considering his time in history, it is admirable that he was able to write with so much clarity.

However, it is not enough for us to establish that the *Gorin-no-sho* is a work that is difficult to understand. It must be admitted that Musashi lacked the ability to organize his knowledge. I do not mean to say that he did not master kendo in an organized fashion; he was able to become an adept of the highest quality because he did master his art in an organized fashion. It is in his way of organizing his knowledge on the art of the sword in a scientific manner that he shows himself lacking in the ability to organize. (10, pp. 96–99)

The difficulties in Musashi's text present themselves all the more acutely when one is translating it. As his critics indicate, repetition, elliptical expressions, and obscure and ambiguous passages are numerous. In a translation into a Western language, because of the logical structure of this language and the precision of its terminology, the risk is double: Sometimes a translation that is too precise, even if it closely follows the text, runs the risk of only partially rendering the meaning; sometimes the meaning is liable to become diluted, giving the impression of very general aphorisms. It is true that Musashi often uses words in a polysemous fashion, but the appearance of empty generality that one can sometimes encounter on a first reading acquires precision, in my experience, when the passage is applied to practice.

The critics just cited seem to have based their remarks on a distortion of the sense of Musashi's work. They consider it as a literary work, the entire sense of which is meant to be communicated by the use of words. In my view, Musashi's text should be understood by seeing its connection to those to whom it was addressed, his students, and by understanding the role its author intended it to play for them—a guide to be used as a complement to shared practice.

At the beginning of the Scroll of Water, Musashi says, "Read this text thinking that it is written for you, do not think that you are reading or learning just written things."

As we practice the martial arts, we feel the need to preserve the know-how we acquire, either in writing or through drawings. When we receive an explanation that makes us truly understand an important aspect of a technique, or when we discover for ourselves a new meaning in a technique, we feel the need to note this down. These notes are often composed in a kind of shorthand, and if another person were to read them, they would probably have a hard time understanding them. But if our experience and our sensations, for us, give substance to this simple notation, it will be enough to preserve the sensations we have felt and the knowledge we have gained.

For example, in my practice notebook, I read the following line: "Do not stay frozen after gripping the adversary's wrist." That is a note I took fifteen years ago in Tokyo when I received instruction from Master Kubota, who taught me gripping techniques in jujutsu. *Itsuku*, "frozen" or "fixed," is an expression frequently used by Musashi. This simple note evokes for me a whole series of exercises that I carried out under the direction of this master. It even evokes for me the pain I felt in my wrist, which became swollen and nearly black from the bruising that resulted from continuous gripping exercises. It is accompanied by these various sensations that I recall Master Kubota's precious teaching, which I could formulate in the following fashion:

When faced with a punching attack, you should never think of gripping the adversary's wrist but, above all, think of parrying. Parrying should always be uppermost in your mind. If you succeed in parrying in the right way, following the pattern of movement of your technique, you will naturally succeed in gripping your opponent's wrist without fail. But once you have gripped his wrist, your hand must not remain frozen (*itsuku*) even for a brief instant. If you stagnate, you will not be able to exert the right pressure with the base of your index finger, and you will lose the entire effectiveness of your grip. Staying stagnant is a disease in the practice of the martial arts. You must avoid stagnation in all techniques, especially in footwork. As soon as your feet freeze or stagnate, you become vulnerable, since at that precise moment you can no longer react appropriately to your opponent's attack. Conversely, you should not let the moment escape when your adversary's feet are about to stagnate. That is the moment when you can attack.

For me, this whole series of teachings I received from that teacher arises out of that little note. The way I read it is very different from how I would read a text by someone else. First, in order to grasp the thought of another, we have to try to understand the thread of their logic. Sometimes, then, our own experience might accord with theirs, and in this case only what they have written can acquire for us a body that is richer than the explicit expression. But this is rather rare; whereas for personal notes, a few written words always serve to evoke a sequence of experiences. But it is possible that a few words written by a master can capture an experience he has shared with his students. For example, Master Kubota, after having shown us a number of gripping and throwing techniques, explained to us that to make these techniques more forceful and effective, the essential point was *sakazuki o nomi hosu*, "empty a glass of sake." This description of a movement and the form one's hand takes in executing it summarized in the best manner the way to execute and work with the grip in order to immobilize the adversary. Later, in a booklet intended for his students, he wrote the following brief description: "After having accomplished the hold, if you make the gesture of emptying a glass of sake, your adversary will be hanging by his wrist like a rag." For those who received his instruction, this text is clear and eloquent. The image he used was a guide that would help them to improve their practice.

In the passage from the Scroll of Water cited above, I believe Musashi was reminding his intended readers, who were his close students, that his text should be read in this way and that everything he had written in his book had already been explained in a richer fashion in the course of his instruction. Thus this was not a work intended to make his strategic thought and his techniques understandable to a reader who was discovering them for the first time. In a certain sense the *Gorin no sho* is a synthesis of the notes that Musashi's students might have taken if they had their master's permission and if they had had writing ability comparable to Musashi's. In any case, Musashi's students certainly did not read this work with the feeling of encountering this material for the first time. Thus Musashi was giving them his teaching in the form of a final synthesis, hoping that his disciples had already assimilated it well and that they would read the text as though they had written it themselves.

Thus reading the *Gorin no sho* as a text that stands by itself would represent a departure from this understanding. There are several possible readings of this work and several possible approaches that a translator could take. I chose to understand the *Gorin no sho* on the basis of my practice, first of all to enrich this practice. I tried to apply Musashi's instructions to barehanded combat and also executed the techniques sword in hand in order to understand them well.

In my translation I have attempted to reconstruct the meaning the text would have when being read in this fashion. I have endeavored to remain faithful to the Japanese text, but sometimes the literal translation seemed to obscure or impoverish the meaning. Particularly for those passages that Japanese authors criticize for their lack of organization or their repetitiveness, I tried to bring out the flow of the author's thought. There was an implied reference here to an experience of the strategy of combat that did not need to be made entirely explicit, because of the style of communication Musashi chose in view of the fact that he was addressing his most advanced students. The difficulty arises in part from the fact that Musashi plays on the multiple meanings of words and often uses the same term in different senses. Two examples are *kokoro* and *michi*. I chose, as I explain below, to translate these terms in various ways. One of the major difficulties was to provide an effective description of movements as well as the dynamic that underlies them; this was difficult because of the inherent differences in the way the body and the mind are represented in the two cultures. Since repetitions of words or expressions in one paragraph were frequent, I tried to render the meaning of the text in the best way and avoided repetitions when they obscured it.

All through the translation, I have tried to maintain the contribution to the overall meaning that comes from putting Musashi's instructions into practice, yet I was constantly vigilant to avoid personal interpretations.

In the *Gorin no sho* there are certain terms that appear frequently that pose particular difficulties for translation. It seems to me necessary to offer some explanation of these.

Some Terms That Create Difficulties for Translation

The meaning of the terms *ku, michi,* and *kokoro* is so broad that they are difficult to render in another language, and moreover, in Musashi's writings their sense varies according to the context. Therefore I made the decision to use several translations for each one of these words and give the Japanese word either in parentheses or in a note.

In addition, certain terms that have no equivalent in English recur frequently in the text. They are *hyoho, hyoshi, ri,* and *toku.* Nevertheless, in order not to make the translation too ponderous, I have systematically used an English term to translate each of them. However, I feel it is indispensable to draw the reader's attention to the disparity in meaning between the Japanese terms and their translation.

Hyoho

For *hyoho* I did not find any expression that renders its precise meaning. After having long hesitated over the possibility of simply keeping the Japanese word in the translation, I decided to translate the word systematically as "strategy." Despite this, however, considering the importance of this word in Musashi's thought, I used the Japanese word *hyoho* in the commentaries.

Hyoho (or *heiho*) means "military method" or "strategy." For Musashi it means a way (*do* or *michi*) that determines the direction of one's whole life. This is the way he followed with perseverance, committing himself to it totally. The term *strategy* is deficient in rendering *hyoho* because, though it does indicate an area of interest and activity, it does not include the dimension of "the way" that is present in the Japanese. Moreover, this term also does not include the dimension of the practice of technique, which for Musashi is central to the conception of *hyoho.*

In the practice of *hyoho,* Musashi distinguishes two levels, which he refers to frequently in the text: *daibun no hyoho* and *ichibun no hyoho. Dai* means "great" and *ichi* means "one." Sometimes he uses the words *tabun* instead of *daibun* and *shobun* instead of *ichibun. Ta* means "many" and *sho* means "small."

For *bun* I give here only the senses that are relevant to the use of the term in our context:

1. Separate part or division of a part, a party, social situation, degree of ability.
2. The position or hierarchical place that corresponds to a particular role.

Since Musashi uses these pairs of terms interchangeably, I conclude that *daibun* and *ichibun,* on one hand, and *tabun* and *shobun,* on the other, have the same sense. What they refer to is something relating to a party composed of a single person and something related to a large or numerous party.

I translated *ichibun* and *shobun* by "individual strategy." It was difficult, without a long paraphrase, to render the sense of "small" that goes with *bun* but does not apply to strategy. "Small-scale strategy" was a possible translation. With the words *daibun* and *tabun,* strategy having to do with large divisions or large parties, Musashi refers not only to the art of leading large groups in combat but also to leading groups in all aspects of life. Two translations struck me as possible—either "large-scale strategy" or "group strategy" as opposed to "individual strategy." I decided on the latter, more concise formulation.

Hyoshi

It seems necessary to explain the precise meaning of *hyoshi,* since this notion is quite complex.

According to the dictionary, it has three main senses:

1. A musical term.
   a. Basic element of a rhythm. Division of a melody arrived at by counting the number of rhythmic elements. The break in a melody made by a rhythmic unit.
   b. Unit of time measure in the performance of music. Powerful drum sound that marks a rhythmic unit in traditional Japanese music (*gagaku*).
   c. Musical instruments of Noh theater.

2. Rhythm, cadence, or momentum in things or in musical expression.
   a. Striking a drum or striking two pieces of wood together to give a signal or a warning.
   b. The momentum or cadence with which things evolve or advance.

      c. The texture of the sensation felt in doing something.

      d. The moment or the occasion when something is accomplished.

3. The wooden blinders attached to the two sides of a horse's head. (99)

Even though *hyoshi* is usually translated "cadence" or "rhythm," these words do not render well the sense the term has in the martial arts. For this reason, I summarize below the essential points of the analysis of *hyoshi* I have given elsewhere:

> In combat, for each movement of evading, blocking, attacking . . . there is a cadence, and this is a constraint for us, just as the cadences of the adversary are. No movement is independent of certain rhythms that are at once physical and mental. Even when we are apparently immobile, just from the rhythmic contraction and relaxation of our muscles, of our breathing, etc., we possess a rhythm that is linked to the movements we are making or are about to make.
>
> The relation between two combatants brings into play the whole set of cadences manifested by each of them: movements, facial expressions, breathing, the ebb and flow of muscular tension, mental state. . . .
>
> In combat, we live each moment in waves of rhythm or cadence. The subjective time of the combatant does not flow in a flat, uniform fashion.
>
> The Japanese notion of *hyoshi* refers to the sequence of spatiotemporal, rhythmic intervals produced by the reciprocal relations of two combatants, and at the same time, to the cadence proper to each of them, which is closely linked to breathing and mental state.
>
> In a more general sense, I would define *hyoshi* this way: It is an integrated set of cadences that link as rhythmic factors several subjects and their surroundings within the framework constituted by a cultural activity. This integrated set of cadences comes to fruition in a balance or an overall harmony. (53, pp. 86–87)

Kokoro

Kokoro designates the functions of the mind, emotional and intellectual. This notion is used in opposition to the body and to an object. Five major meanings are distinguished with variations in subsidiary senses. I summarize those relating to Musashi's use of the term.

1. Spiritual and mental activities as a whole.

      a. The basis of a human being's spiritual activities: reason, knowledge, feeling, will.

    b. The true thought that cannot be grasped on the surface, or the original state of thought.

    c. The innate or acquired tendency of a person's spiritual activity, thus personality or character.

    d. The secret conception of a thought or a feeling. The inside of the mind.

2. One of the following areas of activity of the human mind: knowledge, feeling, will.

    a. The psychological activity that permits one to decide on a behavior through thinking things through in an orderly fashion; discrimination or discernment; detailed thought.

    b. Ability to cope with things according to the situation.

    c. Ability to accept that which is contrary to one's own thought.

    d. That which fluctuates subtly within the subjective process in relation to the external world.

    e. Consideration or feeling with regard to others.

    f. Sensibility that is capable of understanding or giving birth to poetry, literature, or the arts.

    g. Consciousness or feeling that is at the origin of linguistic expression.

    h. Intention.

3. Mental activity that has a profound relationship with human activity, such as religion.

4. Having to do with objects or things by analogy with the human heart.

    a. The essential way of being of things. The central line. The principle of things.

    b. The reason things occur. The principle of things.

5. With regard to the human body or things, the aspect that has to do with the heart or the position that corresponds to the heart.

    a. The center of things.

    b. The heart, the chest. The part of the human body where it was traditionally thought the heart resides.

I have translated *kokoro* by "mind" where it was related to the first group of senses, with accentuations of meaning varying according to the context. I have translated it by "sensation" in sense 2h and in occurrences where it reflected the third and fourth group of senses.

When *kokoro* designated "mind" in a sense in which in the English language there is no distinction between the mind and the person, that is, in cases where mind was indistinguishable from the mere expression of the existence of a subject, I did not use a particular word for *kokoro*.

Ku

Ku presents more than a terminological problem. The difficulty was to render the fullness of the Japanese term in English, in which no equivalent for it exists.

Ku means:

1. Between heaven and earth. Heaven or sky. Space.
2. Emptiness, void.
3. Without foundation.
4. Without interest, without meaning.
5. Buddhist term: all things, from heaven to earth, originate from internal and external causality and are empty of a nature of their own. In reality, *ku* has neither real substance nor natural autonomy. (99)

There are three normal pronunciations of the ideogram *ku*. Pronounced *ku* or *kara*, it tends to mean emptiness; pronounced *sora*, it means heaven or sky, but the two meanings can overlap.

In Musashi's text the ideogram is pronounced *ku*, but Musashi sometimes gives it the first of these two meanings, at other times the second, and sometimes even both at the same time. I have translated this term with one or the other of these two meanings, or else with both at the same time. However, most of the time, especially when it deals with practice and the attitude that underlies it, the sense of the term is "emptiness." In the Scroll of Heaven, the term is taken in its very broadest sense; that is, it takes on the Buddhist meaning.

Michi

Musashi frequently uses the term *michi*.

According to the dictionary, *michi* is composed of the prefix *mi*, "veneration" or "respect," and the noun *chi*, "the god who possesses the way or the road." (99) But this etymology is doubtful.

Michi has two principal meanings:

1. A place where humans pass and phenomena having to do with this passage. In more precise terms:
   a. The line of a journey, road, way on earth; maritime way.
   b. Small road, path (as opposed to a large road or a boulevard).
   c. The region or area one can reach by following a road. The six principal roads (in the *Kojiki*).

    d. The process of a journey or a voyage.

    e. The act of walking or making progress on a road or the route of a journey.

    f. The length of the road or the journey. Unit of measure of the length of a road.

2. The manner in which a person progresses. The guideline for conduct a person should refer to in leading his life. In more precise terms:

    a. The line or direction to follow for each person in accordance with his position or situation. The line or the principle in accordance with which things naturally evolve. The principle or reason of that which is normal and just.

    b. The way or the road indicated by the gods, the Buddha, the saints or sages. Doctrine, dogma, the way of Buddha.

    c. Means, method; way of doing things. The right way of doing things.

    d. A particular domain. A particular direction.

    e. An area of specialization. A special method. An area of art. From the time of the feudal period, *michi* also began to take on the sense of following the way in order to deepen and expand the quality of being human or to edify and educate the human person.

    f. The route or road to take in order to achieve a goal. A process it is necessary to go through in order to attain an objective.

In Musashi's writing, *michi* has several meanings, which vary according to context. For this reason I did not always translate it with the same term. When I translated it by a term other than "way," I have so indicated in a note, or I have given the word *michi* in parentheses after the translation.

Musashi often uses *michi* in sense 2, especially 2b and 2e. In that case I translate it as "way." In several passages in the Scroll of Earth he makes use of the sense of "domain" or "specialization," somewhere between 2b and 2e, to convey the sense of a professional activity. He also often uses sense 2a. In those cases, I translate: "principle *(michi)*."

In descriptions of technique, Musashi frequently uses *michi* in sense 1, especially 1a, 1d, and 1e.

Ri

The pronunciation *ri* corresponds to two ideograms. Musashi uses both of them:

1. Reason, principle.

2A. (a) Very hard-hitting, quite incisive; (b) that which is convenient; (c) effectiveness, utility; (d) the terrain is excellent; (e) victory; (f) interest, advantage, gain. (100)

2B.   (a) Interest, gain; (b) interest (on a sum of money); (c) advantage or opportunity, or domination in combat, victory; (d) that which is convenient, useful; (e) function, effectiveness; (f) quite sharp (for a blade), incisive (for the intelligence). (99)

The meaning of the first ideogram does not cause any problems for translation. But Musashi frequently uses the second ideogram but adds to it the sense of the first one (reason, principle). For example, at the beginning of the Scroll of Water, he writes: *"Tatoe kotoba wa tsuzukazaru to intomo, ri wa onozukara kikoyubeshi."*

Musashi is speaking here to his students, presenting to them his whole approach to the Scroll of Water. In this context the sense of "reason" or "principle" seems to be required. For this reason, I translated: "Even if words are insufficient, you should understand the principle intuitively."

Musashi also employs the second ideogram in the sense of "advantage, effectiveness, opportunity."

Toku

Toku means:

1.   Expression in the action of mastering the way of human beings.
2.   Expression of rightness in action.
3.   The personal ability that makes it possible to decide with certainty in conformity with moral principles or a moral ideal. The habit of deciding on and carrying out a right action. One of the most important conceptions in human ethics.
4.   Rightness. The way of the good.
5.   The force and quality that make someone respected. Virtue.
6.   Innate nature. One's personal quality.
7.   Blessing. Grace.
8.   Wealth.

In this last sense, *toku* can also be written with another ideogram, but Musashi does not use that one. (99, 100)

I translated *toku* as "virtue," the most frequent sense in Musashi's writings. When I used another translation, I so indicated in a note.

NOTES

Introduction

1. Ancient Japanese works were written on long pieces of paper arranged as scrolls. These were progressively unrolled and rolled as they were written or read through. Each scroll was conceived of as a complete entity, either a work in itself or a chapter.

Writings on the Five Elements (*Gorin no sho*)

1. Even the translation of the title poses a problem. It is written *Gorin sho*, but the custom has been established of reading it *Gorin no sho*. *Go* means "five," *sho* means "writing"; but translating the term *rin* is more difficult. The Japanese dictionary (99) gives for the meaning of *rin*: "rounded form," "circle," "ring," "wheel," "fully open flower." The underlying idea comes from Buddhist thought. In the same dictionary, for the expression *gorin*, the following explanation is given: *go* is a simplification of *godai*, "the five elements that constitute the universe"; *rin* means "the acquisition of all the virtues." The universe is composed of five elements: earth, water, fire, wind, and heaven or space. Each one of these possesses a complete abundance of virtues, expressed by a perfectly completed circle, with the rounded form symbolizing perfect unity.

The work is composed of five scrolls, each of which bears the name of one of the elements. Neither the word *circle* nor the word *ring* is satisfactory, because the image providing a figurative representation for either of these words (*gorin soto ba*) is composed of a stack of trimmed stones: a square one for the earth, a spherical one for water, one in the shape of a truncated cone for fire, the section of a sphere for wind, and a stone in the shape of a lotus bud for heaven. I have elected to use the word *element,* which corresponds to the general idea but is not completely satisfactory either, because it does not do justice to the idea of perfect unity.

2. *Niten ichi ryu: ni,* "two"; *ten,* "heaven, universe"; *ichi,* "one"; *ryu,* "school." *Niten* has several senses:

1. Two heavens.
2. The two heavenly bodies, or the moon god and the sun god.
3. Another heaven or another universe that is contrasted with the natural heaven or universe in the following sense: When someone receives a very great favor from a person, that person is considered as a heaven or a universe. (99, 100)

We could translate the name literally as "School of Two Heavenly Bodies United" or "School of Two Heavens United." In the *Gorin no sho,* Musashi designates his school by this name only twice. He usually uses *Nito ichi ryu.* Instead of *ten,* "heaven," he uses *to,* which means "sword," which I have translated as "School of Two Swords." A more literal translation would be "School of the Unity of Two Swords," but this overly long formulation loses the conciseness of the Japanese expression.

The term *niten* evokes two images. We can understand *niten* as a contraction in which the idea of *to,* "sword," is implicit, and this expression then yields the idea of two swords raised toward the sky—or else the two swords, the long and the short, raised toward the sky—symbolizing the two heavenly bodies, or the sun god and the moon god.

Later on, the expression *Niten-sama* (*sama* means "lord") was used as a name for Musashi by his admirers.

3. "Way of strategy": *hyoho no michi.*

4. The province of Higo corresponds roughly to the present-day prefecture of Kumamoto.

5. The name of Musashi's father was very likely Hirata Munisai. He was one of the principal vassals of a minor feudal lord of the mountainous region of Sakushu, west of Kyoto. He was a practitioner of the sword and the *jitte,* a small metal weapon with six hooks on it with which it was possible to parry a sword and potentially immobilize it for a moment.

6. The province of Harima corresponds to a part of the present-day prefecture of Hyogo.

7. As far as Musashi's year of birth is concerned, opinions are divided between 1582 and 1584. I have adopted the second date, which seems the more trustworthy.

8. The province of Tajima corresponds to the current prefecture of Hyogo.

9. Certain duels Musashi fought have remained famous. One of the best known is that in which, all alone, he opposed the adepts of the Yoshioka dojo, one of the most famous of the eight schools of Kyoto. After successively vanquishing the two principal masters of the school in individual combat, Musashi confronted the entire group of the school's practitioners by himself. His victory over the Yoshioka dojo began to solidly establish Musashi's reputation. This combat took place in 1604; Musashi was then twenty years old. At the age of twenty-one, one year after this combat, Musashi wrote "The Mirror of the Way of Strategy" (*Hyodokyo*), which is composed of twenty-eight instructions on strategy. This shows that from the time of his youth he was trying to arrive at a kind of written synthesis of his art. We find in that work a section whose title ("When One Is Fighting against Several Adversaries") recalls this fight against the Yoshioka dojo.

10. Musashi recognized when he was about thirty that despite all the victories he had won up to that point, he had not attained the ultimate level of his art. These victories were only relative ones, since accidental elements—chance, the inadequacy of his opponents, and so forth—were factors in them. For twenty more years he sought after the immutable essence of his art, and it was not until he was around fifty that he believed he had reached a satisfactory state of insight. He expressed this in a poem, as follows:

> I penetrated so deeply into the mountains in my quest,
> Now here I am, come out the other side, so close to human beings.

11. Four-thirty in the morning.

12. "Warrior families," *buke*: This word literally means "family" or "clan," the *ke* of a warrior, *bu*. Here the term is used to refer to the class of warriors in the context of the education that is appropriate for this social group. The term *ke* is also pronounced *ie* and means "house," "family," and also "clan." Here, by an extension of the sense of "clan," it designates the class of warriors. The terms *bushi*, "warriors" or "samurai," and *buke* should be distinguished.

13. *Suki mono* or *suki sha*: from *suki*, "art of living that includes the art of tea," and *mono* or *sha*, "man." This term is no longer in use today.

14. This sentence, like one that comes a bit further on ("Without learning how to handle weapons, without knowing the advantages of each of them, a warrior is lacking somewhat in education") has a tone that is critical toward the warriors of the time. In Musashi's eyes, very few warriors seem to have been worthy of the name. Musashi declared in a previous paragraph, "But very few like the way of strategy." Thus the practice of strategy does not seem to have been easy, even for warriors of this period.

Musashi's attitude will become clearer and clearer as we advance in the *Gorin no sho*. He is trying to find, by means of what he calls *hyoho*, "strategy," a pragmatic approach that is generally applicable. But his pragmatism is not a technique in the Western sense of the term. There is no mind/technique duality. For Musashi, technique is not distinct from mind. Thus mind must be sought for in technique, and the principle of effectiveness is always included in the essential logic of technique. Musashi considers the *hyoho* he practices to be a great principle applicable to all phenomena. He is himself his techniques; the man becomes one with the techniques he applies. Each of the arts can become a path in life if it is understood as a way.

This manner of thinking was reinforced and refined during the Edo period (1603–1867), when Japanese society cut itself off almost entirely from the outside world. Japan fell back on itself and developed a society in which various cultural models came together in their movement toward refinement and formalization. It is only in societies of this type that it is possible to conceive of a principle that is valid for all phenomena, such as the one sought by Musashi.

15. Kantori is presently called Katori and is located in Chiba prefecture. The shrine of Katori is dedicated to Futsunushi no kami, a god of war. (100)

"Kashima" refers to the shrine of Kashima, located in Ibaraki prefecture. According to the *Kojiki* (122, pp. 65–70), Takemikazuchi no Mikoto conquered the country of Ashihara no nakatsu kuni at the command of the goddess Amaterasu. The Kashima shrine is dedicated mainly to Takemikazuchi, a god of war. Hitachi was an ancient province that corresponded to parts of the two present-day prefectures of Chiba and Ibaraki.

When the *sakimori*, soldiers of eastern Japan, moved down into Kyushu to defend it from the invasion of the Koreans and the Chinese, they went to pray to the god of the Kashima shrine. This ritual at the shrine, which was called *kashima dachi*, became established as a custom in the seventh century. Use of the ritual in connection with the recruitment of *sakimori* was abandoned at the beginning of the tenth century, but the cult of the war god of the Kashima shrine continued. It took on greater importance beginning in the Kamakura era, especially for warriors of eastern Japan. The town of Kashima developed along with the shrine.

The two shrines of Katori and Kashima are located on opposite banks of the Tone river. The water god, the god of the river, and the god of the tides are also venerated there. As far as the practice and culture of the martial arts are concerned, the traditions of the two shrines go back to mythological times. Beginning in the fourteenth century, several schools of swordsmanship were founded by priests of these shrines.

The oldest known of these schools was founded by Iizasa Choisai Ienao, a warrior attached to the Katori shrine. (1-b, 1-c, 32, 42) Choisai was experienced in battle and the study of the sword and lived at the Katori shrine while striving to perfect his swordsmanship. He prayed to the war god of the shrine from morning till night and trained with his sword against the trees. At the end of three years of solitary exploration, he received a revelation from the war god and founded the school of the sword known as Tenshi shoden Katori shinto ryu. This school is presently called Shinto ryu. Iizasa Choisai died at the age of a hundred on the fifteenth of the fourth month of the second year of Chokyo (1488).

The school of swordsmanship called Kashima shin ryu or Kashima shin kage ryu was founded by Matsumoto Bizen no kami Masabobu (1468–1524), a student of Iizasa Choisai. The Matsumoto family had been priests of the Shinto shrine of Kashima for generations. Here in brief is the story of Matsumoto Bizen (15, pp. 9–18; 32, pp. 23–29; 42, pp. 276–292) and his student Bokuden (32) as recounted in various chronicles and legends:

Starting from the teachings of Iizasa Choisai, Matsumoto Bizen developed techniques for various weapons, such as the lance, the *naginata*, and the staff. He transmitted the ultimate technique of his school under the name *hitotsu no tachi*, "the single sword." He fought with the lance on the battlefield twenty-three times and killed and beheaded twenty-five famous feudal lords and seventy-six ordinary warriors. He died on the battlefield at the age of fifty-seven.

Matsumoto Bizen transmitted the *hitotsu no tachi* to Tsukahara Bokuden Takamoto (1489–1571), also the son of a family of priests of the Kashima shrine. Having received the teaching of Matsumoto Bizen, Bokuden studied the art of the Katori shinto ryu with his father. In 1505, at the age of seventeen, he fought his first duel with a real sword and killed his opponent. After this he fought nineteen duels and participated in thirty-seven battles. He was wounded only by arrows, six times. The number of enemies he killed reached 212.

He secluded himself in the Kashima shrine for a thousand days and received a revelation related to the art of the sword. Then, with the teachings of Matsumoto Bizen as a basis, he founded the Shinto ryu, whose technique is a revitalized form of the *hitotsu no tachi*. Bokuden traveled through various regions in the course of three journeys, during which he met adepts of various schools and transmitted and spread the art of his own school. Here is a passage from the *Koyo gunkan* recounting his first journey: "On the journey he took to improve his understanding of strategy, Tsukahara Bokuden traveled on horseback with three spare horses, taking along with him three hunting falcons. Eighty men made up his retinue. Thus, with regard to his study of strategy, lords as well as accomplished adepts treated him with respect. Bokuden was a real adept of the art of the sword." (15, p. 10; 32 p. 24)

In Kyoto Bokuden taught his art of swordsmanship to three Ashikaga shoguns in succession: Yoshiharu (1511–1550), Yoshiteru (1536?–1565), and Yoshiaki (1537–1597).

Within the Katori and Kashima traditions, the lineage of Iizasa Choisai, Matsumoto Bizen, and Tsukahara Bokuden Takamoto is the best known. (1-b, 1-c, 15, 32, 42)

The techniques of the schools of swordsmanship that issued from this tradition are forceful and simple, since they were intended to be used on the field of battle, where warriors fought in armor.

In his text Musashi seems to be making an allusion to the manner in which Tsukahara Bokuden propagated his school.

Musashi also wrote that Arima Kihei, his first opponent in a duel, was a practitioner of the Shinto ryu, founded by Tsukahara Bokuden.

16. "The ten talents and the seven arts," *ju no shichi gei:* According to the dictionary (100), *no* and *gei* have the following meanings:

No: (1) The ability to accomplish things; (2) a person who has a talent or who has accomplished things; (3) the technique of an art, ability for technique; (4) effectiveness; (5) Noh theater.

Gei: (1) The technique or the knowledge acquired in a martial science or art; arts, crafts; (2) game technique; (3) technique, work.

17. "Pragmatic domain," *rikata:* Literally, *ri* means (1) trenchant, very sharp; (2) convenient; (3) effective, useful; (4) the terrain is excellent; (5) victory; (6) interest, advantage, gain. *Kata* means "direction," "position," "domain," "means." Thus *rikata* refers to a domain that creates an interest or an advantage and therefore has a concrete usefulness.

18. "The principles," *ri:* Musashi frequently uses the word *ri* in the sense of principle or reason (see page 130).

"The sword": *kenjutsu* literally means "techniques of the sword," hence "the sword," "the art of the sword," or "swordsmanship."

19. During Musashi's time, encounters between schools of the sword were for the most part battles fought without mercy, and taking matters lightly or having the illusion of knowledge could result in death. Thus he recommends not pausing over what is not essential. Musashi's own difficulties show through behind this remark—he never obtained a position of responsibility from a great lord commensurate with the abilities he considered himself to possess.

20. "Four ways": The description of the four ways—warrior, *shi;* peasant, *no;* artisan, *ko;* and merchant, *sho*—does not follow the hierarchical order. This might seem a bit incoherent, but it is doubtless connected with the movement of thought preparing the comparison between the *bushi* and the carpenter.

During the Tensho era (1573–1592), in institutionalizing the existing social hierarchy, Toyotomi Hideyoshi established four feudal classes or orders. This system was reinforced by the Tokugawa regime. Its principal aim was to guarantee the power of the governing class of warriors, which henceforth possessed a monopoly on weapons and benefited from various privileges. Above them, but without effective power, were the nobles who surrounded the emperor. Below these four classes, two other classes existed: *eta* and *himin,* which were considered nonhuman. The *eta* performed various impure manual tasks, notably work with animal skins. The *himin* were beggars and at the same time did work connected with the transport and cleaning of corpses.

The feudal classes were abolished in the Meiji era, but they were replaced by new social classes: *kazoku* (new nobles), *shizoku* (former warriors), and *heimin* (ordinary people). This social classification was abolished by the constitution after the Second World War. But the problem of the *eta* and the *himin* was not resolved in a satisfactory manner. Today tenacious social discrimination against the former *eta* and *himin* still exists, even though these classes no longer exist from a legislative point of view.

"For traversing human life," *hito no yo o wataru koto:* To evoke the situation of human life, Musashi uses the image of a ship crossing. He uses this image again in the Scroll of Fire.

21. *Toku* is most often translated as "virtue" (see page 131), but it also has the sense of "richness." In this passage, *toku* seems to draw on this second set of meanings and indicate the particular qualities, the richness, hidden in each weapon.

22. "Black cords," *sumigane: sumi,* "ink"; *gane* or *kane,* "ruler."

23. "Noble house," *kuge: ku,* "the emperor's court"; *ge,* "house." This refers to the social system of vassalage. "Warrior house," *buke: bu,* "military person," *ke,* the same meaning as *ge.*

In order to understand Musashi's comparison, it should be explained that in Japanese, the same term refers both to the house as a building and to the family that occupies it. The corresponding ideogram is pronounced *ie* when it is alone and *ke* or *ge* when it is combined with another word. For Japanese thought this is not merely a verbal matter but also expresses the profound sense of identity that exists among members of a family and also solidarity among members of a family down through successive generations, both of these being given material expression in the sheltering form of the house. This notion can be expanded to the level of the clan, which is conceived of as a large family, and can then extend beyond that to the solidarity among clans composing the social class of warriors.

Another extension of the term allows it to designate a school of a traditional art; for here, too, the mode of transmission of the school was based mainly on the system of house and family. The relations between the master and his disciples were patterned on the model of the family relationship of father to children. The system of adoption was often utilized to perpetuate the family name that was linked with the knowledge transmitted by a school in a hereditary fashion. The point was for the head of the family to be able to perpetuate his art and perhaps also direct the school. This tendency became more pronounced with time.

Musashi, for his part, maintained the continuity of his family through adoption, but his school was perpetuated independently of his name. It was often the case during the Edo period, and is still often the case today, that when the leadership of a school is determined by family inheritance, the quality of the school declines. What happens in these cases is that the disciple who takes over the succession is not necessarily the best one but the one best placed within the family.

24. "The Four Houses," *shike: shi,* "four"; *ke,* "house" or "family."

Several interpretations of Musashi's use of the word *shike* are possible. The word could refer either to the four Fujiwara families or to the four schools of the tea ceremony; or else it alludes to both of them. In the first sense, *shike* is an abbreviation of Fujiwara *shike* (the four Fujiwara families), which refers to the four main Fujiwara families of the eighth century. The Fujiwara family exercised a very great influence on imperial policy at that time. This family began its rise to importance at the end of the seventh century. After that it divided into numerous branches, some of which were to play an important role in the history of Japan.

The term *shike* can also refer to the four schools of *cha no yu* or *sa do* (tea ceremony). The four schools are the Omote senke, Ura senke, Mushanokoji senke, and Yabunouchike senke.

I have opted for the first interpretation, based on the first paragraph of the introduction to the *Gorin no sho,* where Musashi gives his name as Shinmen Musashi no kami, Fujiwara no Genshin. The family name taken by a *bushi* was, as Musashi's name indicates, a composite form, and often one of the names it included was a reference to a more distant clan than the one with which he was immediately connected. Inclusion of this more-distant clan served to link the individual with the period of the emergence of the *bushi* in Japanese history. In using this name, Musashi was indicating a remote derivation of his family line from the Fujiwara clan.

The other name he used, Shinmen, was that of the feudal lord of whom his family had been vassals for several generations; this is a name Musashi's family would have received authorization to use. Musashi used this name when he wanted to clarify his line of descent. The name Miyamoto does not appear here. This was the name of the village where he spent his youth, and it was not necessary to include it in his official name. Genshin is the Buddhist name that he chose as a participant in that spiritual path. The ideograms composing it can also be pronounced Masanobu. Masana would have been a childhood name.

For a *bushi*, genealogy was of major importance. A sense of honor was always attached to the family name. Although the choice of name was sometimes a matter of circumstance and was flexible, once it was determined, a *bushi* lived and died by his name.

25. "School," *ryu*: "Style," *fu*, can also be read *kaze*, "wind." "House" is *ie*.

26. "In this way the chief carpenter": In Japanese, there are two different ideograms that are pronounced *toryo*.

Toryo: (1) post, beam; (2) he who is in charge of a country; (3) chief; (4) master carpenter.

Toryo: (1) ruling all things; (2) he who rules and directs, presides. (100)

Musashi uses the second ideogram to refer to the chief carpenter as well as the chief warrior, thus stressing the comparison. That is why, in this passage, I translated as "chief carpenter" and not "master carpenter," as in the rest of the text.

I translated as "resemble each other" the expression *onaji*, which literally means "the same, identical."

27. *Shoji*: sliding screens made of stretched, translucent paper.

28. *Tokonoma, toku mawari*: architectural feature at the rear of the main room.

29. "Being vigilant with regard to the surroundings," *monogoto o yurusazaru kato*: *yurusazaru* is used in the sense of *ki o yurusanai*, "not relaxing one's attention and going into detail."

30. "Knowing substance and its function": *taiyu o shiru*. Musashi writes it *tai yu*, in hiragana.

Authors offering commentaries on the *Gorin no sho* are of different opinions on the interpretation of this term, for which four transcriptions into ideograms are possible with the following meanings:

1. "Great courage" or "courage manifested in the accomplishment of an important thing." (10)
2. "Function, effect, use." (13)

3. "Essential point" (11); *Kamata* (4) retains the hiragana and gives an interpretation in his commentary that fits with that.
4. "Substance and its application" (Buddhist term).

Musashi's contemporary, Yagyu Munenori, writes: *"Tai yu* exists in each thing;
when there is *tai,* there is *yu.* For example, the bow is *tai* and the act of aiming, drawing,
and hitting the target is the *yu* of the bow. The lamp is *tai* and the light is *yu.* . . . The
sword is *tai;* slashing and stabbing is *yu.* Thus the essence derives from *tai,* and that
which arises from the essence and moves toward the outside in order to accomplish
different functions is *yu."* (56, p. 102)

Yagyu Munenori developed a theory of the art of the sword based on the practice
of Zen. Musashi also practiced Zen; that is why, in view of Yagyu Munenori's interpretation, I based my translation on the fourth sense of the term.

31. "Ambient energy": I translated the term *ki,* which means "air," "ambience," "vital
energy," this way in order to try to preserve the play on the two aspects of the term's
meaning.

32. Musashi could in fact have been a carpenter and even a master of this discipline.
In the course of his life, he handcrafted works of art as well as weapons and objects of
daily usage for a warrior. His wood sculptures and his paintings are well known, but
he made a great number of ordinary objects whose qualities are also highly esteemed:
wooden swords *(bokken),* saddles, *tsuba* (sword hilts), metal *hunchin* (paperweights for
Chinese ink calligraphies), and so on.

The modern separation of art from handcraft did not exist for Musashi. He was an
artist and artisan at the same time. At the time of his duel with Sasaki Kojiro, it is said
that he made a wooden sword from an oar just before the bout. Later on, when one
of his patrons asked him, "What was the *bokken* like that you used to fight against
Kojiro?" by way of answer, Musashi readily made on the spot a *bokken* of 127 centimeters in length. This *bokken* is still preserved today. (11, p. 37)

33. Musashi writes this *mendo. Mendo* or *medo* refers to "long external corridors." In the
construction of this period, long, raised external corridors linked buildings. To make
it possible to enter inner courtyards on horseback, it was sometimes necessary to
provide passageways by having a corridor that could be raised in the manner of a
drawbridge. This is what was called a *kiri medo* or *medo.* Later on this term came to
refer to the long corridors. (99)

Mendo, written in another way, means "problem of detail." The ideogram is derived from the one for the term above. The business of getting the horses by the *medo*
was a source of problems, hence the emergence of this second sense, which is more

common today. (100) I kept the first interpretation because it fit with the logic of the comparison of strategic qualities to the work of a carpenter.

34. This arrangement might seem puzzling from the point of view of Western logic. It does not have anything to do with an analysis of the techniques. It reflects something that is much more important for Musashi: the state of mind that must dominate each phase of progress along the way. In truth, for Musashi, swordsmanship is not merely a matter of technique but rather—as we have already seen—a way of life. Nevertheless, in the course of this work, the techniques are described with the greatest precision. For Musashi, man and nature are of the same order, both part of the same cosmic entity; this is what is expressed by the orientation of the Scroll of Water.

The explanation of the meaning of the Scroll of Heaven might cause the reader some confusion. This scroll represents the fruition of the process of the way, that is, emptiness, which is not nothingness but rather the origin of existence.

35. "Principle": *ri.*

36. "Model," *kata*, means "form, prototype" or "model for the plastic arts." It is also the word that designates standardized sequences of movements in the physical arts. A *kata* in this sense serves at once as an ideal reference point and as a means of transmission of technical knowledge.

37. "Happens in a short time": this idea also refers to urgent situations.

38. The word *wind* has several metaphorical senses. In the common expressions referred to here, different images are evoked. In the reference to the ancient wind and the modern wind, the image is that of fashion. In the expression "the wind of such and such a family," the meaning is "family tradition."

39. "Deviating from the true way": I translated the word *gedo* in this way, which refers to "religions other than Buddhism (for which the word *naido* is used), heresies, dogmas that are in conflict with the truth, an insult."

40. The word *ku* has several senses: "heaven," "sky," "emptiness," and "space" (see page 129). In the Scroll of Heaven, Musashi uses it in the full range of its meanings, stressing the sense of emptiness. In the text, after having translated it the first two times as "heaven (or emptiness)," I used one translation or another depending on the nuance that seemed to me to be dominant at that point.

41. "Depth," *oku*, and "surface," *kuchi*. *Kuchi* literally means "mouth," hence the image

of a mouth through which entry is made and thence of an entrance or surface in relation to a depth or core. Usually for the dichotomy of "surface" and "depth," the pair of
terms *omote* and *oku* is used.

42. "The principle of the way": *dori*.

43. "High level of ability": *Kidoku*, which today is pronounced *kitoku*, literally means (1)
"extraordinary, marvelous, something rare and strange, the fact of particularly excel-
ling, a strange sign, excellent effectiveness, being deserving of praise"; (2) "the strange
power of God and of Buddha."

44. Musashi called his school Nito ichi ryu. It is possible to interpret *ichi ryu* simply in
the sense of "my school," but in the vocabulary of the martial arts, *ichi* is frequently
used with the connotation of unity, the integration of multiple elements. For example, *ichi ban*, "a single occasion"; *ichi nen*, "a single intention"; and *ippon*, whose meaning I describe more precisely below. *Nito* means "two swords." *Ichi* means "one," and
ryu means "school." To say only "the School of Two Swords," it would be enough to
say *nito ryu*. By combining the two words *nito* and *ichi*, Musashi seems to be expressing
the state of the *bushi* who knows how to use the two swords as one. Thus the meaning
is "School of the Unity of the Two Swords," but so as to stick with a rendering that
reflects the concise rhythm of the name of Musashi's school in Japanese, I am reserv-
ing mention of this nuance for a note only.

To explain further the sense of *ichi*, I will take the example of the term *ippon*
used in all the contemporary Japanese martial arts to indicate a victory. *Ippon* is
a contraction of *ichi hon*, *hon* meaning "fundamental" or "essential." In a training
session or a tournament, it is customary to count the number of bouts won by each
participant. *Ippon* refers to a win obtained through the use of a single technique
within a system of conventions where it is recognized that if the particular movement in question had been fully completed outside the conventional system, the
opponent would have suffered a blow that would have put him out of combat. In
the days when people fought with real swords or with wooden swords, the result
of a duel was most often determined by the use of a single decisive technique.
During the period of Musashi's youth, the result was death. However, in performing
combat exercises within a school, thanks to the conventions that were adopted, the
practitioners could engage in combat repeatedly in a series of many bouts. They
then counted up the number of victories and defeats in terms of units of *hon (ippon)*.
What is sought after in the martial arts is the ideal *ippon*, that is, a victory obtained
through a technique that has an integral connection with that which is fundamental
to the combat.

45. *Ryo koshi* means "two swords." *Ryo* means "two," and *koshi* is the unit used to count swords.

46. The *naginata* is a weapon with a long handle and a thick, curved blade like that of a scythe.

47. *To no momo: To* is currently pronounced *soto* and means "outside"; *mono* means "weapon." Thus the expression means "weapon meant to be used outside," among other places, on the field of battle.

The ideogram *to* or *soto* is also pronounced *hoka*. In that case the meaning is different: "the realm or world that exists outside the ordinary one; a thing that exists outside normal standards; elsewhere, other than." If we interpret it in this sense, then the sword being the normal weapon of the warrior, the lance and the *naginata* are added on to that. We could then translate: "The lance and the *naginata* are weapons of war additional to the sword."

48. It should be noted here that in Musashi's text, the designation for each of the two swords is not consistent. Sometimes he uses *tachi* and *katana* and sometimes *katana* and *wakizashi*. As he himself explained in the previous paragraph, the two expressions mean "the large sword and the small sword," but *katana* refers to the small sword in the first expression and the large one in the second. In Musashi's time, the names of the swords had not yet become altogether fixed.

49. "It is deplorable to . . . ," *hoie ni aru bekarazu:* Hoi is pronounced *honi* at the present time and means (1) "true mind," "spirit," or "intention," "initial intention," "true desire"; (2) true sense, true meaning; (3) that which originally should be, character or manner inherent in a thing.

A literal translation would have been: "It is not in the true spirit to . . . ," but to avoid confusion with the translation of *kokoro,* I decided to avoid the terms *spirit* and *mind.*

50. Clearly there was no idea here of drawing the bow using the left hand alone. What is being talked about is carrying a bow so as to use it at some other moment. It should be noted that in battle, warriors carried several weapons at the same time. In addition to the two swords stuck into the belt on the left side, some warriors carried two or three more on their backs so they could change weapons; and others, as Musashi says, carried a bow, a lance, a *naginata,* and so forth.

51. In spite of what Musashi says, it is extremely difficult to wield a sword easily with

just one hand. Even holding a *shinai* (a bamboo practice sword), which is three to four times lighter than a sword, with just one hand, it is difficult to fight with ease.

Nowadays, there are very few practitioners of kendo who use two *shinai*. The difficulty experienced now must have been much greater when practitioners fought with swords in real combat. The fact is that in sword combat, it is not enough merely to swing the weapon, but one must also be able to parry the attacks of an opponent who is using a heavy sword that he is most often holding with two hands and then be able to slash him. It is not possible to evaluate the difficulty involved in this by fighting with *shinai* alone. "It is impossible to use two swords without having the innate strength of Niten-sama" (Sir Niten, or Master Niten, was the title of respect given to Musashi). This is an adage that is often heard in sword circles. To give you an example of Musashi's strength, I cite here a passage from the *Nitenki*:

> One day Lord Nagaoka asked Musashi: "How should bamboo poles for flags be chosen?"
>
> "Show me the pieces of bamboo you have," replied Musashi.
>
> The Lord had a hundred pieces of bamboo he had ordered for this purpose brought into the garden. Musashi picked up one of the pieces of bamboo, and holding it by the end, made a rapid stroke in the air. He went on to do the same thing with each piece of bamboo. Every one of them broke in half except one, which Musashi gave to the lord, saying, "This one is good."
>
> "That is an absolutely sure way to test them, but it can only be done by you," replied Lord Nagaoka, smiling. (2, p. 181)

52. It might be useful to make clear just how difficult it is to handle a heavy sword. At the present time in kendo, an adult man uses a *shinai* that weighs about 500 grams, a woman one that weighs 420 grams. When practitioners of another discipline, such as karate or judo, use a *shinai* for the first time, they generally have the impression that it is very light. But as they begin to practice kendo, their impression changes very quickly, and they pass through a phase where the *shinai* seems very heavy to them. Practitioners of kendo are very sensitive to the balance and differences in weight of their *shinai*, a difference of 10 or 20 grams being strongly felt. When kendo is practiced using two *shinai* (*nito*), the large *shinai* weighs about 375 grams and the small one 265. But when doing combat exercises, a *shinai* of 375 grams, held with just one hand, seems very heavy, and very few modern kendo practitioners succeed in handling one one-handed with ease.

The large sword that Musashi talks about weighed between 1,200 and 1,500 grams. Thus it was three to four times heavier than the *shinai* currently used in the *nito* (two *shinai*) combat form.

53. Here I decided to translate *hoi* this way because it seemed to me to have the sense of "initial intention."

54. This sentence explains what the way of strategy means for Musashi. It goes far beyond handling a sword. He makes things that others might seek in religion a part of strategy itself.

One anecdote—perhaps romanticized—tells us that on his way to meet a great number of opponents whom he was supposed to face in a fight in which his chances were very poor, Musashi passed by a Shinto shrine. Suddenly becoming aware that he had started to pray with the intention of asking for the protection of the gods, he straightened up and came to his senses, accusing himself of lacking confidence in his strategy, for he should be trusting his fate only to that. (61) This is the sense in which the phrase of Musashi's found in the *Dokkodo* is usually interpreted: "Respect the Buddha and the gods without relying on their help." In this way he expresses incisively and explicitly a tendency that ordinarily underlies the philosophy of *budo* but is left unspoken. Warriors could be practitioners of different religions, but the religions were more a coloration of the way of the warrior than the other way around.

55. *Hyoho futatsu no ji no ri*: Literally, *ri* means "interest, advantage." Musashi often uses *ri* without distinguishing it from its other meaning, "reason, principle, the logic of things, meaning." Here, in connection with "knowing the *ri* of the two ideograms *hyo* and *ho*," it seems more plausible that *ri* has more the sense of "meaning" or "principle" than "interest" or "advantage."

56. Musashi uses the term *bugei* to designate the martial arts in general. It is important to note that Musashi makes a point of the demarcation separating *hyoho* from the other terms. That is why I prefer here to indicate the Japanese term he uses each time rather than to translate them all as "martial arts." We have:

> *hyoho sha:* man of *hyoho*, someone who knows how to handle the sword
> *ite:* archer
> *teppo uchi:* someone who shoots a gun
> *yari tsukai:* expert with a lance
> *naginata tsukai:* expert with the *naginata*
> *tachi tsukai:* expert with the long sword
> *wakizashi tsukai:* expert with the short sword

57. "The virtue of the sword," *tachi no toku:* On the meaning of the word *toku*, see

page 13. I have translated *toku* as "virtue," but this word can also mean "interest" or "advantage." The nuance of "virtue" seemed to me to be present in the sense in which Musashi employs the term here in relation to the sword.

58. "Persevere": in this sentence Musashi uses the term *migaku*, which means "to polish" and which I have translated "to persevere." Musashi frequently uses the term *migaku* in the sense of "persevere, develop oneself, study in depth," and the like. This expression is frequently used in the realm of the arts.

59. "Appropriately": *ideau* or *deau*, meaning "to meet, to face, to coincide, to adjust to, to suit the situation."

60. "If you compare the two . . . ," *yari wa sente nari, naginata wa ushirode nari*: I rendered Musashi's comparison as I did in view of the following:

- *Sente* means "precede somebody in an act, do something before someone else, attack before someone else, fight at the head (of a group), take the initiative by attacking first."
- *Ushirode* or *gote* means "the back of a person or a thing." When it is opposed to *sente*, it designates "someone who lags behind, who lets the other take the initiative."

61. The expression *torikomori mono* could also refer to the opposite situation: "when you are attacking one or more enemies who are shut up in a house" or "whom you have encircled and who are on the defensive."

62. "Indoors": This is the translation of *zashiki*. This refers to training taking place in a covered hall. This phrase confirms that in Musashi's time, the quest for technical subtlety began to be a trend. According to Musashi, this takes you away from the practice of effective combat. This trend was further accentuated later on.

63. "They will not be appropriate . . . The bow is appropriate." In both cases, the verb is *deau*.

64. One *ken* equals 1.8 meters; twenty *ken*, the measure given here, is thus equivalent to 36 meters.

65. "The interest is great": This sentence, which is incomplete in the copy that has come down to us, is written as follows: *Sono ri ooshi*. I think this phrase is a copying

error, taking the place of *sukunashi*. In that case, the translation would be "This does not have much interest." Indeed, in many transcriptions into modern Japanese, this sentence, which does not fit into the context, is dropped; also some texts adopt the sense of *sukunashi*.

For example, Kamiko Tadashi, in his transcription, omits this sentence from his reference edition of the text of the *Gorin no sho*. (5, p. 60) Kamata Shigeo interprets it in the sense of *sukunashi*. He translates it into modern Japanese as *"Sono riten wa sukunai."* (4, p. 81) Terayama Danchu keeps the expression *sono ri ooshi*, but he attaches it to the next sentence. He has *"Sono riten no ooi nodewa jokaku no naka kara no teppo ni masarumono wa nai,"* which translates as "There is nothing more advantageous than shooting guns from the inside of a fortress." (11, p. 113)

66. As Musashi has already said, generally warriors carried two swords, the long and the short. The size of a pair of swords varied according to personal choice. The size of a sword was normally measured by the length of the blade, but to get a real idea of the dimensions of a sword, it was necessary to take into account the thickness, breadth, curve, and form of the edge, which composed the overall form of the blade, as well as the quality of the steel. Among the different possible sizes of pairs of swords, Musashi advises choosing large sizes.

67. "Cadence," *hyoshi*: The notion of *hyoshi* has major importance in the *Gorin no sho*. The term does not have an exact equivalent in English and poses significant translation problems (see page 129).

68. "Musicians with their stringed or wind instruments," *reijin kange*: *Reijin* means "a person who plays music." This word refers in particular to an officer who is a musician playing the traditional official music known as *gagaku* at the court for the nobles and also in shrines and temples. *Kan* refers to stringed instruments and *gen* to wind instruments.

69. "That which does not have a visible form," *ku naru koto*: *Ku* means sky, heaven, emptiness, or space (see page 129).

70. "The concordant cadences and . . . the discordant ones," *hazu no au hyoshi, hazu no chigau hyoshi*: *Hazu* refers to the two ends of a bow where the string is attached. It also refers to the notched end of an arrow that fits onto the bowstring. This is called more precisely the *ya hazu*. On the basis of this image, *hazu* also means "that which is thought will normally happen, that which is reasonable, reason." It is also used in the sense of "plan" or "promise."

71. I will try to convey a more concrete notion of these different forms of cadences or
hyoshi.

- "The striking cadence (or *hyoshi*)": *ataru hyoshi.*
- "The interval cadence," or more precisely, "the *hyoshi* that places you in the
  interval between actions": *ma no hyoshi.* This term refers to all the rhythmic
  elements that can develop in an interval or the moment of void, however
  short it may be, that occurs between two movements or between two phases
  of the breathing process. Such moments of void occur when a person is in
  movement as well as when he is not moving, for example, when he is in a
  guard position. If your level is high enough, you can detect these moments of
  void in your adversary and at this instant attune yourself intentionally to his
  rhythms; and you can also become aware of the moments of void in your own
  actions and fill them with a new rhythm.

    What Musashi means by *ma no hyoshi* will be dealt with later as part of the
  more general notion of *suki,* which refers to a fault or lapse. In the development of technique in the Japanese martial arts, ways of provoking a fault *(suki)*
  in one's opponent play an important role. It is not a matter of finding such a
  fault in your opponent but of creating it in him by exerting various pressures
  through your own technique and through your will to attack.

- "The opposing cadence," *somuku hyoshi: Somuku* means "to turn one's back on
  one direction, to go in the opposite direction, to move away" or "to wrong-
  foot someone." This expression refers to deliberately not matching the other's
  hyoshi in order to forestall an action (either your own or the opponent's). On
  the simplest level, this means knowing how to break the *hyoshi* of an attack
  by backing off. If you are capable of applying this awareness to your own actions, you can realize, at the moment of unleashing them, that certain attacks
  are futile, and you then become capable of dropping them in order to stay
  focused on something more important.

I find a connection between this notion from martial arts practice and Musashi's
fighting style. It is said that Musashi was able to elude the blade of his opponent with
great precision, dodging it by a margin of one and a half centimeters. This quality of
Musashi's perception is called *mikiri.* However, in the documents that are relatively
reliable, we find only a single account that would confirm this capability of Musashi's.
In the *Nitenki* we find the following passage from the account of his duel with Sasaki
Kojiro: "Kojiro's sword cut through the knot of Musashi's headband, and the headband fell to the ground. Musashi also launched his attack at the same moment and his
stroke struck the head of his adversary, who fell immediately." (2, p. 174)

The literal translation of *mikiri* is: *mi*, "to look" or "to see," and *kiri*, "to cut." Hence we may translate the term "to see with cutting minuteness" or "to see all the way with a look"; more precisely, we could say "discerning the state of situations or things with incisive rigor." This incisive rigor is not based just on a static perception of distance, because in the martial arts, distance includes movement—that is why the space of distance becomes fused with cadences. Thus *mikiri* rests on the accuracy of *hyoshi*, especially of the *somuku hyoshi*, which causes the opponent's attack to fail and leads to a sure victory. That is a first dimension of *mikiri*.

According to Musashi's logic, which is now familiar to us, *mikiri* could also be understood on a larger scale. In the course of the numerous combats in which he engaged, Musashi was never once mistaken in his assessment of the strength of his adversaries, which is what made it possible for him to avoid defeat. He never lost a fight and doubtless achieved the highest level of his time. We can also draw the conclusion that if he judged certain opponents to possibly be superior to himself, he avoided fighting with them for as long as he had not succeeded in turning the situation in his favor. For Musashi, discernment of incisive rigor must be the basis of strategy, individual or collective. In the situation of a duel, the *mikiri* of three centimeters determines the *ma* and decides the issue of the bout. *Mikiri* extended to large-scale strategy distills in one word one of the teachings of Sun Tsu: "If you know yourself and you know your enemy, you will not lose one fight in a hundred." This rigorous discernment characterizes the sword of Musashi as well as his artistic expression.

72. "Think of that which is not evil," *yokoshima ni naki koto o omou*: The Japanese expression here contains a nuance of double negation: "Think of that which is not good." Another translation, corresponding to a second sense of the term *yokoshima*, is possible: "Think of that which does not deviate from the way."

73. "Method," *ho*: *Ho* means "law, rule, manner" or "method, model." It is also a Buddhist term meaning "teaching of the Buddha." In this sentence Musashi uses *ho* to refer back to *hyoho*, thus to his teaching as a whole; that is why I translated this term as "method." A bit earlier he uses this term to refer to the precepts he had formulated. The sense of the term being clearly limited there, I translated it "rules."

74. "You maintain your vital energy constantly . . . ," *ki ni hyoho o tacsazu*: A more literal translation would be: "In your *ki*, you do not interrupt strategy." Inversion can serve to reinforce the meaning of an expression.

75. "You have free mastery of your body," *sotai yawaraka nareba*: The more usual reading of the ideograms is *jiyu*, which means "free." But in the text of the *Gorin no sho* handed

down in the Hosokawa family, which is today considered to be the one closest to the original and which I use as my basic text, these ideograms, in this passage, are transcribed without annotation, while in another passage of the Scroll of Water they are accompanied by an annotation in katakana: *yawaraka*.

In the *Ihon gorin no sho* by Yamada Jirokichi, this sentence is written differently: *Sotai yawarakani jiyu ni nari*. (14, p. 365) Thus it contains both the words *yawaraka* and *jiyu*. The meanings of these words are as follows :

- *Jiyu* means "pursuing freedom of the mind or thought." In its Buddhist sense, it means "without any constraint."
- *Yawaraka* means "being flexible, gentle, docile."
- *Yawara* is also pronounced *ju*. It is "the art of flexibility," which was the ancient form of judo. (100)

Although in the dictionaries I consulted I did not find any indication of affinity between these two words, their meanings are often used in association with practical explanations of jujutsu. For example, when I was learning jujutsu under the tutelage of Master Kubota Shozan between 1975 and 1980 in Japan, he explained the meaning of the word *ju* by completing it with the meaning of the word *jiyu*. Following his explanations of technique, he often added, *"Ju wa jiyu. Jiyu deareba yawarakai."* ("Flexibility means freedom. If one is free, one is flexible.") I interpret this as follows: The flexibility of jujutsu aims at the freedom of the body that is derived from perfect mastery of the body. If one is free in the body, the mind is also free. It is at this point that one can acquire true flexibility.

Master Kubota did not invent this association of the words *ju, jiyu,* and *yawaraka*. He himself learned it from his teacher. I have also heard this expression on other occasions, in connection with the practice of the martial arts of *kenjutsu* and karate.

Even though these connections are not reported in the dictionaries, I think it should be pointed out that these ideas are transmitted together in the practice of the martial arts. This helps to clarify Musashi's text.

76. On the sole copy of the *Gorin no sho* that has come down to us today, mention is added of a transmission later in 1667.

77. The work is composed in five scrolls, and each scroll is signed and dated in the same way.

78. "As its fundamental model": *mizu o mototoshi.*

79. "A method of pragmatic effectiveness," *rikata no ho:* For *rikata,* see note 17, page 138; literally, it means "method in a pragmatic domain."

80. *Ri.* See page 130.

81. "Read this text . . .": Let us recall that Musashi is writing for his students by way of complementing the practical exercises they have carried out under his guidance.

82. In the next three paragraphs, Musashi uses the word *kokoro* twenty-four times. See appendix.

83. Musashi here crystallizes his experience of combat in an image, writing that it is necessary to keep one's mind at the center of oneself and at the center of everything, and that the movement of the mind must never stop. When he writes that the mind must not be too much to one side, this means that one must not become attached to anything in a partial manner.

This image translates what he feels at the time of combat, when his body is reacting before any conscious reflection. He is describing a state of mind that permits him to react appropriately to each situation that arises, all the rest being left outside the field of consciousness. This is what we express sometimes in the course of training by saying "Relate to your mind as though you were sleeping"; for at the moment of falling asleep, the various thoughts and preoccupations of daily life that are an obstacle to the emergence of lucidity at the time of combat subside. Ordinary thoughts are like spots on a glass pane—only by wiping them away can we arrive at a clear view. "Relate to your mind as though sleeping" conveys the most accessible technique for attaining this state of mind.

When we attempt to apply Musashi's teaching to the combat situation, we become aware that our consciousness of time changes spontaneously. We move then in a time that is not flowing in a linear fashion but extends out like the universe. This is what I describe as "exploded" or enlarged time. (53, p. 118) This is a matter of perceiving all the aspects of a situation on the same level. The temporality of everyday life in a sense follows the image of speech flowing. Exploded or enlarged time opens one to a multiplicity of simultaneous perceptions and thus distinctly contrasts with the hierarchizing function entailed by speech, which is perpetually classifying, which operates by making the field of consciousness narrower and more precise. The temporality of combat is time during which verbalization (even for oneself) ceases to be a privileged means. The image we use for it has been devised after the fact in an effort to communicate with someone else who has also himself experienced this opening of awareness to simultaneity.

"Situating the mind at the center" describes the attitude acquired in combat of maintaining a sense of direction that underlies consciousness, which guides physical movements. Fixing precisely on an object or an aspect of the situation disrupts the breadth of this opening and puts one back in the channelized structure of everyday time. In this psychic state, neither the body nor consciousness undertakes movements by itself.

84. "Posture in strategy," *hyoho:* The posture that Musashi indicates is close to that used in the standing meditation that is an essential part of certain Chinese martial arts. In these disciplines, practitioners seek through standing meditation to achieve integration of the overall forces of the body and to extend the sensorial field that plays such an essential role in the art of combat. Some kendo masters today practice a similar meditation called *tachi geiko* (standing training) or *ritsu zen* (standing Zen). This posture makes it possible to stimulate and strengthen the various parts of the body and at the same time to enlarge the field of vision. In this exercise they include the instructions Musashi gives on the way of looking and emphasize that to see properly, it is necessary to have correct posture.

In the standing meditation used in the art of the sword, the practitioner tries to arrive at an empty state of mind that augments his lucidity and provides a foundation for exercises with energy. Starting from that, he tries to imagine various movements of technique and movements in the combat situation, without moving. In this way he studies in depth the sensations inherent in the movements so as to arrive at the essence of the movement of the technique. This is the point from which one of the paradoxes of the teaching of *budo* is derived: Speed is not worth as much as slowness; slowness is not worth as much as immobility. To perceive true movement, it is necessary to be immersed in immobility—this is the significance of the exercise of standing Zen.

85. Here Musashi uses the two terms *kan* and *ken,* which I have translated respectively as "looking" and "seeing." *Kan* refers to the "the profound looking that illuminates the essence of things," and *ken* refers to "looking that makes it possible to perceive the surface of things."

86. When we fight with excitement, our eyes are often very wide open. It is not possible to maintain this position for a long time, and we blink. Moreover, when we have our eyes wide open, we do not see distinctly what surrounds us. The way of looking that Musashi describes is close to that of painters who look at objects by squinting. This way of looking in the midst of combat has an influence on our state of mind. By looking in this way, we can curb our excitement and avoid losing our lucidity. Thus it should be understood that this way of looking is the result of the state of mind described by Musashi. That state of mind brings about that way of looking, and that way of looking is conducive to the state of mind of *hyoho.*

87. The term *itsuku* means, in the literal sense, "to establish oneself at the place one

has arrived and remain in place there." I translated this as "to become fixed." This term merits an explanation. It is generally used in the martial arts to describe a negative aspect of the accomplishment of a technique. It has to do with the instant that precedes or follows a movement in which either the body as a whole or a leg or a limb or a weapon remains fixed or frozen. As a result of this stagnation, however brief it may be, the technique loses its effectiveness and one consequently runs the risk of creating a moment of vulnerability vis-à-vis one's adversary.

For example, if after having executed a technique, the body, the arm, or the hand remains at the point reached by the last movement, the realization of the following techniques will be hindered, which brings down the level of one's technical execution as a whole. In the art of the sword, it is said that even if one's movements are correct, if the hands are in a state of *itsuku* (fixation), the sword does not cut well. The degree of effectiveness of sword strikes or punches with the fist is often diminished by this form of stagnation.

The phenomenon of *itsuku* comes from a lack of mastery of the techniques and also from a certain psychological state that is inherent in combat.

An anecdote well known in kendo circles illustrates the complexity of this phenomenon. A practitioner who had attained a high level in the art of the sword underwent his first duel to the death. He defeated his opponent, but from the moment when he cut into his opponent's body, a strange sensation remained in his hands and spread to his entire body. As he looked at the slashed body in front of him and saw the blood gushing from a gaping wound, his hands remained clenched for a moment. He said to himself: "It's fortunate my hands tensed up afterward and not before."

He was able to win because his technique was excellent, but this technique had remained partially abstract and there was no way to get beyond this abstraction other than through the experience of real combat. This is why, during a certain period, the experience of killing and slashing a corpse was a part of the training in technique. For the same reason, at the end of the Edo period, dogs were often found that had been killed or mutilated by sword blows. (94, 123)

88. "Jumping," *tobi ashi;* "with a floating step," *uki ashi;* "stomping heavily," *fumisuyuru ashi.*

89. "The essential instruction . . .": Certain masters of modern kendo insist on movement *suri ashi,* that is, by sliding the feet—lifting the heel and always keeping the same foot forward. This is a contradiction of Musashi's instruction.

What approach is closest to the right one? During the Edo period, the art of the sword was refined and developed through training in dojos, buildings designed for practice, where it was not necessary to worry about the quality of the floor, which was usually a smooth parquet. At the beginning of the Edo period, practitioners—among them Musashi—were preparing themselves for combat on the field of battle. Over time this need disappeared, while at the same time interest in posture and purity of technique increased and developed to the point where they constituted a kind of aesthetic that became a factor in judging a practitioner's progress along the way. Modern kendo took shape as an extension of this system.

Musashi's school developed directly out of his experiences on the battlefield. There the fighting terrain is never even. To move from one place to another, it is indispensable to raise the toes off the ground, because if they run into a stone or a dip in the ground, one runs the risk of twisting one's ankle or falling, which in battle could lead to death.

Also, still today in the teaching of the Jigen ryu, handed down from the seventeenth century to the present day in the fief of Satsuma (which became the prefecture of Kagoshima), a unique method of movement is practiced. Practitioners of this school perform all techniques lifting the foot up with each step. This might appear ridiculous to someone watching a demonstration in an indoor room with a smooth floor if he is unaware of the reasons for the procedure. This mode of movement goes against the grain of the aesthetic of modern kendo. It seems to me it might be interesting for contemporary practitioners of kendo to have a look at their style of footwork with the help of a little historical perspective.

A similar process has occurred in other disciplines. In karate, for example, until the beginning of the twentieth century, training and combat took place outdoors. There were a certain number of foot movements that were intended to throw sand in the face of the opponent or provide stability on uneven or broken ground. Some of these movements have been handed down to the present time and, in the name of tradition, are repeated in rooms with smooth floors without those who are performing them having any idea of their significance. Other movements have been thrown out because they seem irrational to practitioners executing them on a smooth floor without knowing their origin.

For Musashi, the manner of moving the feet is connected to the fundamental basis of strategy and is not merely a technique. Nakazato Kaizan recounts the following anecdote:

> One day a student asked Musashi about the principle that makes it possible to make progress in *hyoho*. Pointing to the edges of the tatami, which were about five centimeters wide, the master told him, "Walk on the edges."
>
> The student did this. Musashi then asked him, "If the edge were two meters high, would you be able to do the same thing?
>
> "That seems like it would be a bit difficult."
>
> "And if it were sixty centimeters wide?"
>
> "In that case, I could do it."
>
> Musashi questioned him again. "If a footbridge sixty centimeters wide

were run between the top of Himeji castle and the summit of Mount Masui-
yama [one league away], would you be able to cross that bridge?"

"I would certainly not be able to do that," replied the student.

Musashi nodded with approval and said, "That is the principle of the practice of the sword. You can easily walk on the edges of a tatami. At a height of
two meters, your mind would be calm if you were on a plank sixty centimeters
wide. Now, if the footbridge were as high in the air as the top of the castle and
the summit of Mount Masui, your mind would not be calm, because you would
be afraid of making a misstep. This fear comes from a lack of training. The beginning is easy, the middle is dangerous, and after the middle, the danger increases further. That is why you must have a confident mind; then you will not
be in danger. If you learn to walk on the edge of the tatami while strengthening
your sensation of vital energy, you will never make a misstep, no matter what
the height of the bridge sixty centimeters wide." (23, pp. 76–78)

90. "Substantial positions, . . . circumstantial ones": Here Musashi uses the expression *tai yu*, written in the hiragana alphabet. The three Japanese editions of the *Gorin
no sho* present different interpretations in ideograms of the opposition *tai yu* (see note
30, page 141).

Tai means "the body," understood as a substance or entity that supports various
functions, or "essence." *Yu* means "to play" or "to move"; written, it means "to use" or
"to employ." *Tai* corresponds to essence or substance and *yu* to an application of *tai*,
which is circumstantial.

91. "The middle-level guard position," *kamae no hoi nari*: Hoi or *honni* means (1) "true
mind" or "intention, initial intention, true desire"; (2) "true sense, true meaning"; (3)
"that which must be originally, character or manner of being inherent in a thing." I
have translated this term as "original."

92. Musashi uses the term *michi* with different meanings. Its meanings include "way,
path, discipline, sphere of activity, route, pathway, trajectory, direction, nature," and
so on. In this text *michi* seems to have four different nuances. This is why I prefer to
express the richness of its meaning by using different terms to translate *michi* while
indicating in parentheses that this is the term being translated. All the same, in this
passage this term most often signifies the "pathway of the sword" in the sense of
the blade's trajectory. Every time I use the word *pathway* here, it is a translation of the
word *michi*.

93. "You must move the sword . . .": In the Scroll of Wind, Musashi criticizes the
school that recommends striking with power. Here, when he writes "powerfully," he

is talking about the power that results from striking in a sweeping manner while extending and stretching the arms, not from an effort made with the intent of striking with power.

94. It is difficult to imagine today the precision that Musashi has in mind when he speaks of the path or pathway of the sword, but this notion can be illustrated by a few anecdotes.

The following is drawn from the work of Ozawa Masao:

One day Musashi was received by Lord Shimamura at Kokura on the island of Kyushu. In the course of their conversation, a servant came in and announced to Musashi that a samurai called Aoki wished to be received by him. He was brought in. After a polite exchange, Musashi asked him:

"What is your progress in strategy?"

Aoki replied, "I persevere in it constantly."

The conversation continued and Musashi said to him, "You can already teach in most dojos." Aoki was very happy about this.

Just as he was about to withdraw, Musashi saw that he was carrying a *bokken* (wooden sword) in a handsome cloth case to which a forearm guard of red leather *(udenuki)* was also attached and asked, "What is that red object?"

Somewhat embarrassed, Aoki replied, "That is what I use when I am forced to fight in the course of my travels through various fiefs," and he showed him his great stick, to the handle of which the guard was attached.

Musashi's mood suddenly changed, and he said: "You are an imbecile. At your level, you are still far from being able to think about the combat of *hyoho*. I complimented you before because I thought you could be a good teacher for beginners. If someone asks you to fight with them, the best thing you can do is to leave immediately. You are still far from the combat of *hyoho*."

Musashi then had a child called who was beginning his apprenticeship in *hyoho*. He pasted a grain of rice on the child's forehead at the point from which his hair was pulled back into a bun and told him to remain standing motionless. Musashi then stood up, took his sword, and bringing it down sharply from above, he precisely cut the grain in half and showed it to Aoki. Then he repeated the action, three times altogether. All those present were impressed, but Musashi said: "Even with a confident technique, it is difficult to defeat an enemy. It is out of the question, at your level, to talk about combat." (9, p. 226)

True or not, this anecdote illustrates the reputation of the extreme precision of Musashi's sword. The example of the grain of rice gives a more concrete sense of what Musashi refers to in his text as "the pathway" or "the way of the sword." The sword's trajectory had to be extremely precise and allow at the same time for the adjustment of the force employed to the resistance of the object to be cut.

The second point to note here is Musashi's scrupulousness and the seriousness of his attitude toward combat.

In the history of the great practitioners of the sword, there are many anecdotes that illustrate the effectiveness of a strike from a sword or a *shinai*. This effectiveness derives not simply from the force of the strike but precisely, as Musashi expresses it, from its path, speed, and force being in conformity with the nature of the sword.

Thus, according to Omori Sogen, Harigaya Sekiun (1592–1662), a master who was a contemporary of Musashi's, one day received a *bushi* who challenged the effectiveness of his stroke:

> "It is said that a strike from your *shinai* can break a steel helmet. Is this true? I have put on a steel helmet. Please be so kind as to strike me."
>
> Sekiun refused, and the *bushi* insisted, thinking he was not capable of doing it. Finally Sekiun said, "All right."
>
> He went out into the garden and picked up a *shinai*. He calmly approached the *bushi*, raised the *shinai*, and struck the helmet from above. Having taken the blow, the *bushi* staggered as far as the foot of a tree and fell to the ground split-ting blood. (26, p. 46)

The following anecdote is frequently recounted by masters of kendo, but I have not been able to find its source.

> In the nineteenth century, Ueda Umanosuke, a practitioner from the Kyoshin meichi ryu, was challenged to a bout by a practitioner named Yoshida, who came from the province of Hyuga. In this practitioner's school, combat was practiced without protective armor. Yoshida said:
>
> "You can put on protective armor, but I will fight without armor, because my body is as tough as steel."
>
> Ueda, irritated by these words, said to him, "I will show you that my *shinai* can break a body, even if it is as tough as steel."
>
> Saying this, he took a particularly thick piece of bamboo armor used to protect the side of the body and attached it to the trunk of a tree. He struck it a blow with his *shinai* and the three thick bamboo strips of the armor were broken. [If you are familiar with kendo armor, you have some idea what this blow must have been like.] Seeing this demonstration, Yoshida paled and also donned a suit of armor.

Finally, in 1887 Sakakibara Kenkichi (1830–1894) performed a demonstration of *kabuto wari* before the emperor. This involved splitting a steel helmet with a sword. The three most famous sword masters attempted this and only Sakakibara succeeded. He split the helmet to a depth of 11.5 centimeters, and his sword blade remained intact. The blades of the two other masters were deformed in the shape of the curvature of the helmet. (120, p. 135)

In the history of the sword, we can find many similar examples. The effectiveness of a strike depends mainly upon the way of holding the sword as it follows a trajectory that is "in conformity with the nature of the sword."

95. "The Series . . . ," *tsutsu no omote no shidai: Shidai* means "the manner of placement within an order, the order, the degree, to classify in accordance with an order, the movement of a situation, a process, the derivation of things." (99, 100) The meaning here is the first one; the order followed is an order of presentation and not a hierarchical order. That is why, in order to avoid any ambiguity, I have translated the word as *series.* In the title of each form, I attempted to render the nuance implicit in *shidai* by adopting an ordinal number (first, second . . .).

Omote refers to a technical form or formula. This term is frequently used in the various disciplines of the Japanese martial arts. The literal sense of the word *omote* is "surface, exterior, external shape, facade," whence the sense, "that which is seen and shown officially on the outside." The facade is something official because it is, and must be, presentable for the outside world, the public. Thus in the martial arts, *omote* refers to the techniques that are officially recognized as being characteristic of a given school. But in signifying "the surface," the term *omote* always presupposes that which is hidden behind the appearances. To every *omote* there is a corresponding *ura,* "behind" or "the other side."

The transmission of a martial art generally takes place by following both sides, *omote* and *ura.* The main substance of an art cannot be transmitted solely through visible forms and formulas, so the transmission relies on what is not visible from the outside, the *ura.* This same procedure is also valuable in preserving the secrecy of a school. When the external appearance is too revealing or there is a competition between schools, the practitioners of an art set up complex codes of transmission and practice following the *omote* and *ura* scheme.

For example, in karate a technique called *shuto uke* is frequently used in the formalized exercises known as katas. This technique is interpreted as a parry carried out with the edge of the hand—parrying a blow of the fist or a kick by the adversary with the edge of the hand. Using the right hand, the practitioner moves the hand forward obliquely to the right, starting from the left shoulder. That is the technique that is shown, *omote,* and this explanation has become the "official" one; it is the explanation known to most karate practitioners. By contrast, in the hidden transmission, *ura,* the final position of the hand is identical to that described above, but the practitioner does not strike only with the edge of his hand. In accordance with the situation, different ways of striking are studied: One can strike with the base of the index finger (which is located on the opposite side of the hand from the edge), with the palm of the hand, with the back of the hand; and one can also use the fingers, poking them into the throat or the eyes of the opponent.

Another technique, called *nukite*, is done by poking with the fingers according to the description in the shown, *omote*, listing of techniques. In the hidden, or *ura*, version, this technique is not performed using the fingers but with the bony part of the forearm, with which the practitioner applies pressure to the arm of the opponent with a movement that is close to the motion of a saw.

In the sword technique of the Komagawa Kaishin ryu that I myself practice, six series of katas exist that are called *omote no kata*. Kuroda Tetsuzan, the principal master of this school, published a book on the techniques of his school in 1992. One of my French students, who does not read Japanese, was looking at a series of photos presented in the chapter called "*Ura no kata*" (115, pp. 356–389) and asked me the following question, "These are examples of bad techniques, aren't they?" Although he had been practicing for only two years, he had a keen awareness of the techniques he was learning and was able to discern small differences from them in the movements shown in "*Ura no kata*." Not knowing about this kind of exercise, he thought these differences represented deformations of the techniques. The *ura* techniques are in fact more refined, but they often appear less elegant to beginners. And for those who have no knowledge of the techniques of a given school, the hidden techniques may look like they are being performed in a sloppier way than the shown ones. Indeed, without an explanation it is difficult to understand the full meaning of these techniques.

Although this duality is customary in the martial arts schools, the notion of *ura*, the hidden part of the art, is often subjected to a kind of mystification for a variety of reasons. With his pragmatic mindset, Musashi shows the essence of his school in this chapter, without mystifying and in simple language. For him the essential can be expressed by means of the *omote* technical form. Nevertheless, as he adds at the end of each section, one must carefully examine and train in what he talks about, because it is impossible to transmit the practice of an art completely in a written piece, even if one is not trying to keep a secret *ura* part in reserve.

Regarding the execution of the five technical forms in Musashi's school today: Musashi's five forms are still practiced today under the same name—*itsutsu no omote*—in the school that hands down his art; however, the techniques as practiced at the present time have diverged from the descriptions Musashi gives of them. This divergence can be explained by involuntary changes that have accumulated over the course of time, since this was a series of techniques that Musashi transmitted in practice before giving them the definitive outlines described in the five forms.

Having witnessed the execution of the five forms by Masayuk Imaii, the tenth lineage successor of the main branch of Musashi's school, for purposes of reference I will describe his executions of each of the five techniques as we come to the description of it given by Musashi.

96. The second part of this sentence poses a problem of interpretation: "When he launches an attack, deflect his sword to your right and, pressing on it, make your attack with the point of your sword." In this sentence Musashi uses the word *noru*, which means "to mount or get in" (a horse or a vehicle); thus this passage has often been understood as meaning "to place your sword above the sword of your opponent." A passage from a work entitled "Writings on the Sword Technique of the Enmei Ryu" *(Enmei ryu kenpo sho)* (1-i) clears up this point. This work, sometimes attributed to Musashi, has been handed down in the School of Musashi of Saga prefecture. Although the general lines of the work are those of Musashi, I do not accept it as being a work by him because it seems to me it was probably composed on the basis of excerpts from the *Gorin no sho* by adepts of the School of Musashi, who have added their interpretations. We find the following sentence there: "*Noru* means neither bringing the sword back toward oneself nor parrying but, rather, rapidly directing the point of the sword upward, then crossing the opponent's sword with it."

I have, however, noted the following in practice: In performing the first form as a linked sequence of three techniques through which one is attempting to place one's sword on that of the opponent, it immediately emerges that our movements are hindered between the first and second techniques. For that reason it was necessary to look for another interpretation. In the practice of the sword, the word *noru* does not necessarily have the sense given above. It can also mean "climb onto the occasion that arises," that is, "seize the occasion or the opportunity to take the initiative." In this interpretation, the instruction given by Musashi is not to put one's sword on top of the opponent's but to strike the opponent on the head, the arm, or the wrist, depending on the opportunity that arises. The technical meaning of the sentence would then be: "When he launches an attack, deflect his sword to the right (so that it is left to cut the air) and, seizing the opportunity, make your attack with the point of your sword."

Even though this second interpretation seems to fit, I have kept the first interpretation because of the text of the Enmei ryu.

97. I translated *kissaki gaeshi* as "turning the point of your sword one quarter of a circle." In the *Enmei ryu kenpo sho* we read the following passage: "The way you turn the point of your sword necessitates a close estimate of the distance away from you your opponent is. When you want to strike an opponent who is far away, you execute a large movement, beginning to turn the point of your sword when your hand is at the height of the right side of your neck." (13, p. 52)

In addition to the issue referred to in note 96, I also differ from the usual interpretation of the overall sense of this paragraph. Usually the situations described are interpreted as a linked sequence taking place in the course of a confrontation and as three exercises to be executed successively.

The three situations described are not necessarily linked. The appropriate way of understanding them is that each situation was to be practiced independently and that the linkage with the following techniques occurred only in the case where the riposte did not succeed. On this basis, we can understand that the idea is first of all to practice dominating the opponent with a single movement in each case, but that the combination is also possible when the counterattack does not succeed.

The first situation is a dodging movement to the left, causing the sword of your adversary to cut the air on your right. You can immediately take the initiative by spontaneously striking the spot that is most exposed at this moment. For this reason Musashi does not say specifically where and how to strike.

If your attack has failed, your opponent will launch another attack, but this situation can also occur in other circumstances. There is no necessary link with the first situation. Musashi provides for the situation in which your counterattack has not succeeded by saying, "strike him from above downward, turning the point of your sword one quarter of a circle, and leave your sword in the position it has reached."

Indeed, in the case where your attack has not succeeded, the position in which your preceding movement of attack has left you can become the optimal preparation for a riposte against another attack on the part of your opponent. For this reason there is a more probable linkage between the second and third situations, but if you execute the third sequence by placing your sword in the low position that corresponds to the situation described, your position will be the low guard position of which Musashi speaks a number of times in this work. Thus you can also execute the third technique independently.

In this sense the three techniques become part of a single form because of sharing the same attitude toward combat: Dominate your adversary at the very moment where he strikes you with his sword. The last two techniques can be a linked sequence, but that is not necessary.

98. The first form as demonstrated by Masayuki Imai: Masayuki Imai calls this guard position *enso no kamae,* and he explains that it is a guard to be related to with a broad and calm mind that contains an entire universe between the two swords. *Enso* means (1) "circular form"; (2) as a Zen Buddhist term, "the circle drawn to symbolize the illumination inherent in the human mind"; at times words or signs are inscribed in this circle to express either a function of the mind or the degree of progress toward illumination; (3) "a circle that surrounds the body of Buddha and the gods." (99)

Masayuki Imai holds the two swords horizontally, with the points pointing at the face of his opponent. This is the middle guard position (*chudan*) with two swords. The blades of both swords are turned outward. The opponent attacks with a stroke of his sword from above downward; Masayuki Imai lowers his two swords and, taking a small step backward, allows the sword of his opponent to cut the air. The opponent launches a fresh attack from above downward; Imai Masayuki stops it this time with his small sword held in his left hand, and he slashes his opponent's arm with his large sword held in his right hand, striking on an angle from the lower left toward the upper right.

This does not correspond exactly to the description Musashi gives (see notes 96 and 97).

99. The second form as demonstrated by Masayuki Imai: Masayuki Imai holds his large sword in the right hand, in the high position, *jodan*, over his right shoulder and his small sword in the middle position, *chudan*, pointing at the face of his opponent. He calls this guard position the "fire guard." The adversary attacks, striking from above downward. Masayuki Imai parries with his large sword and extends the parry into a circular movement that moves the opponent's sword downward by pressing the blade of his sword against the back of the opponent's sword. The adversary pulls his sword back and launches another attack, and Masayuki Imai blocks this by crossing his two swords above his forehead. The blades of the three swords cross for a moment at a single point. But this coming together lasts for only an instant, because immediately Masayuki Imai separates his two swords in a broad movement of a quarter circle, forcing the adversary's sword downward and to the left, and without stopping this circular movement of separation, he strikes the head of his adversary with his large sword, held in the right hand.

100. "A passing cadence," *kosu hyoshi*: This expression comes from the verb *kosu*, which means "to outstrip, travel through, cross (a mountain pass), pass, surpass." This refers to a cadence that makes it possible to turn aside the sword that is trying to knock your own down in the same fashion that one would get over a mountain pass—in the air. The technique can be explained as follows: If your opponent parries and attempts to get your sword down by striking it, you twist your sword aside with a passing cadence, with the result that your opponent cuts the air, and in deflecting his sword you cut his upper arm.

Musashi's original text is written in hiragana without punctuation, which leaves room for a variety of interpretations. That is why, in other interpretations of the *Gorin no sho*, this expression is understood as *okosu hyoshi*. The literal translation of *okosu* is "to wake up, to straighten up or raise (something that has fallen)" or "to begin." The translation would then be a "raised cadence" or "initial cadence." However, this translation seems to me to be wrong, because we nowhere find the expression *okosu hyoshi* in the work of Musashi, whereas he uses *kosu hyoshi* a number of times, for example, in the instruction *"Ni no koshi no hyoshi"* (p. 36 of the cited edition of the *Gorin no sho*) and in the *Hyoho sanju go kajo*. (9, p. 247)

Moreover, the interpretation of "passing cadence" fits with the practical application. This cadence appears at the moment when, during an attack, you strike, and after having hit your opponent's sword, you stop for an instant; your opponent will be drawn into this pause, then you take advantage of this instant of stagnation on his part to strike him.

101. The third form as demonstrated by Masayuki Imai: In this form, Masayuki Imai holds the two swords lowered and pointing toward the ground. He calls this position *ritsu zen* (standing Zen). There exists a self-portrait of Musashi in this posture.

The opponent strikes from above downward. Imai Masayuki stops this with his small sword. This situation is close to the first form, with the difference that the body of Masayuki Imai is somewhat farther from his opponent and therefore his large sword does not reach the arm of his opponent. The opponent attacks again; Masayuki Imai parries with his large sword and presses it against the back of the opponent's sword, which he forces down. He cuts the opponent's arm with the small sword, striking horizontally from left to right and passing above the two swords—his own large one and the opponent's.

102. "Strike . . . with an upward motion," *shita yori haru:* Literally, this means, "You strike starting from the bottom." The literal translation, however, might give the reader the impression that there is a preparatory movement downward, which does not exist. That is why I translated "with an upward motion."

103. The phrase "If he attempts to knock down your upward moving sword, you follow your intention of striking his wrist in accordance with the way of the sword" could more simply be interpreted: "You receive and parry the pathway (*michi*) of your opponent's sword, which is attempting to knock your sword down." In this case the verb *ukeru* is understood purely in the sense of "receiving something materially," that is to say, here, the sword of your adversary, which in effect means parrying. Following this interpretation, we would understand the expression *tachi no michi o uke* as meaning that the pathway of the sword referred to is that of your adversary and not your own.

I translated as "follow" Musashi's term *uke*, which is an inflected form of the verb *ukeru*, which means "to receive." But here "to receive" is employed in the sense of "receiving the right principle in the act of slashing" (an inflection of the sense of *michi* translated by "the way"). In other words, the motion of the sword, moved by this principle, will follow the right trajectory. Thus, in this phrase, *uke* has a double sense. On the basis of testing it in practice, this interpretation seems to me to be the more accurate one and also the one that fits with Musashi's general idea. Musashi is indicating the principle of the sword that ought to be followed by the practitioner rather than developing this notion in relation to the sword of the adversary.

104. "You extend the stroke obliquely up to the height of your own shoulder": This determines the movement as obliquely upward. However, another interpretation is possible: "You slash obliquely to a point above the shoulder of your opponent." The description is ambiguous.

The problem resides in a single word, written as an ideogram by Musashi. Throughout his text, Musashi indicates the subject, that is the speaker, or "I," by the word *ware*. However, frequently I have translated this word as "you," because this "I" is used by Musashi to refer to the person he is addressing, his reader, his disciple. Thus if this ideogram is read *ware*, it becomes the subject, and we must translate here: "You obliquely slash the shoulder of your adversary"; but if you read it *waga (mon)*, we must translate: "You slash obliquely up to the height of your own shoulder." I adopted this interpretation because it is better adapted to the practical situation that is described.

105. The fourth form as demonstrated by Masayuki Imai: Masayuki Imai's small sword is pointed toward the opponent at the middle level (*chudan*), and his large sword, held in the right hand, is placed under his left armpit, pointing backward. His torso is almost in profile in relation to his opponent, whom he looks at over his right shoulder. This is a special position that one would take, for example, in a combat situation where obstacles make it impossible to take the usual position.

The adversary attacks downward from above twice; each time Masayuki Imai parries with the small sword at the same time as he strikes horizontally to the right with his large sword, as though drawing it from the scabbard. His adversary backs off from this movement of attack. After his second horizontal movement of attack from the left to the right, Masayuki Imai extends the movement of his sword up to the level of his right shoulder, and from that point strikes diagonally toward the lower left shoulder of his opponent.

106. The fifth form as demonstrated by Masayuki Imai: Masayuki Imai holds his small sword at the middle level and the large sword at his right hip. Both swords are pointing at the adversary, but the large sword is much farther back. This position is used when there are obstacles or in a special situation.

The opponent attacks downward from above; Masayuki Imai dodges by taking a half step backward, and he parries with his small sword, moving his opponent's sword to the outside, leaving it to cut thin air all the way down. Masayuki Imai immediately strikes the opponent's head with his large sword, taking a half step forward.

107. "Through continuously applying the techniques of these five forms in their full depth," *te o karasu:* Here *te* means "technique"; *karasu* means "dry out by removing the water, draw the water till it runs dry," from which comes the derivative sense of doing something thoroughly and fully or exhaustively. I translated here "applying the techniques . . . in their full depth" in order to retain a trace of the image of getting to the very bottom of the spring or well.

108. Problems posed by these five sections: In Musashi's text, the use of two swords is not apparent. It is simpler to grasp the situation by understanding his text as referring to one sword, because there is no description in which the movements of each of the two swords is explained. Indeed, if this text were read without the reader's knowing that it concerned the School of Two Swords, no one would imagine the presence of a second sword. Why do we have this lack of precision and apparent neglect, even though Musashi insists elsewhere on the importance of two swords in his school? The answer is not simple.

In my view, Musashi describes the essential technique for only one sword because even when using two swords at once, it is with one sword that you slash the opponent. Nevertheless, Musashi stresses the importance of becoming accustomed to handling the sword with just one hand, even to the point of naming his school the School of Two Swords. Taking this into account, I think the movement of the other sword can be regarded as variable; Musashi leaves the second sword freedom of reaction as long as the main action is carried out. Moreover, Musashi speaks only of the main action. For the practitioner who correctly uses the main sword as he describes, the movement of the second sword will be determined spontaneously. An overly detailed description would render too fixed and artificial an exercise that is supposed to be a preparation for real situations. All the same, these technical passages are directly applicable to those who practice the sword holding it in both hands, and they are instructive.

109. "The teaching of the guard without a guard": *uko muko no oshie.*

110. "Depending on the openings furnished by your opponent": *teki no en ni yori.*

111. "All that becomes the occasion for you to strike him," *teki o kiru en nari: En* is a Buddhist term meaning "cause, relation between things, object of thought."

112. "Fixate," *itsuku:* See note 87.

113. "A single cadence for striking your adversary" is the translation of *hitotsu hyoshi no uchi.* In contemporary Japanese, *hitotsu hyoshi* is more commonly read *ichi hyoshi.*

114. "Without moving your body": When you strike from a guard position, making a preparatory movement, as small as it might be, is almost unavoidable. For example, starting from a middle-level guard, to strike a blow to the head of your opponent, you will first have to raise the point of your sword, then strike him. In this case the movement of striking is based on two cadences, that of raising and that of coming down. Even if you execute these movements very rapidly, there are still two cadences there. This is one of the fundamental questions over which a kendo practitioner will pause for a long time. In examining this question the work of Morita Monjuro (19, 20), a kendo master who has devoted a great part of his life to resolving this problem, offers insight.

In the technique described here by Musashi, the pathway of the point of the sword must not show a break into two movements but must describe a curve that forms a circle and does not require two cadences.

115. As I explain on page 126, it is not possible to find a single word in a Western language corresponding to the term *hyoshi*, which contains the idea of cadence, but this does not fully encompass its meaning.

Let us briefly analyze the hyoshi in question here, the single-cadence *(hyoshi)* strike.

Musashi writes: "You strike very rapidly and directly without moving your body, not letting your will to attack become attached anywhere." And about the opponent he says: "Seizing the instant when he does not expect it, you strike him with a single blow just at the instant when he is not even thinking of pulling back his sword or moving it out of the guard position or attacking."

Thus, in order to execute this technique, it is necessary for you to be able to strike quickly without manifesting in any way your will to attack. In general, when a person launches an intentional attack, a manifestation of his will to attack, as minimal as it might be, precedes the attack movement. The more he is caught up in aggression or in his will to attack, the more marked this manifestation is. For this reason, one of the principal efforts on the part of a practitioner in training consists in getting rid of this gap between his own will and the execution of the technique by learning how to make a movement that arises spontaneously.

Let us look into the second part of Musashi's term. The single-cadence strike is not only the description of the cadence of a movement in which you strike without manifesting your will to attack; it describes at the same time a relationship with the inner rhythm of your adversary that allows you to grasp the instant in which he is not able to react. A highly accomplished practitioner is always attentive to the will to attack of his opponent and is easily able to detect it. Even when facing a very rapid attack, if he is able to grasp the instant of the gap or lag between the manifestation of the opponent's will to attack and his attack movement, he will be able to react effectively with a less rapid movement.

We are talking about a state in which will and movement fuse and the technique produced is accurate. It turns out that to arrive at this state, you must not "want to," because the more you want to, the more the will to attack becomes manifest. What is necessary is for the body to move all by itself, choosing the favorable moment. This is a state in which, before noticing it, you have already struck, without anything's having intervened between perception and movement. On the level of perception, the single-cadence strike comes close to the strike of nonthought presented by Musashi two paragraphs farther on.

The difficulty in translating the term *hyoshi* is now easier to understand. In Japanese it is just one *hyoshi*, but it is not just one cadence, because it is the coming together of two cadences, your own and your opponent's.

"Interval," *ma:* Just as with *hyoshi*, the term *ma* does not have an equivalent in English. Generally this term is translated as "distance" or "gap," but it expresses not only a spatial gap (or distance) between objects or persons and a temporal gap (for example, the moment in music when the rhythm changes) but also the dynamic tension of the relationship between two or several persons. It is precisely because they both or all participate in this dynamic of relationship that the two dimensions of *ma* and *hyoshi* are inseparable.

116. There are several problems in this passage regarding the understanding of the Japanese text:

"In two phases": The title reads *ni no koshi no hyoshi*. In the original text, *ni no koshi no* is written in hiragana. *Ni no* seems to have a double meaning, that of "second" in relation to the preceding cadence, which was *ichi*, "one," and that of "two" in the temporal sense, that is, referring to a cadence in two temporal steps or phases; this one is situated in relation to the previous one as *ni*, "two." Thus two translations are possible: "the second passing cadence " or "the passing cadence in two phases." I decided in favor of the latter because *ni no* is repeated later in the same paragraph in relation to the strike, and in this case the temporal sense is mandatory.

"The passing cadence": The most frequent interpretation is based on the transcription of *koshi* as the hips or the small of the back; this yields the reading *ni no koshi no hyoshi*, which means "the second, the *hyoshi* of the hips or the small of the back (*koshi*)." In most of the texts published today, this interpretation is repeated and seems to have become established. However, if we read this phrase attentively and relate it to other sentences of Musashi's, and especially if we practice this teaching, it appears that this interpretation is false.

In my view there are two possible valid interpretations of this phrase. If you read *ni no koshi no hyoshi,* the term *koshi* need not be understood only in the sense of hips or small of the back but can also be understood as the nominative form of the verb *kosu,* which means "to get past," as we saw earlier (see note 100). Indeed, this ideogram is found in the original text of the *Ihon gorin no sho,* the edition by Yamada Jirokichi (14, p. 358), and in the twenty-second article of the *Hyoho sanju go kajo* (9, p. 247), which confirms this interpretation.

I justify this interpretation on the basis of Musashi's explanatory sentence that comes afterward: *teki no hari te tarumu tokoro o uchi, hikite tarumu tokoro o utsu, kore ni no koshi no uchi nari.* Before discussing the possible interpretations of this sentence, we must pause a moment over the expression *hari te tarumu. Hari* comes from the verb *haru,* meaning "to tense up," and *tarumu* means "to relax." The simplest way of interpreting this expression is to apply it to the state of the adversary, who is relaxing after having tensed up, but Musashi frequently uses the term *haru* to refer to one of the parrying techniques. In this sense the expression refers to the moment the adversary relaxes after having made a parrying movement provoked by a feint. This is the interpretation I chose, translating "after having started a parrying movement."

Teki no hari te tarumu tokoro o uchi, hikite tarumu tokoro o utsu, kore ni no koshi no uchi nari: The translation by M. and M. Shibata keeps the sense of "small of the back" for *koshi* and "to relax after having tensed up" for *hari te tarumu.* The result is "Thus the adversary will at first be in a state of tension, but he will relax this afterward. At that moment it is necessary to attack without delay. That is the secondary rhythm of the small of the back." In this translation, as in the other Japanese translations corresponding to it, it is difficult to see the relationship between the small of the back and the logic of the text.

If we translate *kosuhi* as "getting past," the meaning of the sentence becomes "You feint striking him and then actually strike him at the moment when he relaxes after having started a parrying movement *(hari te tarumu)* or after having backed up." If we read *futatsu no koshi no hyoshi* instead of *ni no koshi no hyoshi,* the translation will be "the passing cadence in two phases" or "the two cadences of passing."

Another interpretation of the entire sentence is to read *ni nokoshi* instead of *ni no koshi.* The term *nokoshi* is the nominative form of the verb *nokosu,* meaning "leave out part of something." In this case the sentence would mean "You feint a strike but leave your movement partially incomplete and you actually strike at the moment when he relaxes after having started a parrying movement." I find this interpretation peculiar, and I have not found any other author who shares it. However, during a conversation with Imai Masayuki in 1987, he rejected the interpretation of *koshi* as hips or small of the back and understood the expression as meaning "passing cadence in two phases." When I explained my interpretation to him, he found it as interesting as his own but nevertheless did not withdraw his own.

These two interpretations partially overlap because in both cases a situation is depicted in which you create a void in your opponent by using two *hyoshi* (cadences), which produces a feint in his direction. It is by reading this way that we see the profundity of this technique and we can understand its real relationship with the previous one, which involves a single *hyoshi,* because the second one is created by doubling that *hyoshi.* By contrast, if you go with "the cadence of the small of the back," there is no need to double such a cadence, and we cannot understand what Musashi is describing in a concrete way. In this situation the point is to create a gap or lag in the *hyoshi* (cadences) in which the opponent is at the end of the first cadence, through which his attention and energy have been emptied out creating a void, while you are fully in the midst of the second one. Thus the instruction to double the *hyoshi* (cadence) is clear in the last two interpretations.

I had this passage read by ten advanced practitioners of the Japanese martial arts of kendo, aikido, and karate. All of them at first interpreted *koshi* in the sense of small of the back or hips. I explained my analysis to them and then asked them to read the text attentively again. After due reflection, all of them, without exception, rejected their first interpretation and then hesitated between the two interpretations I proposed.

In conclusion, in this passage and the preceding one, Musashi places first the different striking techniques that each recquire a single *hyoshi* and then second those that require a *hyoshi* in two phases. This is an example of the ambiguity produced in Musashi's text by the syllabic form of writing. This leads to divergences in interpretation that can be worked out only through a thorough reading of the text in association with actual practice. From the literary point of view, all three interpretations are possible, but from the point of view of actual practice, one is wrong and the other two are possible. This long explanation is justified by the fact that this wrong interpretation has come to be almost systematically accepted in contemporary Japanese publications.

117. "The strike of nonthought," *munen muso no uchi: Mu* is "negation"; *nen* means "thought, consideration, what is in the mind, memory of past experience"; *so* means "idea, representation of perceived phenomena." *Munen* is a Buddhist term meaning "without thinking anything, penetrating into the state of nonego." *Muso* as a Buddhist term means "having no form, not being conditioned by form." *Muso* signifies "to empty of all thought, have nothing in the mind." This ideogram is also used in connection with *muso.*

These two ways of writing *muso* used in association with *munen* mean ostensibly the same thing: "not thinking of anything, becoming detached from any idea or thought." I translated this expression as "nonthought."

In practically all schools of the sword, a spontaneous strike is considered the right kind of strike and is a central element in sword technique. It is a strike that arises unconsciously and leads to a positive result. It occurs when your mind, because it is empty, is able to allow itself to be impregnated by the situation and the body comes up with a spontaneous and accurate movement.

To elucidate the idea of striking with an empty mind, I refer to the work "Explanation of the School of Two Swords" (*Nito ryu o kataru*) by Yoshida Seiken: "The term *munen-muso* is widely known, and it seems that one can cut down any opponent if one strikes in this manner. But it should be understood that this strike is viable only under certain conditions. It is viable when you and your opponent are both waiting for the other to attack. During this situation of reciprocal waiting, your strike arises spontaneously if your body and mind are integrated in an attitude of attack." (35, p. 66)

As Musashi says, practitioners often encounter this type of strike, which takes the form of punches and kicks in karate and throwing techniques in judo. In certain sword schools it is one of the ideal goals of technique. Musashi underlines the importance of studying it and training in it consciously. It seems to me that he is emphasizing that to succeed in executing spontaneous and unconscious technique, it is necessary to train in it in a highly conscious fashion.

Apropos of the strike of nonthought, adepts of the martial arts frequently refer to the story of Satori. I will pass on the account of it given by Chiba Shusaku:

> Here is an anecdote. Once when a woodsman was trying to cut a tree in a deep forest, an animal named Satori appeared. The woodsman wanted to catch it, because this animal is rare. Satori then said, "You were thinking about catching me." The woodsman was terribly surprised to hear this. Satori then said, "You are surprised because I know what you're thinking." The woodsman was more and more astonished and thought secretly of killing it with the axe he had in his hand. Satori then said, "You were thinking of killing me." The woodsman thought, "It has the ability to know what I'm thinking. There's nothing I can do." And he went back to cutting the tree. Satori said, "You were thinking that there's nothing you can do against me."
>
> This time the woodsman continued to concentrate on cutting the trunk of the tree, without concerning himself with this animal. The blade of his axe then accidentally came off and planted itself in Satori's head, and Satori died without saying a word. (82, pp. 42–43)

This parable teaches us that even satori can be struck by an axe of nonthought. In *kenjutsu* also, if you are confronting a very advanced practitioner, he will detect your actions as soon as you even think of them. Therefore it is necessary to develop techniques that arise without thought. You must train in this well.

118. "The flowing-water strike": *ryu sui no uchi.*

119. "That seems to be stagnating," *yodomi*: The image is that of flowing water that seems to slow down and stagnate as it passes over a deep spot.

"You strike broadly": This formulation might seem paradoxical. It does not really mean to strike slowly but rather to create a cadence that gives the impression of stagnating. This sentence has to be understood in conjunction with the preceding one, where Musashi asks the practitioner to expand his body and mind. This subjective expansion contains the same latent power as the current when it is passing over a large deep area.

120. "The level of your opponent," *teki no kurai: Kurai* means "position, state, quality, capacity." Thus two translations are possible: "the level of your opponent" or "the position of your opponent." I chose the first because the technique described by Musashi can be carried out only against an opponent whose level is inferior to your own. In sword combat, the result of a bout is not always determined by a difference in level. If his mind is slack, a great master can be killed by a beginner who is determined to die. Musashi's techniques take this fact into account.

121. "The chance-opening blow," *en no atari:* I translated the term *en* as "chance-opening." This term is of Buddhist origin and has four main meanings:

- the secondary cause of a phenomenon or the contingent factors that work in the same direction as the direct cause of the phenomenon
- the relationships between things and phenomena or human actions
- the occasion or the chance of a relationship's arising
- the surroundings of an object

Here I went with the first sense. In Buddhist thought, even when there is no apparent cause, the interdependent links of a cosmic dynamic constitute the hidden cause. In the course of combat, whether this chance that is always there is grasped or allowed to escape will depend on the practitioner's ability. When an opening is offered by chance, if your ability is insufficient, you let it get away. If you have the ability, you can use it. Musashi's teaching here is not to let a chance pass but to transform it into a chance that has been given to you. For someone who does not see, there is in effect no opening for a strike. Being available so that you can grasp the opening is an important ability in *hyoho*.

122. I translated *atari* as "hit" or "blow," *uchi* as "strike." In fact *atari* does contain a nuance of chance. In the title of this section, Musashi uses the term *atari*, but at the end of it he uses *uchi*. Thus he is conveying the idea of transforming a chance situation into something quite clearly evident.

123. "The blow like a spark from a stone": *sekka no atari*.

124. "You must strike quickly . . . ," *ahi mo tsuyoku, mi mo tsuyoku, te mo tsuyoku, mitokoro o motte hayaku utsu beki nari:* This literally means "legs as strongly, body as strongly, hands as strongly, strike quickly with these three parts."

In translating this passage I tried to take into account the logic of Musashi's thought. In fact, the instruction given just before this by Musashi ("strike extremely hard without raising your sword at all") is equivalent in karate to "deliver a powerful punch, beginning your movement just a few centimeters from your opponent's body." So there is no distance for the strike to accelerate in, and it is a very difficult strike to execute. Therefore it is necessary, as Musashi writes here, to mobilize simultaneously the three combined forces of the legs, the body, and the hands and integrate them into one.

125. "The crimson-leaves strike," *momiji no uchi:* Momiji in general refers to a kind of maple that turns crimson in the fall, which is also called *kaede.* In a broader sense, *momiji* refers to leaves that turn color in the fall. But here, in my view, it refers to the leaves of the *momiji* tree that color the Japanese countryside with their magnificent purple hue. These leaves fall readily with the first winds of winter. Here the leaf that falls is a crimson leaf, which also evokes the color of the opponent's blood. Musashi seems to be bringing together these two images in his description of this technique.

126. "You extend the force of your strike," *nebaru kokoro nite:* The term *nebaru* appears several times in Musashi's writings. The primary sense of this verb is "to stick or paste," and the next sense is "to persist." What Musashi is expressing here is a force that persists in its effect as a paste does. This image crops up in most of the Japanese martial arts, with the sense of improving a technique, that is, of making it flexible so it can be more resistant and so its effectiveness can persist or penetrate more deeply.

For example, in sumo, force and the capacity for resistance in the lower part of the body are essential. The term *nebaru* is used as a positive description of this. In judo and in sumo, you resist an attempt on the part of your opponent to throw you with a "small of the back that is sticky or flexible," *nebari goshi.* Conversely, when your opponent attempts to resist your throwing techniques, you can throw him nonetheless because of your flexible or sticky small of the back. In karate the action of sticking (*nebaru*) with the hand is emphasized for parrying techniques that make it possible to absorb the impact of your adversary's attack and repulse it.

127. "The body replacing the sword": *tachi ni kawaru mi.*

128. "A strike and a hit," *utsu to atari:* Throughout this text, I have translated *atari* as "blow" or "hit" and *uchi* as "strike," for *atari* contains a nuance of chance. In this

passage Musashi stresses this distinction. That is why, to make it clearer, I have translated *atari* in the sense of a chance hit and *uchi* in the sense of an intentional strike.

Musashi's technical ideas come out clearly here. If one wishes to make progress in the way of *hyoho*, it is indispensable to distinguish a controlled strike from one that is produced by chance. Nevertheless, training must be carried out in such a way that even a chance hit will be sufficiently effective. For someone seeking to make progress in a martial art, it is indispensable to understand why he has won or lost. The attitude here differs fundamentally from that of sports competition, where the result is what counts, even if it is fortuitous. A win is not necessarily indicative of the level a person has attained. Let us recall what Musashi wrote right at the beginning of this work: "I have fought more than sixty times, but not once was I beaten. All that happened between my thirteenth and my twenty-eighth or twenty-ninth year."

Winning by means of a chance blow does not constitute an objective in training; Musashi by no means excludes it, but he does not accept it as a real victory. What form of victory is he looking for then? That is what he describes next:

> At the age of thirty, I reflected and saw that although I had won, I had done so without having reached the ultimate level of strategy. Perhaps it was because my natural disposition prevented me from straying from universal principles; perhaps it was because my opponents lacked ability in strategy.
>
> I continued to train and to seek from morning till night to attain a deeper principle. When I reached the age of fifty, I naturally found myself on the way of strategy.

His objective is to win deliberately, by creating the incontrovertible conditions of victory. The distinction between the conscious strike and the chance hit is at the root of this quest. This idea is summed up in one of the key maxims of modern kendo: "Strike after having won, don't win after having struck."

129. "The autumn monkey's body," *shuko no mi*: Two interpretations are possible:

- "The autumn monkey's body": In the fall the monkeys come together to warm each other and huddle together, keeping their hands squeezed tight against their bodies; hence the name of the technique.
- "The short-armed monkey."

130. "Getting . . . close," *hairu* or *iru*: Literally, this means "enter into." In connection with combat, the idea is to enter inside your opponent's range of protection, which is that distance apart at which he can attack you. In the martial arts, this verb is commonly used to indicate the idea of crossing this boundary (either going in or coming

out). That is why I have translated it as "getting in close to your opponent" and not "entering into your opponent." On the inside of this range, the closer you get to the adversary, the more the idea is present of entering into his body, *tekini mio iruiru,* to use Musashi's expression, which means to attack him.

131. "Distant": This comes from the verb *tonoku,* which literally means "to move away." The idea expressed here is that if you think of moving your hands forward, which is understood to mean "to execute a technique," the body tends to remain behind, distant from the adversary.

132. "Distance," *aida:* The ideogram can also be read *ma.* It can be interpreted either as a spatial or temporal interval. Therefore two translations are possible: either "at a distance at which" or "at the moment when."

133. "When you are at a distance . . . ," *te nite ukeahasuru hodo no aida niwa:* In this sentence, Musashi uses the word *te,* which means "hand," to refer to the hands holding the sword. This is why the translation is not literal, and the distance is not that at which the hands of the two adversaries are touching but rather that at which the two swords they are holding in their hands can touch each other and exchange blows.

In combat our perception is subject to the pressure of the particular situation, dominated by fear and excitement, especially in sword combat, where a single blow can be fatal. The first adversary is within ourselves, since attachment to life hinders our movements because of our unconscious reaction of fear. Thus the technique of a martial art cannot be related to movements alone. If there is not a psychological foundation sturdy enough to face the situation, no movement will be viable. If a bird is paralyzed, it cannot fly away. His apprenticeship and his study of techniques that basically revolve around the notion of death move the student of *budo* in the direction of introspection. However, this introspection is not metaphysical; rather, it passes through the body. Thus the philosophy of *budo* resides in the technique, in the daily practice of the art.

In the combat situation, the discrepancy or gap between perception and reality is considerable. Consequently, we should not consider the technique of *budo* to be simply technique concerned with movement. Because of this gap, instructions of the following type are given: "If you want to cut down your opponent, think of delivering a blow with your guard position; do not think of slashing with the blade of the sword, think of striking with your guard." These instructions guide the student's subjective sensations and compensate for the gap by shifting perception forward in time; thus an adjustment to the combat situation comes about. Warriors are familiar with this gap and see fear as their greatest enemy.

In this connection, here is an anecdote recounted by Nakazato:

One day a young boy came to see Musashi to ask him for his help. "I asked my lord to allow me to engage in a duel to avenge the honor of my dead father and I have already received his permission. Everything is ready and the dueling site has already been enclosed with a bamboo fence. The duel will take place tomorrow. I would like to ask you to teach me how to win the duel."

In those days, to engage in a duel motivated by vengeance was considered a normal and honorable act, and even a necessary one, in *bushi* families. Sometimes the decision to seek vengeance was up to the discretion of the head of the family; sometimes it was obligatory. For this kind of duel, one had to ask permission of one's liege lord. If a journey was necessary in order to meet one's enemy, someone who took on this duty could forgo providing his services as a vassal for years on end without losing his position. But if he failed to accomplish his initial objective, he was considered unworthy as a *bushi* and risked having his standing revoked. The vengeance duel was thus sometimes essential for both parties.

Musashi replied, "I am touched by your sense of duty. I will teach you a secret technique that will make it possible for you to win without fail. Hold your knife (*tanto*) in your left hand in a horizontal position, and hold your large sword in your right hand. Advance in your opponent's direction quickly, and the instant you meet his attack with your knife, pierce his chest with the sword held in your right hand."

The boy practiced during the night and succeeded in basically learning the technique. Observing the way he executed the technique, Musashi complimented him and added: "Your victory is certain. Also tomorrow morning when you arrive at the place of the duel, take a good look beneath your seat when you sit down; if you see any ants, this will be a sign of victory. I will stay here and pray for you to win, so you will be protected from all sides. Don't worry about a thing."

The following day the boy saw a great number of ants around his feet, and he was greatly encouraged. Confronting his adversary, he did exactly as Musashi had taught him, and he succeeded in killing his enemy, who was quite powerful. He was thus able to fulfill his most weighty obligation. (23, pp. 82–83)

It is worthwhile to analyze the subtlety with which Musashi taught the technique of the autumn monkey's body here. If one of his disciples had been in this situation, Musashi would not have done it this way. It would have been enough for him to say, "Don't forget the autumn monkey's body." That would have been enough to get his disciple to understand the approach he had to take in the duel. Here, by contrast, he was dealing with a young boy for whom the task ahead was an overly heavy one and to whom, moreover, he had to teach a technique that he could apply the following day.

The first thing Musashi tells him is to hold a knife in his left hand, not a *wakizashi* (a small sword about sixty-five centimeters long) but a knife (*tanto*). The technique consists in parrying with the knife, which measured about forty centimeters, which is not easy, but if this succeeds, the distance between the boy and his opponent will be short enough for him to stab him with his large sword. If the boy can get inside his opponent's attack zone, first using only his knife, he will execute the technique of the autumn monkey's body without realizing it.

To get inside his opponent's attack range in this fashion, using only a knife, would be possible only if he was without fear. The technique itself (concentrating on the parry with the knife) helps him to keep from thinking that he is crossing the boundary of his opponent's attack zone, which is the most difficult thing he has to do and the most frightening.

Musashi observes the results of the boy's practice session and comes to the conclusion that he has a chance of making good on his accelerated teaching. At that point he tells him, "Your victory is certain." This statement on the part of the celebrated Musashi does not fail to encourage the boy. Next Musashi speaks of the ants. This connection of the ants and victory in combat is all the more amazing because the boy really does find a lot of ants around his feet—thus Musashi appears to have premonitory power. Now, in fact, Musashi could be certain that the boy would find ants, because except in the winter, in Japan you find ants everywhere. What counted was that the boy was able to see those little ants, the perception of which would elude anyone who had lost his head in the moments before combat. Thus the important thing was not that there were or were not ants but whether he saw them or not. The boy, guided by Musashi's suggestion, put his attention on the ants, and he found them. Finding them, he was reassured once again. On top of that, lowering one's glance to one's feet makes possible stabilizing one's physical equilibrium. Musashi raised his confidence level yet another notch by telling him that at the time of the duel, he would be praying for him.

This kind of skill in teaching was also, for Musashi, part of the way of strategy.

134. "The body of lacquer and paste": *shikko no mi.*

135. "Comparing heights," *take kurabe:* The contemporary expression is *sei kurabe.* In Japan it is traditional to measure children's and teenagers' heights periodically, often by drawing a line on one of the posts of the house. This measurement frequently takes place on Boys' Day. In this comparison with their contemporaries, it is important for them to show how much they have grown since the last measurement.

136. "Making your movements stick," *nebari o kakuru,* from the verb *nebaru* (see note 126). Making one's sword stick to one's opponent's is an important technique in vari-

ous schools of swordsmanship. In the old Kashima school, the Kashima shin ryu (Kashima School of the Gods), this technique was practiced and transmitted under the name *sokui zuke* ("to stick with rice glue"). This technique consists in making your sword stick to your opponent's in a subtle fashion. When he wants to attack, you deflect his sword without letting it come unstuck from yours. When he wants to pull his sword back, you also follow him, not letting the two swords come apart. In this way your adversary will lose the fight. To reach this level, of course, one must be a truly accomplished swordsman.

We could think of the *sokui zuke* technique as a more subtle elaboration of the technique described here by Musashi. A similar technique has been developed in the bare-handed martial arts.

137. "Banging into your opponent," *mi no atari:* The word *atari* is the nominative form of the intransitive verb *ataru,* "to collide with," or the transitive verb *ateru,* "to hit." When the impact is delivered by the whole body, as in this passage, I have translated this as "bang," "knock," or "bang into." When it involves a person using an object, a sword, to hit someone, I have translated *atari* as "blow" or "hit" (for example, *"en no atari"* or *"sekka no atari"*).

138. When you are using just one sword as in modern kendo, the bang is delivered by the right shoulder, which is closer to the opponent, because you are holding the sword with two hands, the right hand forward. But in the School of Two Swords, the bang is delivered as described by Musashi, with the left shoulder, because generally you hold the small sword with the left hand and take the guard position with the left shoulder forward. Regarding this position, Yoshida Seiken writes: "When your opponent attacks on the left side, you parry with a quick movement of the short sword. This parry is very effective, and you slash immediately with the long sword in your right hand. Indeed, for an adept of the two swords, there is no better situation than that in which the adversary launches his attack on the left side. It is as though the adversary were coming to get cut down. That is why those who are familiar with the particulars of the two-swords style do not readily attack on the left side." (35, p. 79)

139. "A cadence of concordance with the breath," *iki au hyoshi:* It is also possible to read *iki ai;* in that case the expression means "with a bound."

140. "Two or three *ken*": 3.6 to 5.4 meters. A *ken* measures about 1. 8 meters.

141. "The three parries": *mittsu no uke.*

142. "Stabbing," *tsuki:* This is the nominative form of the verb *tsuku,* "to stab or pierce

with a pointed object with a violent movement." In the Japanese martial arts, *tsuki* refers, in the art of the sword and kendo, to the movement of stabbing the adversary with a sword. In the bare-handed martial arts (jujutsu, karate), it refers to the movement of punching. It is difficult to translate this word into English with a single word that would designate both techniques. That is why I have translated it "stabbing" when the context was using a sword, and as "punching" in the second part of this text segment, where Musashi explains that the movement is executed with a closed left hand.

143. "For this third parry," *kore mittsu no uke nari*: Because of the last word, *nari*, this expression would normally mean "These are three parries." But what follows ("you should think that you are delivering . . .") would then have no relevance, since according to Musashi's text, it is clear that the first two parries are executed with the large sword held in the right hand. That is why I think we have a transcription error here, and the word *nari* was added by mistake. If we do not take this word into account, which is the choice I have made, then the sense is coherent.

144. Let us look a little more closely at Musashi's description. For the first parry, you take the blade of your opponent's sword on the back of your large sword, and with a movement directed as though to stab him in the eye, you move your sword forward by slightly lifting your wrist, causing his sword, as it slides along the back of your sword, to pass above your right shoulder. This technique can be used even if you are holding your sword in two hands. You can also apply the principle of this technique in the bare-handed martial arts. In karate this technique is called *tsuki uke* or *sashi te*.

The difference between the second parry and the first is that you parry your opponent's attack with the flat of your small sword held in your left hand, pushing slightly downward. The side of your blade will then be resting on the back of his sword. At the same time, you make the movement of stabbing your adversary's right eye, and you will then be in a position where the back of his sword will provide yours, in the manner of a lever, with a support for cutting the right side of his face. You then direct the blade of your sword toward his throat. Thus this parry contains an attack that might be a decisive one. If not, you follow it immediately with an attack with your other sword.

This technique is also applicable when you are holding your sword with two hands and in karate combat. However, in the kendo matches of the present time, very few practitioners are aware of the position and direction of the blade of their sword, because they are accustomed to fighting with a *shinai* (bamboo sword). Since the *shinai* has the form of a round stick, it is difficult to make out the direction and position that the strike would have with a real sword. Let us recall, however, that until the beginning of the twentieth century, the most highly accomplished practitioners of kendo distinguished between false and real victories by determining through the movements of the *shinai* what the direction and position of the blade of a real sword would have been. Such rigor is still necessary today if one wishes to approach through the practice of kendo that which represents the way of the sword in terms of technical precision as well as in the orientation of the mind.

The third parry is more an attack than a parry. In any case, for Musashi no such thing as a parrying technique intended only to achieve a parry exists. We have seen in the instruction of the guardless guard that, for him, a parry is never just a defense but always an opportunity to achieve victory. In this third parry, when you press in as though to stab your opponent's face with your small sword, this technique is not a mere matter of know-how. It also involves the perception and the force of decision that makes it possible to cross the attack zone of your opponent without being overly concerned with the idea of parrying. If you find yourself in a position to stab the face of your opponent with the small sword held in your left hand, the large sword held in the other hand will be in a favorable position to attack.

145. "Piercing the face," *omote o sasu:* *Sasu* means "causing a pointed object to penetrate." What Musashi means by "piercing the face" has been passed down in kendo practice and is expressed today by the terms *seme* and *kizeme.* *Seme* consists in aiming the point of the sword toward the center line of the opponent's body, between his two eyes or in the direction of one of the eyes. During the combat you must try at every moment to strike or stab the adversary. When this clarity of the will is underpinned by real technical ability, the adversary will feel a painful pressure. Projecting toward the adversary the will to stab, prior to any manifestation of technique, is the objective of the teaching on *seme.*

When practitioners of a superior technical level have acquired the ability to project this will and perceive sharply the will of the other, the major part of the combat consists in the confrontation of *seme.*

A high level of mastery of *seme* is called *kizeme.* Thus a high-level combat consists of the interaction of two wills that have taken on a technical form. The two adversaries assume guard positions, and then one of them is repelled without having been able to make a move. The other will already have won before striking—if in this situation a blow is delivered, the victory will be total. Sometimes the bout ends without a blow ever having been struck, but with the result being perfectly clear to practitioners of the same level. It is in this way that the tradition is preserved, and it is also in this way that it is increasingly at variance with today's tendency toward spectacular combat sports.

146. "To repulse," *norasuru:* This is from the verb *noru,* which means (1) "to stretch, elongate"; (2) "to twist, bend over backward"; (3) "the body stretches out to the point of leaning over backward."

The situation depicted by Musashi can be described in the following manner: In taking your combat posture, your body leans slightly forward. When you drive your adversary back, first he stretches his torso upward and loses the stability of his stance, and then if the pressure continues, he leans his torso backward and is then forced to back up.

147. "Piercing the heart," *shin o sasu*: In the transcriptions of this text (4, 11, 13), the authors give the pronunciation *mune* for this ideogram instead of the usual pronunciation *shin*, which is what I have used.

Shin or *kokoro* means "chest, center" and also "heart" or "mind." In Musashi's text, the idea of chest is often equivalent to the idea of the center of the body. In fact, the technique he is describing is usually associated, in the teaching of kendo and swordsmanship, with aiming at the central line of the adversary's body. *Shin* is often used to refer to the central axis, as in a toy top. Here I have translated *shin* as "heart" in order to differentiate it from the expression employed a little farther on, *mune o tsuke* (see note 149).

148. "The back of your sword," *tachi no mune*: Here *mune* means "the back of the blade," that is to say, the part located opposite the edge.

149. "Stab him in the chest," *mune o tsuke*: To designate the chest, Musashi uses the word *mune*.

150. *Katsu-totsu*:
Katsu! This word, pronounced with a very heavily stressed open *a*, is a cry that is used in Zen, sometimes to communicate a function of the mind difficult to express in speech, sometimes to encourage the disciple or to strike him with an intuitive criticism. It is also used to guide the mind of a dead person to the way of Buddha.

Totsu! This word is pronounced with a short stressed *o* and is an exclamation expressing displeasure or the command to stop. But here the word is used as an echo of *katsu!* Musashi uses the sound of the two exclamations to express the immediacy of the linkage of the two movements that form the technique. What is actually pronounced is *ka-tot*, which mimics the resonance of a sound bouncing off a wall.

These sounds, which come from Sanskrit through the intermediary of Chinese, produce an evocative image for the Japanese. When they are used by Western practitioners of the martial arts or Zen, who know them through a retranscription, the sounds are deformed and lose their evocative force and their rhythm. In that case, they can become a braking force on a movement, because the cry associated with a martial arts technique is generally a single syllable, and when there are two syllables, one is dominant and the other almost swallowed.

151. "The parry with the flat of the sword," *hariuke*: *Hari* comes from the verb *haru*, (99) which means (1) "to stretch a thread, a cord, a piece of cloth, or a net so that there is no fold in it"; (2) "to paste something that is flat"; (3) "to stretch by expanding the elbow, arm, shoulder, or chest"; (4) "to strike with a horizontal movement with the palm, the open hand."

The verb *haru* is used here in senses 2 and 4. The idea expressed is parrying with a slap of the side of your sword, which plays the role of the hand in sense 4 of the term, by pasting it against the side of your opponent's sword (in sense 2 of the term).

At the end of the text, *haru* is used in the expression *haru kokoro areba*, which I translated "with the sensation of stretching your arm," since the verb *haru* applies here to a person and therefore expresses sense 4.

152. *Totan-totan* is an onomatopoeic expression used by Musashi to express the *hyoshi* (cadence) in a situation in which the attacks and parries of two combatants have become repetitive and in which the combat situation has stagnated.

153. To parry a rapid and powerful attack on the part of your opponent, you need not necessarily employ as much speed and power—on the condition that the force applied is sufficiently flexible and powerful to absorb the shock at the moment of taking the strike, because you can back off slightly without letting yourself be driven back completely. This works both for sword and bare-handed combat. The force applied in this parry should not be confused with that of a simple rigid contraction. It implies suppleness and flexibility at the same time as force. It makes it possible to catch and control the adversary's strike and render it ineffective, and he will find himself for an instant with a disconcerting sensation that will place him in a position of vulnerability. Taking the initiative by means of this parry means forcing your opponent into a situation where he momentarily loses the cadence of his movements.

154. "Conduct against many adversaries," *tateki no kurai*: Musashi fought against more than one opponent a number of times. This passage evokes his combat against the Yoshioka clan, where for the first time, other than on the battlefield, he had to confront a large number of opponents. The number of the Yoshioka clan that he faced alone varies, depending on which document you rely on, from tens (*Nitenki*, 2) to several hundred (*Kokura hibun*, 17; *Honcho bugei shoden*, 1-b). Musashi was then twenty years old (1604).

According to the *Hyoho senshi denki*: "When a large number of students of [Yoshioka] Kenpo surrounded the master, sword in hand, to kill him, the master drew both his swords, and cutting down his opponents, he escaped by getting over a hedge. He fought with great courage, and on the basis of this experience, he elaborated his school's strategy for fighting many adversaries." (9, p. 225)

155. "The principle of combat," *uchiai no ri: Uchi ai* means "to strike each other," which expresses the notion of combat in a concrete manner. In Japanese the idea of combat is expressed by various terms:

- *shobu:* "the idea of victory or defeat"
- *tatakai:* "the idea of fighting or confronting one another"
- *uchi ai:* "the idea of exchanging blows"
- *shiai:* "the idea of a mutual confrontation testing skill or art. Today this word is frequently used to refer to a martial arts tournament or sports competition."

Ri means "advantage" or "profit." Here Musashi uses the ideogram *ri* in the sense of "principle, reason."

156. "Transmitted orally," *kuden:* Written transmission plays only a very minor role in the martial arts. In this respect, Musashi's work is an exception. Often it was even prohibited to take notes during teaching.

157. "The single strike," *hitotsu no uchi:* What Musashi describes here is the original form of the notion of *ippon,* which is present today in most of the Japanese martial arts. *Ippon* means "a single essential blow." It is a contraction of *ichi,* "a single one," and *hon,* "origin, root, essence." *Ippon* has become the criterion for a win in competition in martial arts such as kendo, judo, and karate. In that context it has the sense of the decisive point that puts an end to a bout and qualifies a technique as successful. It is in kendo that the application of the notion of *ippon* is least removed from its origin. In kendo the practitioner seeks a victory through a blow that "resounds in the heart of the mind that receives it and also the mind that delivers it." We find this expression in almost every book on the practice of kendo published in Japan.

This notion originally corresponded to the state of mind, described by Musashi, that has as its aim to achieve victory through a single technique. It is this state of mind that guides the search for development and perfection in the Japanese martial arts. All the mental techniques described by Musashi converge toward this state of mind. For example, in order to "stab your opponent in the face," it is essential to seek to win by "a single strike."

158. Direct communication," *jiki tsu no kurai:* The term *jiki tsu* is problematic, and its use seems to be restricted to Musashi alone. It is most often understood in the sense of "direct communication" or "penetration of mind," but these interpretations leave room for ambiguity.

Both of these words has several meanings. I have chosen the ones that are most compatible with Musashi's text. *Jiki* means "direct, straight, honest, rapidly, immediately, communication, quite soon." *Tsu* means "communication, without any stagnation, capacity for supernatural energy, supernatural, to be informed."

An important key here is found in the oral transmission of the *jiki do no kurai* of one of the branches of Musashi's school, the Enmei ryu. According to Yoshida Seiken, the content of this oral transmission *(kuden)* is as follows:

> Your guard position must arise in response to your opponent. That is why, if you take up a guard position, it is based on your opponent, and your guard position is formless like water. Once you are face-to-face with an opponent, a guard position appears spontaneously in accordance with that of the other. For example, if he assumes a high guard, you are in a middle-level guard, and if he is in a middle-level guard, you are in a high guard or a middle one. Thus your guard is the one that makes it possible to naturally dominate the other. You must learn through diligent training to discern the guard position of the adversary so that you can take up a guard position that is suitable and consistent. It is in this way that you will be able to attain direct communication. (35, p. 103)

Based on these elements, I interpret the expression *jiki tsu* in the sense of "direct communication that leads to victory." In my view this involves not only a guard position determined in an effective manner by responding to that of the adversary but also a way of being in combat that is linked to the perception of the adversary and to what Musashi made his adversary feel that permitted him to have direct access to victory.

Yoshida Seiken puts forward another explanation: "The sense of *jiki do no kurai* is a direct path in the mind, that is to say, a state that makes it possible for us to turn ourselves toward the direct way. In other words, it has to do with our own guard position responding directly and correctly to the guard position of the adversary in order to defeat him. I think it would be more appropriate to call this state *jiki do* rather than *jiki tsu*, as Musashi does." Thus, for Yoshida, the two terms *jiki tsu* and *jiki do* express the same state.

Let us note that the reason the teaching of *jiki do no kurai* exists in the Enmei ryu is that Musashi used this term. In the thirty-fifth article of his work *Hyoho sanju go kajo*, he writes, "In my school there exists an ultimate technique that I call *jiki do*." Given the very close meanings of the two phrases, we can either surmise that Musashi uses the two closely related ideograms *do* and *tsu* interchangeably or hypothesize a copying error, since, written with a brush, these two ideograms resemble each other a great deal.

159. "Even if you gain victory . . .": This sentence refers directly to the beginning of the Scroll of Earth. The principle of victory that Musashi is seeking is the principle of

hyoho. Victory must proceed from this principle, which extends to all domains. In this way seeking victory in combat leads to philosophical reflection.

160. "This scroll of fire": *hi no maki* or *ka no maki.*

161. "An area of the wrist . . . ," *tekubi gosun sanzun:* Literally, this means "five or three *sun* (fifteen or nine centimeters) of the area of the wrist." This is a reference to the flexible area of the wrist, which corresponds roughly to this length. The numbers express the idea of the ridiculously trivial aspect of things and have no importance as actual measures.

162. "*Shinai*": Kamiizumi Nobutsuna (c. 1508–c. 1577) invented the bamboo *shinai* as a weapon to be used for exercises. (15, 32, 41) Until that time, training in swordsmanship was carried out mainly with the *bokken* (wooden sword). However, exercising with the *bokken* involved a great number of accidents once training took on a form close to that of the duel. The story of Musashi is an illustration of this—in the majority of his duels, using only a *bokken* himself, he fought an opponent armed with a real sword whom he vanquished and often killed.

Kamiizumi Nobutsuna, wishing to avoid accidents, devised the *fukuro shinai,* or *hikihada shinai,* which is composed of a piece of bamboo left whole at the grip, split into thin strips in the area corresponding to the blade of a sword, and sheathed in a scabbard of lacquered leather. The lacquer reinforced the leather and made it shrink, giving it the appearance of a frog's skin scabbard, hence the name *hikihada shinai.* The length of the *shinai* was the same as a sword's. This *shinai* is still used today in the traditional Yagyu shin kage ryu. The commonly used *shinai* is also derived from it.

With the *shinai* one could exercise with less concern, and this made it possible to develop technical subtleties. Musashi criticizes this tendency, seeing it as a superficial development. In Musashi's time, most of the schools of swordsmanship used wooden swords for training. Toward the middle of the eighteenth century, practitioners of various schools introduced the use of the *shinai* along with protective armor. The best-known of these innovators are Yamada Zaemon and Naganuma Shirozaemeon of the Jiki shin kage ryu and Nakanishi Chubei of the Itto ryu. Sword training with a *shinai* and protective armor is called *shinai uchi kenjutsu* or *gekiken* or *gekken.* With this form of training, which became dominant in the course of the nineteenth century, technique diversified and became more subtle.

163. "The meaning of the edge and the back of the sword," *katana no hamune no michi:* Literally, this means "the way of the back and edge of the sword," which refers in concrete terms to exact trajectories of the blade and precision of technique related to that. It is impossible to slash properly without mastering with precision the pathway

of the blade and therefore without having an awareness of the back and edge of the sword.

164. "Armor," *rokugu:* In the *Ihon gorin no sho,* this is rendered by the term *hyogu.* (14)

165. "The way of my strategy . . .": In this sentence, the term *michi* is used twice, the first time in the sense of "way"; the second time it is applied to that which makes it possible to attain victory. In that case I therefore translated it "principle."

166. "The principle of the way," *dori:* This has the sense of principle, but to distinguish it from the terms *do* or *michi* or *ri* (which Musashi uses alone in the sense of "principle"), I have translated this expression "the principle of the way."

167. "To win against any person," *ban nin ni katsu: Ban nin* literally means "ten thousand men." In this context, the sense is "all persons, whoever they might be, anybody."

168. "Direct communication," *jiki do:* See the last section of the Scroll of Water ("Direct Communication").

169. "Supernatural power," *tsuriki fushigi: Tsuriki* is a Buddhist term meaning "subtle and excellent force or power which is free and effective and applies to every thing and every phenomenon"; *fushigi* is a Buddhist term meaning "that which is unfathomable, that which is beyond the capacity of human thought and reason."

Musashi is considered to be highly pragmatic. In his writings he confines himself in general to the realm of the tangible, but here he mentions a "supernatural power." In the anecdotes about Musashi, we find a number of descriptions of "supernatural abilities," which might be interpreted as an exaggeration. Nevertheless, still today in Japanese martial arts circles, "supernatural" phenomena are spoken of, that is, phenomena that are difficult to explain, such as causing opponents to fall down from a distance or communicating by telepathy.

In the course of my practice, I have had a few experiences of this nature. For example, a master caused me to feel a strange pressure in the course of combat exercises, as if the air were pushing me backward. I felt this physically, but I was able to resist this pressure because I refused to enter into collusion with the energy of it. His regular students were thrown spectacularly without the master's ever touching them. I concluded from this experience that emanation of a strange energy does indeed exist. In this particular case, this energy did not seem sufficiently strong to throw someone without there being a master-student relationship to create and hold a certain psychological synchronization. If the energy emanated in this way were stronger and the person emanating it were capable of imposing this kind of synchronization on his opponent, then it would be possible to understand the accounts relating to the end of Musashi's life in which he drove opponents back or made them collapse without touching them.

170. "Vital essence," *iki:* literally, "breath."

171. "Regarding the place of combat," *ba no shidai.*

172. With two swords, the most advantageous situation is to have your opponent on your left and avoid being attacked on the right, because the longer sword, held in the right hand, is always ready to attack.

173. Musashi uses the term *kamiza,* which literally means "the high place." In traditional architecture, the *kamiza* is situated at the rear of a room. The most important person or a guest is placed there. At a gathering, the places people receive are hierarchically arranged starting from the *kamiza.* In general this is the location of the *tokonoma,* a small, slightly elevated alcove in which an ornamental arrangement of some type is placed.

174. "Three ways of taking the initiative," *mittsu no sen:* The term *sen* is often used in teaching techniques of swordsmanship. *Sen* means "to precede." Here the term indicates the need to act first in situations of combat, that is, to take a step forward and thus to take the initiative.

175. *Ken* means "attack, assault." Musashi employs this term in the sense of "connect the will to attack with your own mind," that is, "prepare to attack." *Ken no sen* can thus be translated, "to take the initiative in a situation where you attack first or in which you are in a position to launch an attack." In this case it is your initial disposition that determines how the combat unfolds. In an attempt to conserve the brevity of the Japanese formulation, I have translated *ken no sen* as "attacking before your opponent."

176. "As soon as you near . . . ," *hayaku momitatsuru sen:* This passage contains an ambiguity. In general it is read *hayaku* (fast) *momitatsuru* (to attack), and then translated "to attack fast." However, this passage can also be read *hayakumo* (fast) *mitatsuru* (to discern), the verb then being *mitatsuru,* "to discern." The word *mitatsuru* is connected with the term *mikiri,* often used to refer to the particular sharpness of Musashi's perception. Both interpretations are compatible with the combat situation.

177. "An untroubled mind," *kokoro hanatsu:* Literally, this means "to let go of the mind." In a synoptic text, *Nito ichi ryu gokui jojo,* written up from his notes by a student of Musashi's, we find the following sentence: "What is called 'letting go of the mind' is part of the domain of mental techniques; it means to cut and clear away various thoughts, troubles, hesitations, fear or hate, and so forth, in order to be able to establish a serene and immutable mind." (6, p. 31)

Kokoro hanatsu is often simply translated "to let go of the mind" in the sense of "to relax"; however, here the text permits us to home in on the meaning more precisely. Hence the translation "preserve an untroubled mind."

178. The term *tai* means "to wait." *Tai no sen* therefore means "to take the initiative, having waited for the attack of the adversary," or more simply, "when the adversary attacks." For the sake of keeping the brevity of the Japanese formulation, I translated *tai no sen* as "taking the initiative at the time of an attack."

179. It should be noted that the term *tai* has two distinct meanings. Musashi writes *tai* in the syllabic alphabet (*hiragana*) to express it in the sense of "to wait" and *tai-tai sen* in ideograms to express the sense of "to clash" or "to oppose." *Tai-tai* expresses a situation where two adversaries are ready to attack each other. For the sake of keeping the brevity of the Japanese formulation, I translated *tai-tai no sen* as "taking the initiative at the time of a reciprocal attack." The sense of *tai* as it is used here is therefore different from the previous use. This explanation is necessary for a Western practitioner who might tend to draw a conclusion about the sense of the word on the basis of the phonetic system of the language. In fact, differences in linguistic systems are often the cause of errors of understanding and communication for Western practitioners of the Japanese martial arts. Musashi uses three words here: *ken, tai,* and another *tai.* The sense of the third term, *tai,* is more or less the same as that of the first term, *ken.* Thus Musashi could have written *ken-ken no sen* instead of *tai-tai no sen,* which would have made it possible to avoid confusion here, even for Japanese practitioners.

180. On *sen,* see my *Miyamoto Musashi: His Life and Writings,* "*Sen*—Taking the Initiative: A Central Notion in Musashi's Practice."

181. "Holding down on the headrest," *makura o sayuru:* The image is to prevent a movement beginning with the head, that is, from the moment it starts.

The usual sense of *makura* is "headrest," but this term also means "he who is at the origin of things, the preface or the prologue of a story or tale." Thus another image is possible—that of exercising a pressure that prevents someone from getting started on the main story.

182. Musashi indicated in this passage, as though it were obvious, that it is necessary to perceive the will of your opponent. However, trying to perceive the will of an adversary before he makes a move is one of the most important and difficult points in the practice of the martial arts. In all the schools, the most secret teaching revolves around how it is possible to acquire this ability.

Musashi is writing for someone who may have acquired this ability. It is for such a person that the instruction "holding down on the headrest" takes on meaning. In practice, it is incomprehensible for those who have not mastered sufficiently the technique of a martial art. More than anything else, this fashion of expressing himself bears witness to the very high level of Musashi's martial arts practice, and this text, for me, evokes an emotion of a different order from the kind of emotion that can be aroused by literary images.

An equivalent attitude is expressed in kendo today by the expression "giving your opponent a train ticket." That means that you know what station he is going to get off at and you are waiting for him at the exit, holding your *shinai* over your head. You strike him a blow before he can even take a step toward the outside.

183. "Getting over a critical passage": *to o kosu.*

184. "Traversing life," *hito no yo o wataru koto:* To evoke human life, Musashi uses the image of a ship crossing. He has already made use of this image at the beginning of the Scroll of Earth.

185. "This event is unique," *ichidaiji:* This is a term of Buddhist origin that means "a great event, the birth of the Buddha; a thought of unique importance, an affair of great importance."

186. "Realizing the situation": *keiki o shiru.*

187. "Have knowledge . . . ," *teki no nagare o wakimaru: Nagare* (current), which can also be pronounced *ryu,* comes from the verb *nagareru,* which means "to flow." A school of an art is expressed as a current of water that perpetuates itself by traversing time from the past to the present to the future. It is on the basis of this image that *ryu* became a suffix that is frequently added to the name of a school.

188. "Use tactics . . . ," *teki no keshiki ni chigau tokoro o shikake:* Another possible translation of this phrase is "Use different tactics by following his reactions." In fact, the term *keshiki* means (1) "the external form of things, the sensation that one feels based on a vision of things or a situation, a facial expression; (2) the movement of the mind that it is possible to observe from the outside, the confidential expression of a secret thought."

I chose the first sense, since it corresponds best to the overall sense of the paragraph and to Musashi's strategy.

189. "Crushing the sword with your foot," *ken o fumu*: Musashi uses here the term *ken* to mean "sword," but this term also expresses an allusion to another word *ken*, which means "a place difficult to get past," or "difficulty."

Fumu means "walk on, bring the foot down from above and pressing down on the top of something; pressing on the ground with the foot in order to walk."

I translated *fumu* "crush with the foot," although it literally means "to walk on." I rejected "stamp" and "trample," because the sense is that of a single powerful act and not of a repetition. "Crushing the sword with your foot" designates an attitude that consists in facing a situation of combat and directly confronting the decisive moment. This moment represents a difficulty that is such that if you dominate it, you can win as though you had broken the sword of your opponent with your foot.

The image of treading on something evokes power in combat. The more serious the combat is, the more we tend to make the tension rise toward the upper part of our body and lose the strength in our legs and feet. The teaching of breaking with the foot contains the instruction to stabilize your force during combat.

190. "Repetition of the same cadences": This is the way I translated the onomatopoeic expression *totan-totan* that Musashi uses to express a technical exchange carried out according to a repetitive cadence that has led to a situation where the combat stagnates (see "The Parry with the Flat of the Sword," page 59).

191. "Crush (*fumu*) with your body": We have seen that the term *fumu* has to do with the state of mind of combat and indicates the force rather than the concrete technique of crushing with your foot. Thus Musashi uses this expression with regard to the body, the mind, and the sword to express the attitude in which one places the totality of one's body above the object to be crushed. Therefore in this sentence I translated the word *fumu* as "crush" rather than "crush with the foot."

192. "You act at the same time . . .": I propose the following interpretation of this sentence. In order to crush the sword of your opponent, that is to say, to crush the action of his technique, it is necessary to act at the same time as he does and not after, but this does not mean knocking into him, because if you collide with him, he will be thrown backward. On the contrary, you meet him at the same time that he is advancing, and without pushing him back, you act as though to absorb the impact of the encounter with the sensation of following his action. This will allow you to crush him rather than throw him backward.

193. "Recognizing the instant of collapse": *kuzure o shiru.*

194. Let us recall that *hyoshi* is the entire set of cadences that constitute a phenome-non. To replace this term with a single word such as *cadence* necessarily involves a shift in the meaning (see page 126).

195. "This strike that causes the blow to carry a long way," *uchi hanasu: Uchi* means "a strike"; *hanasu* means "to separate two connected things, to move away, to distance oneself, to free."

According to the dictionary, *uchi hanasu* means "to kill by cutting down force-fully." (99) However, when the dictionary uses this term to describe a technique, it does not indicate killing but rather describes a technique that, when it is applied to the utmost extent, is capable of killing. That is why I settled on the translation "strike that causes the blow to carry a long way."

We are talking here about a way of striking whose effect on the adversary goes well beyond the direct impact of the landed blow, and this increases the effect of the blow. Even if your opponent resists, he will have trouble pulling himself back to-gether in order to riposte. The sensation is not that of striking powerfully or fully but of striking in such a way that your force carries a lot farther than the spot you hit. Your opponent has the impression that the power of the strike covers his whole body and goes beyond that. In this situation, even if there is no repetition of several strikes, he has the impression of being under the pressure of an ongoing series of strikes. Your opponent will then have the impression of being dominated by a force that is greatly superior to him.

196. "If you do not put some distance . . .": *hanare zareba shidaruki kokoro ari.* Another translation is possible: "If you do not drive your opponent back with this strike, the combat will be in danger of stagnating." The first translation makes more sense in connection with the whole technique. When executing it, one realizes that it is a nec-essary step to place oneself at a certain distance from the adversary.

197. "Becoming your opponent": *teki ni naru.*

198. "Undoing four hands," *yotsu de o hanasu:* This expression is still in use today in traditional Japanese wrestling, which is called sumo. *Yotsu ni kumu,* "to take a four-hands position," refers to the situation in which, in full body contact, each of the two combatants has grabbed hold of the belt of his opponent with both hands. In sumo, the two wrestlers begin by pushing each other or banging into each other, and some-times one of them wins the victory with these techniques. But if the two wrestlers move on to putting holds on each other, the combat has passed into another phase.

The four-hands position, *yotsu*, is a position from which new exchanges of technique can begin.

In contemporary Japanese speech, the expression "to take a four-hands position" means "to fight on an equal footing."

Musashi's expression is easier to understand if we keep the sumo idea in mind. Sumo has long been one of the foundations of the physical education of warriors, and thus it underlies all the techniques of the martial arts. For example, Chiba Shusaku (1794–1855) took the classification of sumo techniques as his point of departure when in the nineteenth century he systematized the technique of swordsmanship into sixty-eight techniques *(kenjutsu rokuju hatte)*. (82, pp. 47–63) Sumo is also a popular pastime, and sumo matches take place on holidays. Musashi, raised in the country, certainly practiced sumo from the time of his childhood. In the West, sumo evokes the image of enormous wrestlers, but those are the professionals. It should be pointed out that until quite recently, the nonprofessional practice of sumo was widespread in Japan.

Musashi, who created his school on the basis of his own experience, is using an expression here whose significance is plain to anyone who has practiced sumo. What he means to indicate is that one must avoid placing oneself on an equal footing with one's opponent.

In my experience, if a practitioner trains in combat only within a confined group, his way of fighting is relatively limited because of the small range of adversaries he faces. When he fights a new opponent, he might well not defeat a person of inferior ability, because he is thrown off by a style of combat he has not yet encountered. He will have an impression of an absence of synchronization, for example, that the two adversaries are attacking and backing off at the same time. He might well lose a bout if his opponent, even one of lesser ability, surpasses him in fighting spirit. By contrast, someone who is accustomed to fighting with a variety of opponents will be able to get out of this kind of situation more easily by modifying his techniques and his cadence.

199. "Moving your shadow," *kage o ugokasu:* What Musashi is referring to in this description corresponds in part to what is practiced in modern kendo under the name of *seme*. At the simplest level, this means a feinted attack used to make an opponent who has taken up a solid guard position make a move. When he reacts to your feint, he reveals his hidden intentions and he has a moment of vacillation that renders him vulnerable.

At a higher level, a practitioner, without making any visible movement, emanates a threat of attack in response to which his opponent is forced to reveal his veiled intentions. This is the moment to launch your actual attack.

If the disparity in ability is considerable, hindered in his action, the adversary will be disconcerted and forced back away from this implicit threat. This situation is an example of the combat of *kizeme.*

200. "Effective means," *ri: Ri* is understood here in its second series of senses: "effectiveness, advantage, interest" (see page 130). I usually translate it "advantage," but in this context the idea of effectiveness seemed to be dominant.

201. In Musashi's time the schools of swordsmanship had not yet stabilized, and there were certainly guard positions in use that today's practitioners cannot even conceive of. Today in the practice of kendo, we cannot find an equivalent of taking up a "guard position with his sword held back." The way of moving the feet and the places to which strikes are directed are considerably different from what they were in Musashi's time. In the practice of swordsmanship *(kenjutsu)*, there is in use today a side-guard position called *waki gamae.* This is a guard position that is taken to the right side with the right foot back, the torso turned sideways—nearly in profile—and the point of the sword directed downward and back. With this guard the adversary is unable to get an idea of the length of the sword, and when the sword is held completely back, he cannot even tell what the nature of the weapon is.

202. "Constricting the shadow": *kage o osayuru.*

203. "Taking the initiative ...": The term used by Musashi, *ku,* means at the same time "emptiness," "sky or heaven," and "space." The sense here is "emptiness," designating a state of mind that is undistorted, that reflects a spontaneous wisdom. This notion is close to that of nonthought in Zen. We find this idea explored more deeply in the Scroll of Heaven.

204. "Infecting," *utsurakasu* (transitive), *utsura-kasu: Kasu* is a suffix that strengthens the transitive sense of a verb. The meaning of this word is almost the same as that of *utsura-seru,* which is used more often. (99) It is the transitive form of the intransitive verb *utsuru,* which means "to transfer, change position or situation" for an object or a person. From this three meanings are derived: (1) "to be contagious" (for an illness); (2) referring to time, "to pass, pass by"; (3) "change in the situation or character of a thing."

Here Musashi plays on a double meaning of the word. Written with another ideogram, which develops its main sense, *utsuru* means "to reflect" in the sense of the shadow or the light of a thing resting on another—its form or its shadow being reflected on something. In this passage Musashi plays on senses 1 and 2 of the term. Several times already we have encountered Musashi playing on a single pronunciation attached to different ideograms that have different meanings in order to give an idea more texture and relief. His play on its pronunciation extends a term's field of meaning.

If a disposition or a sensation is transferred to another being, that is "infecting." If time moves on from one instant to the next, it passes. The time of combat contains all these dynamics—that is why Musashi introduces time in his first list of examples in this section.

205. "And this goes for time too": *toki no utsuru mo ari.*

206. "Irritating your adversary": *mukatsukasuru.*

207. "Before their minds . . . ," *teki no kokoro no kiwamarazaru uchi ni:* Another possible translation would be "before they realize what the situation is."

208. "Without slacking off even to the slightest extent," *iki o nukasazu:* Another possible translation would be "without letting your adversaries breathe for an instant."

209. "Frightening," *obiyakasu:* literally, "to frighten by means of a threatening act."

210. "Coating," *maburuu:* This word comes from *mamireru,* which means "to dirty the whole body with blood, sweat, mud, or dust." The contemporary form is *mabusu,* which is often used as a cooking term, referring, for example, to rolling a fritter in flour.

211. "Hitting a corner," *kado ni sawaru:* In combat position, knees and feet are among the protruding "corners" Musashi is talking about. In modern kendo, only four parts of the body are attacked: the head (*men*), the side (*do*), the wrist (*kote*), and the throat (*tsuki*). Attacks directed at other parts of the body do not count. Matches with adepts of the *naginata* (mainly women)—a discipline in which the shins are also attacked—show plainly the major difficulty encountered by practitioners of kendo resulting from attacks for which they are not prepared.

At the end of the Edo period, the sword had attained a very high level, but at the same time, a certain standardization had distanced the art from situations of combat. When warriors once again found themselves involved in a period of sword combat, between 1850 and 1870, the Ryugo ryu was greatly celebrated for its effectiveness, which resulted from attacks to all parts of the body, notably the shins.

212. "Troubling": *uromekasu.*

213. "The three types of cries," *mittsu no koe:* Left over from the wave of karate and kung fu films is the expression "the cry that kills." And if you attend a competition or

a training session of these disciplines, you will certainly hear cries, but they are far from killing; rather, they approximate the cries of animals, accompanied by grimaces.

Musashi clearly says: "Do not sound a great cry at the same time as you strike with your sword."

This teaching differs from the custom that has become the usual one in kendo, of crying out *kiai* and announcing the part to which you are delivering your blow (*men, do, kote, tsuki*) at the same time as you strike. This custom has been inherited from training sessions of former times, where a wooden sword or sometimes even a real sword was used, during which, to avoid accidents, the attacker called out what part of the body he was about to strike. The controlled movement of attack followed immediately after. With this method, the attacker sought to score a sure victory, that is, to attack when he was sure his strike was going to hit home. This is what is called *ki-ken-tai*, which means the simultaneous coming together of *ki*, the sword, and the body at the moment of the strike. In kendo this is a way of ruling out a win by a chance blow and of trying for fullness, a kind of existential sensation, in the act of striking.

The difference between this and the swordsmanship of Musashi is clear. Musashi situated himself first and foremost within an overall strategy of combat in which the life of the combatant was at risk. In modern kendo, defeat can be a challenging moment that can lead to progress. In this context it is necessary to have many experiences of defeat in order to make progress, whereas for Musashi, a single defeat meant death. Another attempt was thus not a viable notion.

214. "As loudly as possible," *ikahodo mo kasa kakete:* This literally means "exaggeratedly, to an unimaginable degree." The expression is composed of

> *ikahodo:* (1) "how much, to what degree"; (2) "the degree, the quantity, and the value are so great that they cannot be assessed"
> *kasa:* (1) "dimension, height, size of superimposed objects; quantity of things"; (2) "height, high part, upper part"; (3) "weight, dignity, talent"; (4) "energy that repels the adversary"
> *kasa o kakeru:* to express exaggeratedly, multiply the dimensions.

215. According to Yoshida Seiken, in Musashi's time the two series of cries that were most common in the schools of swordsmanship were *ei, o, to* and *ei, ya, to.* (35, p. 130)

Tominaga Kengo writes:

> In the practice of the Niten ryu, different cries exist. During training, most often these three cries are used: *ya, ei, to.* Some groups use *shi, ei, to, ho, yo, ya,* and sometimes another cry is added: *sore.* According to an ancient teaching of this

school, the cries are defined by the seven sounds: *ei, to, shi, ho, yo, ya,* and *sore,* and there are no others. Today in the Niten ryu there are masters who use cries and others who do not. Some use a long cry: *u, to;* and others: *ei, ha, to.*

In certain schools it is said that at the moment of a fight to the death, it is not possible to emit a cry, and therefore, it is better not to train in this. In other schools full cries and empty cries are distinguished, with the empty cries considered to be bad and the full cries to be good. In the Jigen ryu they have just one cry: *chie.* (12, p. 205)

216. "Cries of before and after": *sen go koe.*

217. "Concealing yourself," *magiruru.* This comes from *magireru,* which means (1) to blend in, become lost by mixing with a large number; (2) difficult to distinguish because of their resemblance; (3) to hide oneself, conceal oneself; (4) to try to remain unseen; (5) to clutter up.

218. "Zigzagging down a slope" is expressed by *tsuzura-ori,* which means "a road going down a slope in zigzags." This term is also used in Japanese equitation to refer to the technique that is used to go down a slope in a zigzag fashion on horseback.

219. "This strategy can also be applied . . .": Musashi does not give any further explanation of this point. I interpret this sentence in the following way: When your opponent is powerful, you must not have the slightest thought of backing off and must attack with force, varying your attacks from the head down to the feet of your opponent. In this way you can create an opportunity to defeat him without sticking to a particular technique; for if your opponent is strong, he will be able to counter any definite technique. Thus it is important for you to create a diversion at the moment of each of your attacks, continually varying your techniques. This is what Musashi calls "concealing yourself," that is, concealing your intentions behind your acts.

220. "Smashing": *hishigu.*

221. "Determinedly considering him . . .": We find the same sort of teaching in the Chinese method known as *da cheng quan,* which is based mainly on standing meditation. In this method the practitioner practices various bodily sensations, guiding himself with various images. In the course of my practice of this, during a visit to China in 1991, I received from Master Yu Yong the following instruction: "You imagine yourself as a powerful giant while imagining your opponent and everything that surrounds you as small. You are infinitely larger and stronger than they are and you dominate them." The point is to create a psychological state that increases your combativeness.

222. "Starting with the head . . . ," *kashira yori kasa o kakete:*

- *kasa:* (1) "dimension, height, size of superimposed objects; quantity of things"; (2) "height, high part, upper part"; (3) "weight, dignity, talent"; (4) "energy that oppresses the adversary".
- *kakeru:* (1) to hang; (2) to put on top of, to cover; (3) add force or quantities.

The expression *kasa o kakeru* means "to express exaggeratedly, multiply the dimensions." I translated it more literally as "adding *(o kakete)* an oppressive burst of energy *(kasa).*"

223. "Change from the Mountain to the Sea," *san kai no kawari:* Musashi seems in this title to be making a little play on words. *San* means "mountain," and *kai* means "sea," but another pair of ideograms also pronounced *san* and *kai* mean "three" and "times," which makes "three times." This expression is also used in this sense in the text.

224. "Ripping out the bottom," *soko o nuku:* The image is that of a full barrel from which one brutally removes the bottom. The liquid will completely run out of it; that is, the adversary will feel himself to have lost completely, as though he had been emptied of his contents. This image contains the violence of combat, which is why I translated as "ripping out."

225. Musashi uses the preceding image here again: "he feels completely defeated," *soko yori makuru kokoro ni.* Musashi seems to have used this manner of "ripping out the bottom" as a criterion of victory in his duels. He did not consider himself to have won a bout until he had struck his opponent a blow of his sword in the middle of his forehead, between the brows, which generally brought about his death. If not, this way of striking at least ripped out "the bottom," and his adversary was no longer capable of putting up a fight.

226. "Renewing yourself": *arata ni naru.*

227. I understand this passage from my experience in karate combat. In the beginning, when the development of a combat stagnated, my tendency was to make an all-out effort, straining to the point of exhaustion. In such a situation I had the impression of letting myself slide down a slope, slipping lower and lower. I then had to climb back up at any price, like someone who is drowning. In a case like that, even if I did end up with the win, I expended a great deal of energy and felt exhausted. Around the age of twenty-seven, with the help of this passage in the *Gorin no sho,* I learned to renew myself when the combat was stagnating. It seems that it is necessary, in order

to learn to renew oneself in combat, to have accumulated concrete combat experiences and also to have observed a large number of bouts. Otherwise, even if you understand this passage intellectually, you will not be able to put it into practice, because you will not be capable of assuming the necessary distance from your experience of the moment, from your own sensations. In combat you are doubtless caught up in a particular field of tension, and renewing yourself means resituating yourself in a different type of field of tension. To do this it is indispensable to detach yourself from the initial tension, and this requires a maturity that has been enriched by experience.

228. "A bull's neck," *soto goshu:* I translated the ideogram that appears in both copies of Musashi's text as "bull." This ideogram, pronounced *go* or *uma*, means "horse." The related ideogram is pronounced *go* or *ushi* and means "bull" or "ox."

In practice in the schools that have issued from Musashi, the image comparing the bull and the mouse is one that is used by the masters. Moreover, in the training of warriors, the following aphorism has been in use: "A warrior must have the meticulous attention of the mouse and at the same time the courage of the bull." Thus all commentators adopt the second interpretation, with the idea that some change has occurred in the original ideogram. I follow the same approach.

229. "The general knows his soldiers": *sho sotsu o shiru.*

230. To put this teaching into practice, one has to be a very highly accomplished practitioner. All the same, this teaching can serve as a guide in combat exercises for the state of mind of practitioners who have attained a certain level. This also involves trying to take the initiative, which is a central point in Musashi's strategy.

231. "Letting go of the sword handle," *tsuka o hanasu:* At first blush, this phrase communicates the notion of combat techniques that do not use the sword, but it should rather be understood as an instruction on the state of mind of combat. Even if one is fighting with a sword, one must not be attached to one's weapon. It is important to let go of the sword handle mentally, while still using it. Detachment of this kind makes it possible to free the mind and to expand one's vision in the midst of combat.

To refer to my combat experience in karate, when I am close to my opponent, it sometimes occurs that I become detached from the techniques even as I am using them. The point is that in combat, when you become attached to your techniques, sometimes they become a kind of barrier between the two opponents. If you are using a sword, it is the sword that becomes this kind of block; if you are fighting barehanded, it is your fists, your arms, your legs. When I succeed in detaching myself from my techniques, I have the impression of being able to penetrate directly into the mind of my opponent, and that it is the force of my mind that makes it possible for me to win. Even though it is through the techniques that you gain the victory, attachment to the techniques hinders this mental effort. Nevertheless, you must realize that it takes an enormous amount of work and accumulation of technique to detach yourself from your techniques in a way that is not haphazard or by chance. I think this is the meaning of the notion widely taught in the Japanese martial arts that it is necessary to go beyond technique.

232. "The body of a rock," *iwao no mi:* Musashi explains in his work "Thirty-five Instructions on Strategy" *(Hyoho sanju go kajo)* (see page 102): "The body of a rock is a great and powerful mind that is completely unmoving."
    Here is an anecdote about the body of a rock:

> One day Lord Hosokawa was asking Musashi about the body like a rock. Musashi asked him to send for Terao Motomenosuke, one of his vassals who was a disciple of Musashi's.
>   As soon as Terao arrived, Musashi said to him, "Terao Motomenosuke, by your lord's command, you will kill yourself by seppuku here and now!"
>   Terao greeted him calmly and said: "I thank you for this order. Kindly give me just the time to make preparations." Then he withdrew calmly into the next room to prepare to die, without showing the slightest disturbance.
>   Looking at the back of his disciple who was walking as though nothing had happened, Musashi said, "My lord, that is the body of a rock." (5, p. 180)

That is the end of the story, but we should add that the order given to Terao was immediately withdrawn.
    This anecdote shows that "body of a rock" expresses the attitude of a *bushi* who has passed beyond attachment to life and death. This refers to a way of existing without moving body or mind even if "the earth shakes and the sky falls." The body in question here could be better understood as a state of mind, but it is significant that Musashi expresses this attitude by "the body of a rock," which naturally also includes the mind.
    "The body of a rock," which characterizes the strategy and the life of Musashi, is the last instruction in the Scroll of Fire.

233. "The Scroll of Wind": *kaze no maki* or *fu no maki.*

234. "Surface training and depth training": This translation relates to the opposition *omote/oku,* literally meaning "entry" or "surface" or "facade" as opposed to "depth" or "core." The opposition surface/depth corresponds to an image in the English language, but this image does not properly take into account the Japanese image of an

entry as opposed to an interior depth, which in the case of the martial arts, also contains a reference to that with which one begins as opposed to that which is more profound (see the more detailed note on the last article of this scroll, "Schools That Distinguish between Depth and Surface").

235. "The art of the sword": *kenjutsu.*

236. "My School of Two Swords": *nito ichi ryu.*

237. "A particularly long large sword," *okinaru tachi: Tachi* designates "a large sword"; the literal translation would be "a large large sword."

238. "The longer one's limbs are, the better it is," *issun te masari:* Literally, this means, "a hand longer than one *sun." Masari* means "that which is superior or which is dominant." Since *masari* here has the double sense of "longer limbs" and "that which is superior," I gave this idea twice in the translation.

239. "A small sword," *wakizashi:* Musashi uses two names to designate the small sword: *kowakizashi* and *wakizashi.*

A warrior customarily carried two swords: the large sword, a long one, and another that was shorter. In general the blade of the long sword measured 80 to 90 centimeters and that of the small sword 50 to 60 centimeters. Toward the end of the Edo period, the length of swords diminished, with the blade of the long sword varying in the area around 80 centimeters. One of Musashi's swords has been preserved, and its blade measures 93.3 centimeters, which is within the normal range for his time. During the period of feudal wars, some warriors used swords that were 2 meters long. (41, p. 6)

In the handling of swords, a difference of a few centimeters is significant. Today practitioners of *iai* (the art of drawing the sword) practice with swords whose blades usually measure 75 centimeters (2.5 *shaku*) for practitioners who are 1.7 to 1.8 meters tall. The difficulty of the practice increases considerably if the blade is 1.5 centimeters longer. Today practitioners of *iai* capable of using a sword greater than 80 centimeters long are rare.

240. "The sword with brute force": *tsuyomi no tachi.*

241. "If you try to cut through . . .": Musashi is saying that the cutting quality of the sword is not directly proportional to the strength or weakness of the strike. There is a common expression for denoting the quality of a blade, *kire aji,* which means "cutting quality." As we saw in the Scroll of Water, implementation of this quality belongs to

a domain that is quite different from that of brute force. For example, kendo practitioners practice repetitive strikes in the air with a heavy wooden sword in order to gain mastery of their normal sword, which is much lighter. They must also practice striking with a light wooden sword as though it were heavy. And indeed, when you take a *shinai* blow from a truly accomplished practitioner, even if the blow appears to be light and slow, you feel the impact of a strike delivered with a heavy object. This does not result from the mere force of the blow but from the fact that the practitioner has struck you holding the sword correctly and following the correct blade path. This is what is usually described as *te no uchi*.

242. "A mortal enemy," *kataki: Kataki uchi* denotes an act of vengeance against an enemy who has killed a warrior's lord or a member of his family. During the Edo period, even though duels based on personal conflicts were prohibited, those that were regarded as acts of vengeance were encouraged and were part of the ethics of a warrior. Such acts of vengeance were carried out on all social levels. They were then prohibited at the beginning of the Meiji period, in 1873.

243. "If you slap . . . forcefully in making a parry . . .": The verb I translated as "slap" is *haru;* it is connected with *hariuke,* "a parry effectuated by slapping with the flat of the sword" (see note 151, page 183).

244. "Your sword might break in two": This passage poses a problem. In the text that I use as my reference standard (10), it is written *okuretakuru.* Takayanagi Mitsutoshi points out that another reading is possible: *okuretagaru.* In this case the sense would be "your sword will have a tendency to lag behind."

    In the *Ihon gorin no sho* (14), this word is written *orekudakeru,* which means "to break in pieces."

    Even though Watanabe Ichiro (13) uses the same original text as does Takayanagi Mitsutoshi, he writes *orekudakeru* as in the *Ihon gorin no sho.* Following the logic of the text, I also adopt this interpretation.

245. "The principle of the way": *dori.*

246. "In the way of my school": In the copy of Musashi's text (10), there is a gap, a word missing, that I fill in with "way." My supposition here is based on the *Ihon gorin no sho* (14), which in this passage has the ideogram *michi.*

247. "The short sword," *mijikaki tachi:* Farther on in this passage, Musashi speaks of *tachi* (translated as "large sword") and *katana* (translated as "small sword"). In Musashi's time, the names of the large and small swords were not rigorously fixed; the distinction was nevertheless indicated by using *tachi* for the large sword and *katana* for the

small sword, or by using *katana* for the large sword and *wakizashi* for the small sword. In general, *tachi* referred to a sword whose blade measured more than 3 *shaku* (ninety centimeters). The *katana* measured 2 to 3 *shaku* (sixty to ninety centimeters), and the *wakizashi* less than 1.8 *shaku* (fifty-four centimeters).

248. "*Naginata*": In the most widely used version (13), the term used is *nagatachi*, literally, "particularly long large sword." In another version (14), the term is *naginata*. In view of the context, *naginata* is the right choice.

249. "Submitting to the initiative of the other," *gote* or *ushirode:* These ideograms, when pronounced *gote*, mean "put oneself in a passive situation," because one has let the other take the initiative. This term is the contrary of *sente* (on *sen;* see note 174, page 188, and my *Miyamoto Musashi: His Life and Writings,* "*Sen*—Taking the Initiative: A Central Notion in Musashi's Practice.") These ideograms can also be pronounced *ushirode,* the sense then being "that which is behind" or "the back of things."

250. "When facing many opponents," *taiteki no naka: Taiteki* has two senses: (1) a formidable adversary; (2) many adversaries. *No naka* means "in." The whole expression means "in the number of the adversary," hence my translation.

251. "Close enough": In the practice of the small sword called *kodachi,* one holds the handle of the sword with one hand. Sometimes one grabs hold of the wrist, the sleeve, or the collar of one's opponent as one comes in quite close in order to use one's small sword more effectively.

252. "Driving them back all of a sudden," *yaniwani shioshi: Yaniwani* means "all of a sudden." For *shioshi* or *shihoshi,* Takayanagi gives the ideograms that mean "way of doing" or "method." (10) Watanabe gives two other possible ideograms that mean "push" or "drive back" and "encircle the four sides." In view of the logic of the text, I translated "driving back."

253. "Your mind will be steered by these ways of doing things *(michi),*" *kokoro nichi ni hikasarete:* The term *michi* (in senses 2 and 3, see page 129) means "way of doing." In this case, it refers back to the list that precedes it; hence the translation "these ways of doing things."

254. "A large number of sword techniques," *tachi kazu ooki:* Musashi's critique is directly applicable to the martial arts of the present period. Let us cite, for example, a passage from a book written in 1963 by So Doshin, founder of a martial art called *shorinji kenpo,* which has many practitioners in Japan: "One of the technical particularities of

shorinji kenpo is the aesthetics of its style and a speed of execution that can be found in no other discipline in the realm of *budo*. You will appreciate the thrilling charm of its highly refined techniques, which are derived from tradition. Moreover, the number of its secret techniques comes to well over six hundred. Thus you can continue to train for a long time without losing interest." (51, p. 37)

Ueshiba Kisshomaru, the successor of his father, Ueshiba Morihei, the founder of aikido, wrote in 1972: "The founder of aikido, Ueshiba Morihei, mainly practiced the jujutsu of the Daito ryu, which includes as many as 2,664 techniques. In addition to this, Ueshiba Morihei practiced the jujutsu of the Shin kage ryu, Aioi ryu, and other schools, and he developed his own techniques on the basis of the secret techniques he had learned. That is why the techniques of aikido today are innumerable." (55, p. 21)

He wrote in another work: "There are several thousand techniques in aikido, and they can be classified into three categories: throwing techniques, immobilization techniques, and techniques of immobilization following a throw. In addition, there are two ways—*omote* and *ura*—of performing each technique." (54, p. 57)

Making a display in this fashion of a large number of techniques is a fitting target for Musashi's criticism; however, in the Daito ryu, this was also a way of discouraging potential novices at the beginning, so that they would end up having to accept only people of great determination.

The techniques in any *budo* discipline are innumerable, but at the same time it could be said that they are few. It all depends on one's point of view concerning technique. For Musashi, who attempts to discern and teach the essential, the fundamental techniques are not numerous. At the same time, he could have said that there were thousands of techniques in his school, since if you count up all the technical variations, they are indeed innumerable in every *budo* discipline, and the School of Musashi was no exception. From the point of view of teaching, the important thing is to distill the essence from the complexity of the techniques in order to provide a structure for the learning process and not to proliferate names of variations, which only creates confusion. As to the essence, the techniques are neither complex nor numerous. What is needed is to develop the insight that can perceive what is essential in a phenomenon whose appearance is complex, and then to teach this. Just through modifications of a single striking technique, one can produce scores of different techniques. However, as a working method, rather than studying scores of variants of a technique in order to get at the primary technique, it is more effective to work on a main technique and study its variants afterward. It seems to me that Musashi's approach is close to this.

255. "Pulling back," *hiraki*: from *hiraku*, which means "moving the body backward while taking up a guard position," or "dodge by means of a movement of the body," or "to flee" (99)—all in response to an attack by an opponent.

256. "Guard position in the art of the sword," *tachi no kamae.*

257. "In this world . . .": This sentence and the next one mean "one does not establish laws except when society has become stable." One does not establish laws in the midst of important events; it is after the fact, in retrospect, that society establishes customs and laws. A society that is looking back in this way is not in the heat of facing the event. For example, in Japan certain measures have been taken to deal with earthquakes, lightning, and fires. These measures were taken in periods of calm. They thus represent a guard position that was assumed at a time when there was no adversary.

   In the art of combat, this sort of distance and looking back is not possible because the temporality involved is of another order. It is therefore not possible, as Musashi makes clear all through the text, to rely on a guard position worked out in a rigid fashion, in the manner of a law. In combat, as he explains in the Scroll of Water, fundamentally the guard is made up of positions that enable one to respond in the best way to any form of attack one's opponent might make. This is the idea of the "guard without a guard" recommended by Musashi.

258. "The guard without a guard," *uko muko:* This has been literally translated.

259. "*Naginata*": In the most widely used version of the *Gorin no sho* (13), the term used is *nagatachi*, literally, "particularly long large sword." In Yamada Jirokichi's version (14), the term is *naginata*. In view of the context, *naginata* is the right choice.

260. "Moving a lance or a *naginata* about in such a way as to set up a barrier," *saku ni furitaru: Saku* means "a fence made of bamboo or wood." Kamata Shigeo (4), Terayama Danchu (11), and Watanabe Ichiro (13) interpret this: "to use the lance or the *naginata* across a barrier." Kamiko Tadashi (5) has: "That comes to the same thing as setting up the lance and the *naginata* rigidly as a barrier." For my part, I interpret *saku ni* as an adverbial phrase expressing the movement of the weapons that continues the sequence expressed in the previous sentence.

261. "Particular ways of gazing": *metsuke.*

262. "Someone playing ball": This refers to an ancient game called *kemari*, from *ke*, meaning "kick," and *mari*, meaning "ball." It was initially called *kumaeri* or *marikoyu*, and then later the name *kemari* was established. The same ideogram can also be pronounced *shukiku.*

   This game was initially played by the nobles at the emperor's court. The ball was made from stag skin, and its diameter was about twenty-one centimeters. (99) It was played with eight players, and the players wore leather shoes. The game consisted in striking the ball with the instep. Sometimes a player tried to pass the ball to his partners, sometimes to keep kicking it as long as possible without letting it touch the ground. In this game, elegance of form in body and movements as well as in the curve of the ball's trajectory was sought after. The playing field was a square of approximately fourteen meters on a side. At each corner of the field a tree was planted (a cherry, a willow, a pine, and a maple). The rules of the game were systematized during the Kamakura period (1185–1333), and several schools were founded. The game was played regularly until the Edo period. (99, 104)

263. "Stroking his temples," *hinsuri* or *binsuri*: *Bin* refers to "the hair growing near the ears"; *suru* means "to rub" or "to stroke." Literally, the phrase means "to stroke the hair near the ears."

264. "Acrobat": the translation of *hoka*; *hokashi*, "magician," "acrobat." *Hoka* means (1) to throw something; (2) "to drop"; (3) an art practiced in the Middle Ages, mainly by monks, which consisted in singing while dancing and performing acrobatics and magic tricks.

265. "While balancing a door over his nose," *tobira o hana ni tate*: literally, "while resting a door on his nose," in fact, on the lower part of the forehead.

266. "In strategy you place your gaze . . .": Certain schools or certain masters placed great importance on fixing the gaze and on the places it was considered suitable to fix it. For example, Chiba Shusaku (1794–1855), the master who founded the Hokushin Itto ryu, taught two ways of gazing, defensive and offensive. (82, p. 17)

The defensive gaze, according to his teaching, should be fixed on the point of the adversary's sword and on his fist simultaneously. He explains: "Imagine a keg of sake. If the cork is missing from the tap, it is difficult to keep the sake from running out. It suffices to stop up the tap to block this flow." According to Chiba, keeping the gaze simultaneously on the sword point and the fist of the adversary is equivalent to stopping up the tap of the keg.

For the offensive gaze, he teaches that the gaze should be placed *obi no kane*, literally, "one measure from the belt sash." If the opponent is of a superior level of accomplishment, instead of looking at his eyes, one should look at his belt, which will make it possible to camouflage one's own intention of attacking.

According to the teaching of the Nen ryu, one should look simultaneously at the face and the fist of the adversary. The Yagyu shin kage ryu says one should look in one direction at the same time as looking in another, *futame tsukai*, and also look slyly while pretending to look at something else, *chugan*.

Musashi says, "In strategy, you place your gaze on the mind of your opponent." The different techniques of gazing I have referred to above represent reference points for discovering the mind of one's opponent. Thus Chiba Shusaku explains that all the gazes he describes should be executed by the eyes of the mind (*mokushin*).

In order "to look at the mind of one's adversary," it is necessary to have a mental gaze directed on oneself. Under the influence of Zen, this idea has increased in importance all through the history of the Japanese sword. The ability to perceive the essence of phenomena is called *shin-gan* ("the eyes of the mind").

267. "Looking and seeing": See the Scroll of Water, "The Way of Looking in Strategy."

268. "Various kinds of footwork": *ashi tsukai.*

269. "Floating foot," *uki ashi*: You keep one of your feet, most often the front foot, floating, touching the ground only with the base of the toes, the heel slightly lifted. You can almost move the foot forward in a floating manner as you look for the right distance from which to attack.

"Leaping foot," *tobi ashi*; "hopping foot," *hanuru ashi*; "stamping foot," *fumitsumuru ashi.*

"Crow's foot," *karasu ashi*: Terayama gives a brief commentary, without citing any source, on this kind of movement, describing it as "moving with small steps." (11) In the documents I consulted, I found no further description of this kind of movement. I questioned several sword masters, but none of them could give me an explanation of this expression. I think this was a term used in Musashi's time that did not continue to be used later on.

270. "A movement to dampen the impact . . . that holds the body back": *tobi te itsuku kokoro ari.*

271 "It involves a wait," *tai no ashi*: Literally, this means "feet in a waiting attitude, an attitude that puts you on the defensive."

272. "In my strategy . . .": We are reminded here of a passage in the Scroll of Water: "To move from one place to another, you slightly raise your toes and push off your foot from the heel, forcefully." Here Musashi stresses again: "In my strategy the way of moving is no different from normal walking on a road."

Movements from place to place in modern kendo differ from Musashi's description. In kendo, in general the movement used is one in which the right foot is kept forward and the left foot back, with the heel slightly lifted off the ground.

Musashi also writes in the Scroll of Water, "You should not move just one foot.... You must always move the right and left feet alternately. You must never move only one foot."

The principle of not moving one foot alone is respected in modern kendo but in a different form, since at the end of each movement from place to place, the distance between the feet remains the same. Thus you move right-left or left-right, but without alternating the front foot.

Today the principal of moving the feet described by Musashi is applied primarily in the schools of the ancient art of the sword. These schools transmit the classic art of swordsmanship. Very rarely, some contemporary kendo masters use this type of movement.

273. "If your steps are too slow," *ashi bumi shizuka nite wa*: *Ashi bumi* means "step, gait."

274. "Stress speed": *hayaki o mochiiru.*

275. "A lag has occurred," *ma ni awazaru*: "Lagging behind" is expressed by *ma ni awanai*, literally, "not adjusting to the *ma*" (temporal, spatial, or psychological interval). For Musashi, speed and slowness are produced by a deviation in relation to the proper cadence.

276. The art of Noh drumming is extremely difficult. During a visit to Japan, I was struck by an interview with a young woman of twenty-three, the descendant of a family of traditional Noh theater drummers. She said: "I have been practicing the drum since I was three years old. For a long time I was not considered to be someone who really played. When I was twenty, my father told me with a satisfied expression, 'You have finally become bad.' Before that my level was such that I could not even be considered."

277. "Oimatsu" is a Noh theater song composed by Zeami (1363–1443)—the spirit of an old pine tree appears in order to celebrate springtime in a peaceful world. Later on, the music of this piece was adapted to be played at wedding celebrations or other happy events.

278. "Takasago" is also a song composed by Zeami. Its subject is the journey of a Shinto priest who is traveling from a province on the island of Kyushu to Kyoto. As he is admiring the countryside near the bay of Takasago (in Hyogo prefecture), two old men appear and recount the story of two old pine trees, of which one was located here, at Takasago, and the other at Sumiyoshi (Osaka). These two pines were called *aioi no matsu*, which means "the pines of Aioi" (the name of a place); but at the same time, through a pun, it also means " two pines (*matsu*) getting old (*oi*) together (*ai*)."

After telling him this story, the two old men disappear. When the priest gets to Sumiyoshi, the spirit of a god appears and does a dance in honor of the emperor. Today "Takasago" is a classic song played at weddings.

279. "What is meant by . . .": The opposition here is between *oku* and *omote*, as in the title of the section.

280. "The depth from the entry," *oku guchi*: A possible translation is "the entry door that opens to the transmission of the depth"; however, it seems more accurate to separate *oku* and *guchi* and thus to translate the two words separately.

281. "The ultimate teaching," *gokui*; "the secret transmission," *hiden*: In the text, the two terms are connected (*gokui-hiden*) to form a whole, since the ultimate teaching is generally transmitted secretly.

282. "The degree of their advancement," *kokoro o hodokuru*: *Hodokuru* is an ancient form of *hodokeru*, which means (1) a knot that is coming undone, (2) capable of understanding, (3) softening the feeling. The sense here relates to the knot of the mind coming undone, which means that the capacity for understanding increases. Thus I translated as "the degree of their advancement," which fit with the meaning of the previous sentences.

283. "Mountains": Musashi uses the term *yama*, which is translated as "mountains." But in Western terms, the mountains mentioned here would be regarded as wooded hills. The situation described by Musashi is similar to one in which someone taking a walk penetrates into the midst of a forest and ends up coming out on a different side, a way out that could also be a way in.

284. "It might turn out . . .": Musashi is opposed to a rigid distinction between *oku* and *kuchi*. Different levels were distinguished among students of schools of the martial arts, generally: beginners, intermediates, advanced students, and ultimate-transmission students. In the course of the Edo period, these divisions increased in number, and at each promotion to a higher level, the students had to pay the master something.

In Musashi's school there was also a distinction between depth and entry, but he was opposed to systematizing the teaching in terms of levels.

It is possible to teach the same technique at a rudimentary level or a more advanced one. In the beginning the accent is placed on the correct assimilation of different parts of the movement, which tends to get divided into several sequences. With more advanced students, the component elements of a gesture must be fused together, and the movement is executed in a more fluid manner. Thus, with the same technique, there is a change of cadence as it is executed in a more and more advanced style. When a technique becomes fixed in the form of a kata, these two forms of execution are designated *omote no kata* and *oku no kata*.

With regard to the ultimate transmission and the secret teaching, the transmission of what is most important is often accompanied by poems. Here are three such poems that are part of the tradition of swordsmanship and are quoted in several schools, though the authors are unknown:

> The ultimate transmission is like your own eyelid,
> It is so close, but you don't see it.

> The ultimate teaching is just below the surface,
> Why push yourself to look for it so deep?

> Sea wind, powerful waves on the beach,
> The moon is one, its reflections appear many and violently agitated.
>   (9, pp. 88–89)

In the last poem, the agitated mind of the practitioner prevents him from discovering the essence. His mind is refracted into multiple reflections, like the image of the moon on a choppy sea. All that is necessary is for the waters to become calm for them to reflect the single image of the moon. In the same way, a calm mind can reflect the essence of the teaching.

285. I do not have written oaths . . .": Musashi refers here to the custom, common in schools of martial arts during the feudal period, of taking an oath at the time of admission. The oath document often had on it, next to the signature, a fingerprint of the student in his own blood, which signified that he was committing himself to keep this oath at the price of his very life. In the text of the oath it was common to mention the penalties that could be imposed by the other members of the school and to make reference to the gods or other supernatural powers with whom the master was associated.

Oaths were generally also found on certificates of transmission. The master pledged before the gods to have communicated the essence of his school. It was customary to add: "He who has studied in my school must never study in another school." The student swore never to reveal the secrets of the school to anyone, not even to his parents or his brothers.

286. "The five or six bad ways," *godo rikudo*: *Godo* is written *go*, "five," and *do*, "way." *Rikudo* can also be pronounced *rokudo* and is written: *riku*, "six," *do*, "way." Both terms

come from Buddhism. The first refers to the five different worlds into which a living being can fall after his death. These are hell (*jigoku*), the world of the hungry beings (*gaki*), the animal worlds (*chikusho*), the human world (*ningen*), and the world of heaven (*tenjo*). The second term, *rikudo*, denotes the five worlds of *godo*, and in addition, another world in which the titans, the enemies of the gods (*ashura*), live.

Musashi's expression is ambiguous. One might think he is using this image in an ironic sense, connecting the many schools with hell and the other lower worlds. At the same time, this imagery borrowed from Buddhist thought reminds us that Musashi conceives of his strategy as a whole that contains both good and evil, and he stresses the importance of doing away with the evil in order to attain the ideal of strategy.

287. "Scroll of heaven," *ku no maki:* In the title, I translated the term *ku* as "heaven," in view of the preceding scrolls each being named after one of the five elements: earth, water, fire, wind, and therefore heaven. However, the term *ku* has a much more complex meaning. Its principal senses are "heaven" (or "sky"), "emptiness," and "space." This ideogram has three common pronunciations. Pronounced *ku* or *kara* it tends to mean "emptiness"; pronounced *sora* it means "heaven" (or "sky"). However, these two meanings (emptiness and heaven/sky) can both be present at the same time. In Musashi's text this ideogram is pronounced *ku*, but Musashi at certain times gives it any one of the three meanings (heaven/sky, emptiness, space) and sometimes all three meanings at once.

In this passage I have translated it by one or another of these terms, depending on the sense of the text. At the end of the text, *ku* seems to be used in a more philosophical sense, thus I translated it as "void."

288. Musashi finished composing the *Gorin no sho* during the second month of the same year, and in anticipation of his death, he gave it to his disciples. The original of this work has never been found. We know it today through a copy made by Furuhashi Sozaemon, one of Musashi's three closest disciples.

Why was Musashi's own manuscript not handed down from generation to generation?

One week before his death, Musashi bequeathed the *Gorin no sho* to one of his disciples, Terao Magonojo. The two names that appear at the end of Musashi's text (Terao Magonojo and Terao Musei Katsunobu) refer to the same person. The first is a commonly used name—doubtless this was the name by which Musashi called his disciple. The second is an official warrior name. Terao signed with his official name to formally bestow the *Gorin no sho* on his disciple Yamamoto Gensuke. "Musei Katsunobu" corresponds, for Terao Magonojo, to "Fujiwara no Genshin" for Miyamoto Musashi.

Musashi led a settled existence the last ten years of his life. When he moved into the cave called Reigando, he doubtless knew that his life was drawing to a close. Indeed, he fell ill several times in the course of composing the *Gorin no sho*. He spent the last two years of his life partly at Reigando, partly at his house in town. Musashi died three months after completing this major work.

This scroll appears as the conclusion of the *Gorin no sho.* Translating and interpreting its meaning are particularly difficult.

Takayanagi Mitsutoshi, a contemporary man of letters, gives the following analysis of the *Gorin no sho:*

> Musashi . . . was able to become a practitioner of the highest quality because he mastered his art in an organized manner. . . . We must admit that Musashi lacked the capacity to organize his knowledge. . . .
>
> His text is organized in the following manner: the main outlines in the Scroll of Earth, his own techniques in the Scroll of Water, combat in the Scroll of Fire, the other schools in the Scroll of Wind, and the conclusion in the Scroll of Heaven.
>
> For Musashi the Scroll of Earth comes first because he is preparing the ground on which he can plot a straight way. The Scroll of Water comes second because water follows the form of the vessel, square or round: it is a drop, it is also an ocean; the color of the deep is pure green. He says that he wrote this scroll on the inspiration of the purity of water. In third place comes war, in the Scroll of Fire, because fire symbolizes the fiery spirit. In fourth place comes the Scroll of Wind, written on the subject of the other schools, following the traditional expressions, the old wind, the modern wind, and the wind of such and such a family. Within an organization such as this, the need to classify one's thought into five parts and call them *Gorin* is not imperative. It is entirely a religious way of proceeding. The name *Gorin* contains within it a religious attitude. The text of the Scroll of Heaven, the fifth, is entirely religious and is without any scientific character. But we must accept this fact, for we are dealing with the work of a person who lived during a period in which there was not an adequate distinction between religion and science. . . . I think this is the main reason the text of the *Gorin no sho* is difficult to understand. (10, pp. 98–99)

This assessment of the Scroll of Heaven is debatable. It seems, rather, that in this brief text Musashi is sharing with us his deepest thoughts on the notion of emptiness. Put in the final position, this scroll appears as a conclusion. What is in question here is the practice of strategy, which advances ever further into a dimension of increasing profundity the more one progresses in it. The method here is different from that of a theoretical or scientific work, where we are accustomed to a progression in which, the further we go, the more precise the vision of the domain in question becomes, and the more definite the objective of the inquiry becomes.

In the way of the martial arts, by contrast, we go forward by a process of learning a body of technique that is composed of precise and concrete movements. But the further we advance, the more the vision of the practice comes to include a broad area of life that tends to become inseparable from a vast ungraspable space. This is because through the technique we learn to see ourselves and others, and then the world that surrounds us. According to the logic of the Japanese martial arts, the principle in accordance with which we create technique for ourselves must coincide with the principle of the universe. Starting with technique, Musashi studies and comes to a deeper understanding of this idea, and he writes this down in the last scroll. Thus Musashi's procedure is a logical one, but this is not the logic of science.

The conclusion is the part that appears the most confused. All through the *Gorin no sho*, Musashi organizes his writing on the basis of concrete things, and in this last scroll, he ends up with an abstraction. This process is comparable to the process of a painter who begins with concrete and precise drawings and in the course of a work's evolution and development, introduces elements of abstraction that, in some cases, are all that is left in the final picture.

Musashi sometimes gives up on the writing process, saying it is not possible to give the details in writing. He knows the limitations of words when it comes to conveying meaning about bodily technique.

In its method of explanation, the Scroll of Heaven offers an example of a different approach to writing that might be a little bit perplexing for us today. Here the role of words is to point out a distinct placement within a great space that is emptiness and also heaven, or the sky. Its words form a constellation if we are capable of connecting them in the empty space that separates them by filling it with our imagination and our intuition. This method would have been an obvious one for the disciples of Musashi to whom this text was addressed.

Musashi's poems are part and parcel of this kind of communication. They are transmitted in his school as an accompaniment to the teaching of his art.

Under the raised sword, it is hell,
If you go one step forward, it is paradise.

After having recognized all the principles, comes the clarity of the light of the
full moon,
I was ignorant of it before; I had nothing.

The current of a river in winter reflects the moon,
Like a mirror, it is transparent.

If you see the earth and the universe as you see a garden,
I live outside this universe. (9, pp. 88–89)

BIBLIOGRAPHY

In the references below, Japanese authors are referred to by their family name followed by their given name or initial.

Editions of Texts Written by Miyamoto Musashi

1. Budho sho Kankokai (collective authorship). *Bujutsu sosho* (Collection of Texts on the Martial Arts). Tokyo: Jinbutsu orai sha, 1968. See item 1 under "General Works of the Martial Arts" below for an itemization of the texts in this collection.
2. Fukuhara Josen. *Miyamoto Musashi no tankyu* (Study in Depth of Miyamoto Musashi). Okayama, Japan: Miyamoto Musashi Kenshin Gorin no kai, 1978.
3. Imai Masayuki. *Niten ichi-ryu seiho.* Oita, Japan: M. Imai, 1987.
4. Kamata Shigeo. *Gorin-no-sho.* (Edited with commentary). Tokyo: Kodansha, 1986.
5. Kamiko Tadashi. *Gorin-no-sho.* (Edited with commentary). Tokyo: Tokuma shoten, 1963.
6. Mitsuhashi Kanichiro. *Kendo hiyo* (The Essential Secret of Kendo). (Editions with commentary of several texts by Miyamoto Musashi). Kyoto: Butokushi Hakkosho, 1901.
7. Miyamoto Musashi Kenshokai (collective authorship). *Shin Miyamoto Musashi ko* (A Further Study on Miyamoto Musashi). Tokyo: Miyamoto Musashi Kenshokai, 1977.
8. Nakanishi Seizo. *Miyamoto Musashi no shogai* (The Life of Miyamoto Musashi). Tokyo: Shin jinbutsu orai sha, 1975.

9. Ozawa Masao. *Miyamoto Musashi.* Tokyo: Yoshikawa Kobun kan, 1986.

10. Takayanagi Mitsutoshi. *Gorin-no-sho.* (Edited with commentary). Tokyo: Iwanami, 1942; rev. ed., 1969.

11. Terayama Danchu. *Gorin-no-sho: Miyamoto Musashi no waza to michi* (*Gorin no sho:* The Techniques and the Way of Miyamoto Musashi). (Edited with commentary). Tokyo: Kodansha, 1984.

12. Tominaga Kengo. *Shijitsu Miyamoto Musashi.* Tokyo: Hyakusen shobo, 1969.

13. Watanabe Ichiro. *Gorin-no-sho.* (Edited with commentary). Tokyo: Iwanami, 1985.

14. Yamada Jirokichi. *Kendo shugi* (Compilation of Kendo Transmissions). Collection of texts, 2 vols. Tokyo: Hitotsubashi kenyu kai, 1922. See item 14 under "General Works of the Martial Arts" below for an itemization of the texts in this collection.

Contemporary Works on the Life and Work of Musashi

15. Ezaki Shunpei. *Nihon kengo retsuden* (Writings on the Great Adepts of the Japanese Sword). Tokyo: Gendai kyoyo bunko, 1970.

16. Fukuhara Josen. *Miyamoto Iori no gisho* (The False Testimony of Miyamoto Iori). Okayama, Japan: Josen Fukuhara, 1984.

17. Harada Mukashi. *Shinsetsu Miyamoto Musashi* (The Truth about Miyamoto Musashi). Fukuoka: Ashi shobo, 1984.

18. Ishioka Hisao. *Hyoho sha no seikatsu* (The Life of the Warrior Adepts of the Sword). Tokyo: Yazankaku, 1981.

19. Morita Monjuro. *Kendo zen to kako no jutsu* (Kendo Zen and the Technique of the Past). Tokyo: Shimazu shobo, 1988.

20. ———. *Koshi to tanden de okonau kendo* (Kendo Based on the Small of the Back and the Tanden). Tokyo: Shimazu shobo, 1987.

21. Muneta Hiroshi. *Miyamoto Musashi.* Tokyo: Shin jinbutsu orai sha, 1976.

22. Nakanishi Seizo. *Miyamoto Musashi no saigo* (The Death of Miyamoto Musashi). Tokyo: Nihon Shuppan hoso kikaku, 1987.

23. Nakazato Kaizan. *Nihon bujutsu shinmyo ki* (Extraordinary Tales from the Japanese Martial Arts). Tokyo: Kawade-shobo, 1985.

24. Naramoto Tatsuya. *Gorin-no-sho nyumon* (Initiation into the *Gorin no sho*). Tokyo: Tokuma shoten, 1984.

25. Nippon Hoso Kyokai (collective authorship). *Miyamoto Musashi.* Tokyo: NHK, 1989.

26. Omori Sogen. *Ken to zen* (The Sword and Zen). Tokyo: Shunju-sha, 1973.

27. Okada Kazuo and Kato Hiroshi (editors of a work of collective authorship).

Miyamoto Musashi no subete (Everything about Miyamoto Musashi). Tokyo: Shin jinbutsu orai sha, 1983.

28. Saotome Mitsugu. *Jitsuroku Miyamoto Musashi* (The Historical Truth about Miyamoto Musashi). Tokyo: PHP Bunko, 1989.

29. Shiba Ryotaro. *Nihon kenkyaku den* (The Story of the Adepts of the Japanese Sword). Vol. 2. Tokyo: Asahi shinbun-sha, 1982.

30. ———. *Shin setsu Miyamoto Musashi* (The Truth about Miyamoto Musashi). Tokyo: Asahi shinbun-sha, 1983.

31. Tobe Shinichiro. *Kosho Miyamoto Musashi* (Study of Miyamoto Musashi). Tokyo: Fukosha, 1984.

32. Watanuki Kiyoshi. *Nihon kengo hyakusen* (One Hundred Great Adepts of the Japanese Sword). Tokyo: Akita shoten, 1971.

33. Watanabe Ichiro, ed. *Budo no meicho* (Masterpieces of Budo). Tokyo: Tokyo copi, 1979.

34. Yamada Jirokichi. *Nihon kendo shi* (The History of the Way of the Sword in Japan). Tokyo: Hitotsubashi kenyu kai, 1977.

35. Yoshida Seiken. *Nito ryu o kataru* (Explanation of the School of Two Swords). Tokyo: Kyozaisha, 1941.

36 Yoshida Yutaka, ed. *Budo hiden sho* (Secret Book of Budo). Tokyo: Tokuma shoten, 1973.

General Works on the Martial Arts

The first two works given below (numbers 1 and 14, cited in full in the first section above) are collections of ancient works. I indicate below their titles the main texts I consulted in them.

1. Budo sho Kankokai (collective authorship), *Bujutsu sosho* (Collection of Texts on the Martial Arts)
    a. Miyamoto Musashi. *Hyoho sanju-go-kajo* and *Enmei ryu kenpo sho*. Written in the seventeenth century.
    b. Hinatsu Shigetaka. *Honcho bugei shoden* (Little Tales of the Martial Arts in Japan). Written in 1715.
    c. Aoyama Takanao. *Shinsen bujutsu ryuso roku* (On the Founders of the School of the Martial Arts). Written in 1843.
    d. Itsusai Chozanshi. *Tengu geijutsu ron* (Discourse of the God Tengu on the Art of the Sword). Written in 1729.
    e. Kotoda Toshisada. *Ittosai sensei kenpo sho* (The Teaching of Master Ittosai). Written in the seventeenth century.

f. Minamoto Tokushu. *Gekiken sodan* (Treatise on Schools of Swordsmanship). Written in 1843. Minamoto Tokushu was a sword master and traveled about for more than ten years visiting different schools of swordsmanship. This work gives an account of the documents he collected.

g. Hirayama Shiryu-gyozo. *Kensetsu* (Discourse on the Swords). Hirayama lived from 1759 to 1828 and was a master of the sword.

h. Matsuura Seizan. *Joseishi kendan* (Joseishi's Philosophy of Swordsmanship). Written at the end of the eighteenth century.

i. *Enmei ryu kenpo sho* (Writings on the Sword Technique of the Enmei Ryu).

14. Yamada Jirokichi. *Kendo shugi* (Compilation of Kendo Transmissions)
a. Hinatsu Shigetaka. *Gajo shoden* (Text on the Traditions of the Various Schools of the Martial Arts). Written in the eighteenth century.

b. Kubota Seion. *Keijo ki* (On the Various Techniques of the Art of the Sword); *Kenpo yogaku denju* (Teaching the Sword to Beginners); *Kenpo chotan ron* (The Characteristics of Long and Short Swords); and *Kenpo ryakki* (The Main Outlines of the Techniques of Swordsmanship). Written at the beginning of the nineteenth century.

c. Miyamoto Musashi. *Gorin-no-sho* and *Hyoho-sanju-go-kajo*.

37. Domoto Akihiko. *Kendo kojutsu shi* (Collection of the Talks of Master Hakudo Nakayama on Kendo). Tokyo: Ski janal, 1988.

38. Hasegawa Junzo. *Kano Jigoro no kyoiku to shiso* (Education and Ideology According to Kano Jigoro). Tokyo: Meiji shoin, 1981.

39. Kato Jinpei. *Kano Jigoro* (A Study of Kano Jigoro). Tokyo: Shoyo shoten, 1964.

40. Katsube Mitake. *Bushido* (Dialogue between Tesshu Yamaoka and Katsu Kaishu). Tokyo: Kadokawa, 1971.

41. Mitsuhashi Shuzo. *Kendo*. Tokyo: Taishukan, 1972.

42. Mori Shohei. *Dai Nippon kendo shi* (The History of Japanese Kendo). Osaka: Kendo sho kankokai, 1934.

43. Nakayama Hakudo. *Kendo kowa* (Discourse on Kendo). Tokyo: Yushinkan dojo, 1937.

44. Naramoto Tatsuya. *Bushido no keifu* (Bushido Genealogies). Tokyo: Chuo koron, 1975.

45. Nitobe Inazo. *Bushido*. Tokyo: Iwanami, 1938.

46. Omori Sogen. *Sho to zen* (Calligraphy and Zen). Tokyo: Shunjusha, 1973.

47. ———. *Zen no koso* (The Great Zen Monks). Tokyo: Shunjusha, 1979.

48. Ozawa Chikamitsu. *Ken shin itchi* (Sword and Mind Becoming One). Tokyo: Jutaku shinpo, 1978.

49. Sugimoto Sannojo. *Watanabe Koan taiwa* (Conversation with Watanabe Koan). Watanabe was a samurai who was born in 1582 and died in 1711 at the age of 129. When Watanabe was 127, on the command of Lord Kaga, Sugimoto collected and wrote down his stories as an expression of living history. Watanabe actually knew Musashi, whence the interest of this document.

50. Sasamori Junzo. *Itto-ryu-gokui* (The Supreme Teaching of the Itto Ryu). Tokyo: Reigakudo, 1986.

51. So Doshin. *Shorinji Kenpo*. Tokyo: Kobunsha, 1963.

52. Tokitsu Kenji. "Étude sur le rôle et les transformations de la culture traditionelle dans la societé contemporaire Japonaise" (Study on the Role and the Transformations of Traditional Culture in Contemporary japanese Society). Third-cycle doctorate thesis in sociology (director, G. Balandier), Université René Descartes, 1982.

53. ———. *La voie du karaté, pour une théorie des arts martiaux japonais* (The Way of Karate: Toward a Theory of the Japanese Martial Arts). Paris: Éditions du Seuil, 1979.

54. Ueshiba Kisshomaru. *Aikido hiyo* (The Essence of Aikido). Tokyo: Tokyo shoten, 1972.

55. ———. *Aikido nyumon* (Initiation into Aikido). Tokyo: Kobunsha, 1972.

56. Yagyu Munenori. *Hyoho kadensho* (The Family Transmission of Hyoho). Tokyo: Iwanami, 1985. Written during the same period as the *Gorin no sho*.

57. Shiragami Ikkuken. Article on his school, the Shirai ryu. *Kendo Nippon* 8 (1978). Tokyo: Ski-journal, 1978.

Essays on Miyamoto Musashi

58. Naramoto Tatsuya. *Gorin-no-sho-nyumon*. Tokyo: Tokuma bunko, 1985.

59. Saotome Mitsugu. *Jitsoruku Miyamoto Musashi*. Tokyo: PHP bunko, 1989.

60. NHK (collective work). *Jitsuzo Miyamoto Musashi*. Tokyo: NHK, 1989.

Novels

61. Yoshikawa Eiji. *Miyamoto Musashi*. Tokyo: Kodansha, 1970.

62. ———. *La pierre et le sabre* (The Stone and the Sword), vol. 1; and *La parfaite lumière* (Perfect Light), vol. 2 (the French translation of *Miyamoto Musashi*,

immediately above). Paris: Éditions Balland, 1983. English translation: Eiji Yoshikawa. *Musashi*. New York: Harper and Row, 1981.

General Works on the History of Japan

63.   Collective work. *Nihon no rekishi* (The History of Japan). 32 vols. Tokyo: Shogakukan, 1975.

64.   Collective work. *Nihon no rekishi* (The History of Japan). 26 vols. Tokyo: Chuokoron, 1974.

65.   Collective work. *Nihonshi no kiso chishiki* (Basic Facts of the History of Japan). Tokyo: Yuhikaku, 1974.

66.   Collective work (Takayanagi M., director). *Dictionary of the History of Japan*. Tokyo: Kadokawa, 1982.

67.   Kyokai. *Nihon ryoi ki* (Book of Strange Events of Japanese History). 3 vols. Tokyo: Kodansha, 1978.Written by the monk Kyokai in the eighth century.

68.   Mishima Yukio. *Hagakure nyumon* (Initiation into the *Hagakure* [Book of the Samurai]). Tokyo: Kobunsha, 1967.

69.   Mori Mikisaburo. *Na to haji no bunka* (The Culture of Honor and Shame). Tokyo: Kodansha, 1971.

70.   Nakamura Kichiji. *Buke no rekishi* (The History of the Bushi). Tokyo: Iwanami, 1967.

71.   Terada Toru. *Do no shiso* (The Ideology of Do). Tokyo: Sobunsha, 1978.

72.   Tokutomi Soho. *Kinsei Nihon kokumin shi* (History of the Japanese Population in the Modern Period). 30 vols. Tokyo: Kodansha, 1982.

73.   Yasuda Takashi. *Kata no Nihon bunka* (The Japanese Culture of Katas). Tokyo: Asahi Shinbun, 1984.

Before the Edo Period

74.   Hayashiya Tatsusaburo. *Chusei geinoshi no kenkyu* (Study on the History of the Arts in the Middle Ages). Tokyo: Iwanami, 1960.

75.   Miki Seiichiro. *Teppo to sono jisai* (The Introduction of the Gun and Its Epoch). Tokyo: Kyoikusha, 1981.

76.   Owada Tetsuo. *Sengoku busho* (The Generals of the Period of Feudal Wars). Tokyo: Chuo koron, 1981.

77.   Sakai Tadakutsu, ed. *Sekigahara kassen shimatsuki* (Writings on the Battle of Sekigahara). Tokyo: Kyoiku sha, 1991. Writings from the beginning of the seventeenth century.

78. Yamazaki Masakazu. *Muromachi ki* (Writings on the Muromachi Period). Tokyo: Asahi shinbun, 1974.

79. Yasuda Motohisa. *Bushi sekai no jomaku* (The Beginning of the World of the Bushi). Tokyo: Yoshikawa kobunsha, 1973.

80. Yoshida Yutaka, comp. and commentator. *Zohyo monogatari* (The History of the Soldiers of the Period of Feudal Wars). Tokyo: Kyoikusha, 1980.

81. Yuasa Jozan. *Jozan kidan* (The Writings of Jozan). Tokyo: Iwanami, 1939. Anecdotes and writings on the particular modes of behavior of the *bushi* of the sixteenth and seventeenth centuries.

Edo Period

82. Chiba Eiichiro. *Chiba Shusaku iko.* Tokyo: Taiiko to spotsu, 1982.

83. Collective work. "On the Individual and the Collective in the Edo Period." *Rekishi koron* (On History) 106 (1984). Tokyo: Yuzankaku.

84. Ezaki Junpei. *Yagyu Munenori.* Tokyo: Shakai shiso sa, 1971.

85. Hasegawa Shin, comp. *Nihon adauchi iso* (Strange Stories of Vengeance in Japan of the Edo Period). Tokyo: Chuo koron, 1974.

86. Hino Tatsuo. *Edojin to yutopia* (The Men of the Edo Period and Utopia). Tokyo: Asahi shinbun, 1977.

87. Imano Nobuo. *Edo no tabi* (The Edo Journey). Tokyo: Iwanami, 1986.

88. Inagaki Fumio. *Kosho Edo kibun* (Study on Strange Events in Edo). Tokyo: Kawade shobo, 1984.

89. Inagaki Shisei. *Adauchi o kosho suru* (Study on Japanese Acts of Vengeance). Tokyo: Obunsha, 1987.

90. Kitajima Masamoto. *Edo jidai* (The Edo Period). Tokyo: Iwanami, 1958.

91. Nakano Mitsutoshi. *Edo meibutsu hyohan ki* (Tourist Guide to Edo). Tokyo: Iwanami, 1985.

92. Nishiyama M. and Ogi S. *Edo sanbyaku nen* (The Three Hundred Years of the Edo Period). 3 vols. Tokyo: Kodansha, 1975.

93. Okubo Hikozaemon. *Mikawa monogatari* (The History of Mikawa: The Beginning of the Founding of the Tokugawa Shogunate). Tokyo: Kyoikusha, 1980.

94. Shimozawa Kan. *Shinsengumi ibun* (On the Shinsengumi [the Shogunate police]). Tokyo: Chuo koron, 1977.

95. Takayanagi Kaneyoshi. *Edo no kakyu bushi* (The Warriors from the Bottom of the Hierarchy during the Edo Period). Tokyo: Kashiwa shobo, 1980.

96. Tanizaki Junichiro, comp. and trans. *Bushuko hiwa* (Esoteric Anecdotes of the Bushu Region from the Edo Period). Tokyo: Chuo koron, 1984.

97. Watsuji Tetsuro. *Sakoku.* Tokyo: Chikuma shobo, 1963.

98.   Yamamoto Jocho. *Hagakure* (Text Written behind the Bower Wall: Treatise on the Conduct of Warriors). Tokyo: Chuo koron, 1966.

Dictionaries

Reference Dictionaries

99.   *Kokugo dai jiten.* Tokyo: Shogakukan, 1982.
100. *Kojien.* Tokyo: Iwanami, 1967.

Other Dictionaries

101. *Kokugo jiten.* Tokyo: Iwanami, 1963.
102. *Jigen.* Tokyo: Kadokawa, 1955.
103. *Shin kanwa chujiten.* Tokyo: Sanseido, 1967.
104. *Shokai kanwa dai jiten.* Tokyo: Fuzanbo, 1977.
105. *Kogo jiten.* Tokyo: Sanseido, 1962.
106. *Nihonshi jiten.* Tokyo: Kadokawa, 1982.
107. *Edogo no jiten.* Tokyo: Kodansha, 1979.
108. *Kanji no gogen.* Tokyo: Kadokawa, 1977.
109. *Koji to kotowaza no jiten.* Tokyo: Haga shoten, 1968.

Complementary Works

110. Fujiwara R. *Shinto-yoshin-ryu no rekishi to giho* (The History and Technique of the Shinto Yoshin Ryu). Tokyo: Sozo, 1983.
111. Gima S. and Fujiwara R. *Kindai karate-do no rekishi o kataru* (Conversation on the Modern History of the Karate Do). Tokyo: Besubol-magazin, 1986.
112. Hokama Tetsuhiro. *Okinawa karate-do no ayumi* (The Progress of the Karate Do in Okinawa). Naha, Japan: Minami P., 1984.
113. Kono Y. and Yoro T. *Kobujutsu no hakken* (Discovery of the Classical Japanese Martial Arts). Tokyo: Kobun sha, 1993.
114. Kuroda Tetsuzan. *Iai jutsu seigi* (Treatise on the Art of Iai). Saitama, Japan: Sojin sha, 1991.
115. ———. *Kenjutsu seigi* (Treatise on the Art of Kenjutsu). Saitama, Japan: Sojin sha, 1992.
116. Matsuda Ryuchi. *Chugoku bujutsu* (On the Chinese Martial Arts). Tokyo: Shin jinbutsu orai sha, 1975.
117. ———. *Chugoku bujutsu shi* (On the History of the Chinese Martial Arts). Tokyo: Shin jinbutsu orai sha, 1976.

118.　──. *Hiden Nihon jujutsu* (Secret Transmission of Japanese Jujutsu). Tokyo: Shin jinbutsu orai sha, 1978.

119.　Nagamine Shoshin. *Okinawa no karate sumo meijin den* (The History of the Adepts of Karate and Sumo in Okinawa). Tokyo: Shin jinbutsu orai sha, 1986.

120.　Onishi Hidetaka. *Yamada Jirokichi sensei no shogai* (The Life of Master Yamada Jirokichi). Tokyo: Hitotsubashi kenyu-kai, 1956.

121.　Ono Kazufusa. *Kokoro no hyoho* (Strategy of the Mind: On the Yagyu Shin Kage Ryu of Today). Tokyo: Roppo-shuppan, 1982.

122.　Ota Yoshimaro. *Kojiki monogatari* (The History of the Kojiki). Tokyo: Shakai shiso sha, 1971.

123.　Collective work. *Shinsengumi taishi retsuden* (On the Members of the Shinsengumi [the Shogunate police]). Tokyo: Shin jinbutsu orai sha, 1972.

124.　Jiguang Qi. *Ji xiao xin shu.* Taipei: Hualian, 1983. Sixteenth-century treatise on the Chinese martial arts.

125.　Nango T. *Budo towa nanika* (What Is Budo?). Tokyo: Sanichi-shobo, 1977.

126.　Gurvitch, G. *La vocation actuelle de la sociologie* (The Current Calling of Sociology). Paris: Éditions Presses Universitaires de France, 1969.